DISCOVER THE REAL MAGIC
OF WAYNE DYER!

On self-improvement . . .
If you find yourself believing that you must always be the way you have always been, you are arguing against growth. You must know that you have the power to create whatever kind of person you want to become, in all aspects of your humanity.

On relationships . . .
Relinquish your need to be right. This is the single greatest cause of difficulties and deterioration in relationships. The spiritual partnership is a relationship of equals. No one needs to be proved wrong. Stifle the need to make the other person wrong or to make yourself right, and you have created a miracle.

On spirituality . . .
Spend some time every day in awe, in total, complete awe. Be thankful for your hands, your invisible, incomprehensibly awesome mind. Treat all life with reverence and awe, and know that it is all working purposefully. A few minutes a day in total awe will contribute to your spiritual awakening faster than any metaphysics course.

ALSO BY WAYNE W. DYER

Wisdom of the Ages
Manifest Your Destiny
Your Sacred Self
A Promise Is a Promise
You'll See It When You Believe It
What Do You Really Want for Your Children?
No More Holiday Blues
Gifts from Eykis
The Sky's the Limit
Pulling Your Own Strings
Your Erroneous Zones
Everyday Wisdom
Staying on the Path

REAL

MAGIC

Creating Miracles in Everyday Life

WAYNE W. DYER

Quill

An Imprint of HarperCollins*Publishers*

Grateful acknowledgment is made to the Associated Press for permission to reprint an excerpt from an article by Hal Bock which appeared in the *Maui News,* June 23, 1991. Excerpt from *The Prophet,* by Kahlil Gibran, copyright © 1923 by Kahlil Gibran and renewed 1951 by Administrators C.T.A. of Kahlil Gibran Estate and Mary G. Gibran. Reprinted by permission of Alfred A. Knopf, Inc. Excerpt from *Healers on Healing,* edited by Richard Carlson and Benjamin Shield, copyright © 1989. Reprinted by arrangement with Jeremy P. Tarcher, Inc.

A hardcover edition of this book was published in 1992 by HarperCollins Publishers.

HarperCollins books may be purchased for educational, business, or sales promotional use. For information please write: Special Markets Department, HarperCollins Publishers Inc., 10 East 53rd Street, New York, New York 10022.

First Quill edition published 2001.

Designed by Jessica Shatan

Library of Congress Cataloging-in-Publication Data

Dyer, Wayne W.
    Real magic : creating miracles in everyday life / Wayne W. Dyer.
      p. cm.
    Originally published: 1992
    Includes index.
    ISBN 0-06-093582-0 (pbk.)
      1. Success—Psychological aspects.   I. Title.

BF637.S8 D94 2000
158.1—dc21

00-054115

02 03 04 05 RRD 10 9 8 7 6 5 4 3 2

To our own spiritual miracle who showed up as our daughter against all odds, and is pure bliss in action,
Saje Eykis Irene Dyer.

And to my two very special friends:

Deepak Chopra, M.D., my spiritual brother who links arms with me in love as we bring our limitless vision to the world.

Michael Jackson, whose words, music, and love remind us that it is only through giving that we are saving our own lives.

I love you all!

What if you slept?
And what if,
in your sleep
you dreamed?
And what if,
in your dream,
you went to heaven
and there plucked
a strange and
beautiful flower?
And what if,
when you awoke,
you had the flower
in your hand?

—Samuel Taylor Coleridge

Contents

INTRODUCTION

This is a book about miracles. It is not a book about other people's miracles, but about you, the reader, and how you can create miracles for yourself in your own life. It is not about luck nor is it about being one of a chosen few who have had miracles show up in their lives. This book was written with the express purpose of showing you the way to create what you may have previously thought to be impossible in your life.

This is a very personal book. I have seen the way to real magic in my own life and I have taken great care to detail what I believe to be the essential ingredients for creating a life filled with miracles. I have gone beyond "believing" in miracles, to a place that I call "knowing."

"Knowing" in this sense is something we all have experienced. For instance, if I stay away from my bicycle for several months, I become aware of my knowingness of riding when I next go for a bicycle ride. I pump up the tires and off I go, balancing myself perfectly on those thin wheels and moving effortlessly through the streets, riding "no-handed" with full confidence, turning corners sharply and generally maneuvering my way through the streets with complete abandon. When I get on my bicycle, I do not have a *goal* of being able to balance myself again after all those months, I do not have a *belief* I can ride it, I have an internal *knowing*, and I proceed to act based upon that powerful knowing.

I feel the very same way about your ability to manifest miracles in your life. You can learn to go way beyond believing and goal setting, to a new place within yourself: the place of knowing. It is in this realm of your mind that miracles are produced.

Deep within you is a unified field of limitless possibilities. When you become competent at going to this wondrous place you will discover an entirely new realm of human experience where all things are possible. It is here that real magic takes place and you can begin to manifest all you seek in your physical world. Limits simply do not exist, and you seem always to be at the right place at precisely the right time. It is here that you make synchronistic "unbelievable" connections with others and can almost read the thoughts of those around you. It is here that you are capable of meeting exactly the right person to help you on your own personal path at exactly the right time. It is here that whatever or whoever is necessary to create prosperity and abundance in your life appears. It is here that the precise cure for your ailments shows up, or the right book or tape arrives into your life as if guided to you by some invisible, mysterious force.

In this place of higher awareness, the mystery begins to disappear and your purpose in life becomes very clear to you. Your relationships miraculously shift to new levels of spiritual partnership. Your business endeavors begin to "flow" and you start to make decisions with less and less effort. You begin to rid yourself of toxins and get your physical life on a healthy rather than a disease plane.

This book is my effort to show you how to go about creating this higher level of awareness. I have written what I consider a blueprint to assist you in developing this awareness and applying it to all aspects of your life, including your personal relationships and your relationship to the larger world.

The plan of nature seems to be nothing more than a slow and steady unfoldment of consciousness. A stone is alive with atoms, just like you are, but it has no perceptible awareness. It is immune to feeling kicked or pulverized. It appears to be unaware. A plant is aware of the conditions of the soil, the seasons and the humidity, and it will bloom with the spring sunlight. It is aware but very limited.

Animals, when compared with minerals and vegetables, have more developed levels of awareness. Many animals exhibit an awareness of the seasons in their ability to migrate, of danger in their ability to elude predators, and of deep caring and love in relationships with their mates and their young.

And then there are humans, who have the ultimate awareness of choice. We can choose to function at a lower level of awareness and simply exist, caring for our possessions, eating, drinking, sleeping and managing in the world as pawns of the elements, or we can soar to new and higher levels of awareness allowing ourselves to transcend our environment and literally create a world of our own—a world of real magic. Within each of us is the ultimate awareness offering a certain kind of victory over the material world: the capability of finding equilibrium in every set of circumstances. The lesson of this book is very simple—*you are capable of achieving perfect equilibrium of the mind*. The path requires a commitment to your own inner transformation.

Your inner transformation cannot be completed from an intellectual or scientific perspective. Instruments of limitation will not reveal the limitless. This is a job for your mind and your soul, the invisible segment of you that is always there but often ignored in favor of that which you can grasp with your senses.

The first part of this book provides the foundation for realigning yourself in the invisible world. It is here that you will gain mastery over your mind and set the stage for manifesting miracles in that highest stage of awareness which is yours for the knowing. Once you have learned to realign yourself, you begin the process of experimenting with this new miracle mind-set and watching with awe as your world begins falling into perfect order.

The second part of this book focuses on putting into practice that which you have committed yourself to in your mind. It guides you in the actual manifestation of miracles, and in living your daily life at the highest state of equilibrium. Here I have concluded each chapter with a section on specific suggestions for accessing miracles in your life.

During the early years of the U.S. space program Wernher von Braun encouraged Space Center employees to *know* that "there is perfect order in the universe. Mankind and mankind alone can understand that order." This thought was a powerful stimulus when problems seemed insurmountable. You, as a part of mankind, can understand this perfect order and actually choose to align yourself with it. This is the context of *Real Magic*. I know about that perfect order and I want you to experience it too.

The way to understanding is through your willingness to reach your own highest state of awareness, using that awareness to get your life on purpose, and radiating that awareness to everyone in your life. It is primarily a mental trip so powerful that it can affect the material world with its miraculous magical powers. But you must be willing to go within and discover it for yourself. My words will not make it true. Only experiencing what I am writing about will make it your reality.

This invisible mental trip involves dispelling some powerful misperceptions and arriving at a new set of *knowings*. With your new awareness *you will shift* from

• Knowing you are limited *to knowing that ultimate reality and your own potential are unlimited.*

- Knowing you are controlled by heredity, the environment and supernatural forces *to knowing you create your own reality and that inborn and divine forces work with you rather than independently of you.*

- Knowing knowledge and experience are available exclusively through your five senses *to knowing that an intuitive, invisible guidance is available to you when you reach a higher state of awareness.*

- Knowing human existence is dangerous and evil *to knowing all experience is blessed and for a greater good.*

- Knowing some people are luckier than others *to knowing you can create your own luck and that all experience contains a valuable lesson.*

- Knowing life is chaotic *to knowing there is order in chaos and there are no accidents in a universe that is in perfect order.*

I know the things I have written about in this book will be shocking to some and rejected by many. So be it. They are truth as I live it and they come from my heart. I know there is divine order in this universe, from the tiniest cell to the entire galaxy and beyond. That magnificent awareness is our birthright, and it is a part of each and every one of us.

Take these ideas and make them work, first in your own life, then with your immediate family and circle of acquaintances, and ultimately with the entire world. Once you discover the capacity for real magic within you, you will want to share this knowing with others and empower the entire world with this awareness. I trust this book will be helpful in this endeavor. It has been a joy to write about. I wish you the same real magic in your life. God bless you.

PART I

CREATING AN INNER PATH FOR REAL MAGIC

I

A TRANSCENDENT VIEW OF MAGIC AND MIRACLES

I have been all things unholy; if God can work
through me, he can work through anyone.

—St. Francis of Assisi

According to the illustrious magician Harry Houdini,
magic is achieved through illusion. A simple example
is an illusion created by using smoke and mirrors. The illusion is called magic simply because it *appears* to be unexplainable. Late in his career, though, Houdini alluded to
something that he experienced which he called "real magic."
He apparently had acquired the ability to produce results that
were in fact unexplainable. These magical results could not be
accounted for even as the product of illusion.

I chose the title of this book because I became attracted to
the paradox inherent in those two words, *real magic*. You, like
most people, are probably convinced that if something is real
it cannot be magic, and if it is magic it cannot be real. However, it is my belief that when we get caught in this paradox

we are inhibited from experiencing our magical dimensions. I believe that we experience real magic when we transcend the paradox and that the transcendent view encompasses the experience of real magic as indeed very real, and also magical.

In the past several years my life has undergone a magnificent transformation. I find myself on a path leading to levels of awareness and results that I can only describe as miraculous. They are simply unexplainable in any other terms. I am convinced that there is another realm to experience when we are ready to go beyond this life to which we have become accustomed. This other realm defies our laws of science and logic. It is a place within each of us that is free of ordinary boundaries, rules and limitations. This is not some wonderland that is available only in imagination. It is magically real and available to each person when he or she is ready.

I cannot explain how or why I have arrived at this place in my life. I am surprised I am talking about it! It simply feels as if experiencing and writing about real magic is my purpose or mission at this time in my life. Regardless of explanations, I find that I am filled with awe and respect for this unexpected part of my life path.

I am intrigued with Leo Tolstoy, in part because of what I see as parallels between his life and mine. He was a famous author during his lifetime and a man who had spent much of his life in hedonistic pursuits, one who had no spiritual bent in his early writings but witnessed in his own life a shift that seemed to be happening to him without his consent. His writing began to reflect a spiritual quality, and he wrote of the journey of the soul and the world of real magic. Yet he was uncertain about why or how this transformation had taken place.

Recently a copy of a handwritten portion of Tolstoy's will, written by him twenty years before his death, was given to me by a woman who is one of the world's leading experts on Russian literature. In this will Tolstoy described how he felt about his life's work, which is precisely how I feel as I contemplate my own:

> Furthermore, and in particular, I ask all people near and far not to praise me. (I know they will do so because they have done so in my lifetime in the most unseemly way.) But if they want to study my writings, let them look carefully at those passages in them in which I know the power of God spoke through me, and make use of them for their own lives. There have been times when I felt I was becoming the bearer of God's will. I have often been so impure, so full of personal passions, that the light of this truth has been obscured by my own darkness, but nevertheless this truth has sometimes passed through me, and these have been the happiest moments of my life. God grant that these truths should not have been defiled in passing through me, and that people might feed on them, despite the superficial and impure form which I have given them.

And so too this unexpected turn that my own life has taken has occurred almost without my consent. I had no grand plan. I had no such goals or objectives for my life. What I did have was a willingness, an openness to seeing things another way. Now that I have been a witness to miracles in my own personal life, I feel compelled to share this new magical awareness. Perhaps you have been drawn to this book by the same natural flow of life that has motivated me to write about real magic.

THREE PATHS TOWARD ENLIGHTENMENT

As I look back at the entire tapestry of my life I can see from the perspective of the present moment that every aspect of my life was necessary and perfect. Each step led eventually to a higher place, even though these steps often felt like obstacles or painful experiences. Every successful, truly happy person that I have encountered has confirmed their knowing that there simply are no accidents. They see the universe as all-purposeful, including the so-called accidents. All agree that every unique happening in our lives leads us to a higher place. As Henry Miller said, "The world is *not* to be put in order, the world *is* order incarnate. It is for us to put ourselves in unison with this order."

Begin right now to reconsider your entire life experience as a beautiful tapestry or journey toward greater awareness. A simple way to do this is to envision your life as a journey with three ascending paths.

1. ENLIGHTENMENT THROUGH SUFFERING On the first path of your journey, you learn through a process I call *enlightenment through suffering*. At this time of life, which has nothing to do with chronological age, you ask, "Why me?" when something occurs that is painful or difficult. If it involves, for instance, the unwanted breakup of a relationship, you spend your present moments suffering and wondering how and why such a disaster could have befallen you. After a while, as you recover, you are able to look back and say, "Now I know why I had to go through that breakup," and you see, with the benefit of hindsight and suffering, that it allowed you to move on to another life experience of great value. From the perspective of looking backward, you realize that you had to experience the pain in order to transcend it.

This is the pattern of growth for many people: events occur, suffering takes place, and then the light appears. These events can happen in virtually all areas of one's life: addictions, bankruptcies, illnesses, spiritual emptiness, layoffs, tax problems and anything in between. The experience is one of learning through hindsight by repeating this pattern of suffering over and over. Some people continue this cycle throughout their entire lifetime. They never move up from the first path and never experience the higher ground of enlightenment. They literally spend their lives suffering and then, a long time down the road, they may or may not see that an event was necessary and that it was a test for them at the time. They never seem to get the message that life gives exams and unless you learn from your mistakes you are doomed to repeat them. For some, life is spent in asking, "Why me, God? Why is this happening to me?" For persons in this category, real magic remains unavailable.

2. ENLIGHTENMENT THROUGH OUTCOME If you recognize the first path as a pattern in your own life, then you probably have moved past suffering as your means to learning, to *enlightenment through outcome*. At this level you learn to stop asking, "Why me, God?" You develop a knowing that says, "There are no accidents, everything I am experiencing is in some way necessary for me to move ahead to the next step." Rather than asking the "Why me?" question, you begin to ask, "What is in this experience that I can use in a beneficial way, even if I don't understand why it is happening right now?"

This is a shift of paramount significance. When you are focused in your mind on what you can learn from an experience, your mind cannot dwell on thoughts that will lead to your suffering, thoughts such as "Why me?" "Isn't this terrible!" and "I'm so unlucky." The shift in your mind allows you to look at the outcome of an event or experience and what you can learn from it. Instead of a poor-me approach, you shift to a learning approach. You ask yourself, "How can I create the outcome that I want with this illness that I am presently experiencing?" or "What can I learn about myself and how much strength can I muster to deal effectively with this problem?"

Many people spend their entire lifetime on this second path. They are beyond suffering as a life-style. They are always asking, "What will the outcome be for me?" These are the goal-oriented people focused on quotas and specific ambitions, which they work toward assiduously. They see obstacles as opportunities. Living at outcome is far superior to living at suffering. It gives one's life focus and keeps one motivated to set higher and higher goals. It virtually eliminates the suffering born of self-pity. For many people who are living their lives at outcome, there can be no higher place. They are centered on outcome, and when it is achieved they look for newer and grander results. What is missing in their lives, however, is the possibility of experiencing real magic, and the ability to make miracles happen. For this, one needs to go to the third path on this metaphoric journey.

3. ENLIGHTENMENT THROUGH PURPOSE "Nothing is more likely to help a person overcome or endure troubles than the consciousness of having a task in life." Victor Frankl wrote those words as he endured the insanity and brutality of a Nazi concentration camp at Auschwitz during the Second World War. Learning that you have a heroic mission and getting in step with that mission is the third path I am encouraging you to take as you begin to introduce real magic into your life. I call this path *enlightenment through purpose.*

Everything in the universe has a purpose. Indeed, the invisible intelligence that flows through everything in a purposeful fashion is also flowing through you. In order to experience real magic it is necessary to make a dramatic shift from outcome to purpose. You begin accomplishing this by viewing your presence here from a new perspective. Give this new way of thinking about yourself a brief try and see if it makes sense and feels right. If you feel this is absurd and not something that works for you, go back to outcome or learning via suffering.

GETTING TO PURPOSE

Here is one way to begin the process of getting to purpose. First think about the concept of eternity. Admittedly this is a mind-boggling notion, but just consider what eternity means. No beginning, no end, just like the concept of God or nature or the universe. Only always. As you contemplate this business of eternity, keep in mind that you are doing so from within a physical form, your body, that did begin and will end. This physical self can *consider* a concept that defies beginnings and ends but cannot *experience* it directly. This must be left to your mind. Still, the concept of eternity is something that you can accept. You know the universe doesn't end at any particular place. You know that there was something called life that existed before your conception. If you can consider eternity from within your noneternal body, it must be due to something within your nonphysical self.

Try thinking of your life as a parenthesis in eternity. The parenthesis opens at the moment of your conception and closes at the instant of your death. The space within this parenthesis is your life, surrounded by something called eternity. That something which we label eternity is not experienced physically, yet it exists in some mysterious way within the mind. There is something that is very much a part of us that is invisible. Call it mind, thoughts, consciousness, soul, even Louise if you like. How you spell it doesn't matter. The invisible self, the part that is not your physical sensory self, is the part that can contemplate eternity. If you even mildly accept the notion of eternity, then it is real for you. If you can live with the idea of eternity, then the idea is yours to explore. And if you are at the point where you can consider eternity or endlessness as, at the very least, a curiosity, then you can use this curiosity to help get your life on purpose. Here is how.

First remind yourself that everything exists for some reason as a part of the perfect intelligence that is the universe. Next, in your mind, right here and now, whatever age you are, think back ten years and imagine yourself at that age. Examine what you thought about at that time, how you dressed, what you felt, whom you admired. How much of what you experienced then led you to where you are today? Now, go back ten more years in your mind and see how each and every experience and learning led you to the next place and the next place, until you again arrive at today.

If you are candid, you will discover that each experience in your life was absolutely necessary in order to have gotten you to the next place, and the next, up until this very moment. This mental exercise is very useful in developing your ability to contemplate and meditate. Ultimately you can go back to being a child again in your mind. You will see that the childhood experiences, whatever they were, helped that little person you were to become a bigger person and eventually the adult that you are today. I am not asking you to judge, to like or dislike, to approve or disapprove. Simply see that each experience led to the next and offered you something to either grow on or not grow on. You had to have those experiences, and the evidence for that point of view is that you did. Pure and simple. You did! Then you moved to the next experience and the next, all intertwined in some invisible way, and all leading to now. You may have been at suffering, you may have been at outcome, but you still had those experiences, and nothing can ever change that.

As you go backward in your mind to your childhood, from the perspective of the present moment, and earnestly look at all of your life experiences, the good and the bad, the terrible and the ecstatic, you begin to know right in this moment that there is some kind of invisible force running through your physical life that connects it all together. There is meaning in there someplace, and every single event of your life is in some way related to the next event. There is the person who seemed to come into your life in some coincidental way, who introduced you to someone else, who led you to something that turned your entire life around. You realize that without that coincidental stranger you would not have met your lifetime partner, or created the children that you did, or gone to the school that you went to, or entered the business that became your way of life, or whatever. Little, seemingly unconnected and meaningless events, viewed from the perspective of now, all led you to this very moment reading these words.

As you travel in your mind, you can go all the way back to your infancy, right back to your very beginning. You know in your rational mind that there was an instant, a speck of time, in which you were conceived. Keeping in mind the two essential components of this exercise—that eternity is a concept you can contemplate in a noneternal body and that the universe is purposeful and perfect—mentally contemplate the speck of time immediately preceding your conception when you were still part of eternity, the instant in eternity just before your parenthesis opened. There had to be such an instant when, for whatever reason, you came from what we call nothingness (no boundaries, no rules, no limits, no form) to somethingness. The question I pose to you is "Why?" Why would you go from formlessness to form and show up in this human body to live for a period of time and then go back into eternity, or formlessness?

One could speculate all day on why such a journey is undertaken. Some believe that they made the choice to enter the physical world of limits and boundaries. Others see it as God's will. Still others see it as a monstrous, meaningless accident, simply a cosmic coincidence. But whatever you choose to believe, you know it did happen. I suggest that your presence in the world of form has a grand mission and that you can discover and begin thinking, feeling and behaving in ways consistent with that mission.

I, Wayne W. Dyer, have gone back in my meditations and discovered why I showed up in form, was conceived, back in 1939. It seems very clear to me. I have asked God (or whatever you call that invisible part of ourselves) and I have received answers. I know my grand mission and what it is about for me. I accept that I was born in 1940 to accomplish certain things, and that each and every experience of my life since conception has led me to this purpose. I believe that I had and still have the power to choose to align myself with this perfect order, and that while I was misaligned I was that way for a reason as well.

My purpose has been clearly revealed to me through the process of prayer and meditation. It matters not at all to me how others view my behavior in getting to purpose in my life. The knowing that I have has been revealed to me in the clearest and most profound manner. My purpose is to give, to serve, to promote peace and prosperity and to become totally, unconditionally loving to all people. Willa Cather summarizes what I am writing about:

Where there is great love there are always miracles. Miracles rest not so much upon faces or voices or healing power coming to us from afar off, but on our perceptions being made finer, so that for a moment our eyes can see and our ears can hear what is there about us always.

Yes, something is there about us always.

Getting to purpose in life—by going within and discovering that purpose is about loving unconditionally and serving, and making contact with what is there about us always—alters one's worldview dramatically. Miracle making is then just around the corner. Suffering decreases measurably because the emphasis ceases to be "Why me?" You know that what you are experiencing is necessary and valuable in a way that you likely do not understand at the time it is happening. Nevertheless you still go with it. If I could define enlightenment briefly I would say it is "the quiet acceptance of what is." No judgment, no anger or bitterness, no hostility or remorse but a quiet willingness to go with it rather than to fight it.

When you go beyond outcome in life you find yourself unconcerned about what is in it for you. Thoughts, feelings and behavior focus more and more on the fulfillment of your purpose. You go beyond success, achievement and performance as indications of your life's mission. Instead every moment is lived fully and lovingly. Material possessions cease to dominate your thoughts, which is not to say that they disappear. They simply cease to be the focus of life. Instead, your purpose takes hold, and you gain a sense of joy and inner harmony knowing that you are divinely fulfilling your reason for being here. As Michel de Montaigne put it so succinctly: "The great and glorious masterpiece of man is how to live with purpose."

There is an enormous irony that comes with reaching purpose in your life. The things that you previously believed to be so significant lose their allure. You no longer care about what is coming your way, yet lo and behold you find that those very things arrive in your life in larger and larger amounts. Joy, however, is not found in the arrival of those "rewards" but in the experience of thinking and acting purposefully. Giving becomes more important than getting because giving is in alignment with your purpose. You no longer want the burden of collecting, categorizing, insuring and worrying about possessions. You know the meaning of Satya Sai Baba's pronouncement, "Man's many desires are like the small metal coins he carries about in his pocket. The more he has, the more they weigh him down." You absolutely know when you have reached purpose. No one has to tell you. You know because you no longer question the meaning of your life. You know that all that you do is synchronized with God's work, because you are at harmony and every single activity of your life is involved in the fulfillment of your purpose.

Are you willing to get your life to purpose? Are you prepared to go back in your mind to the moment before you came into form to ask your higher self, "Why did I come here?" When you receive the answer, which will be about giving rather than receiving, regardless of your vocation, you will automatically begin to shift your life energy from suffering to purpose. Once you begin the journey toward a life on purpose, you enter the realm of real magic.

REAL MAGIC, MIRACLES AND PURPOSE

When you are at purpose you are truly flowing with life, experiencing a kind of harmony that comes from not having to strive for something else. In short, you lighten up, figuratively and literally. This comes from the new knowing that enables you to go about your life's work free of worrisome thoughts. You sense that you are being watched over, and your actions come from this inner beatitude of rightness or centeredness. When you are acting out of that inner knowing which constantly reminds you that you are on purpose and that you trust yourself to act out of that purpose, the right thing is all that you can do.

The holiest book of the Hindu faith is called the Bhagavad Gita (the Song of the Lord). It is the story of Arjuna, the most renowned warrior of his time, and Krishna (God), who appears to Arjuna on the battlefield as Arjuna prepares to do battle. Krishna appears in the physical form of Arjuna's charioteer. In eighteen short chapters Krishna talks with Arjuna about the essence of being a divine and purposeful human being. This is the book on which Mahatma Gandhi modeled his life. Summarized briefly the Gita's message is: Behave in ways consistent with love and harmony and do not be attached in any way to the fruits of your labor. If you can attain this state of grace your life will become miraculously peaceful. Live your life entirely on purpose and renounce any and all credit that may come your way from your actions. Be consistently aware of the need to serve God and to serve others in any and all of your actions. This is the way of the miracle worker.

You may be thinking that this is a nice philosophy but one that is too simplistic in the dog-eat-dog, competitive world of the twentieth century. I acknowledge and respect your reservations. In fact, I lived with similar skepticism for the larger portion of my life. I had to go through suffering in order to learn life's lessons; I was totally focused on outcomes and was not a believer in matters metaphysical, nor was I interested in hearing about being detached from the results of my labors. I was in it for the results. I was focused on my destination, not the journey. The issues of my life concerned rewards, money, prestige and accomplishments. While I was certainly a "success" in conventional ways, I had no idea about going beyond these extreme indices, or about real magic. I can only say that miracles and real magic began to show up in my life when I got myself to purpose. Only when I stopped being concerned about what was coming to me was I able to be in a state of grace.

Here is a portion of a letter I received recently from a reader in Goodlettsville, Tennessee, that describes the experience of readiness to discover one's life purpose.

Dear Wayne:

As I sit by the fire in my den, my favorite room, I feel so peaceful. All the usual things are happening. Nine P.M., three children going off to bed, my husband packing his bags for this Phoenix trip, etc.

I sit here in the same room, the same clothes. I know I look the same and yet I am not the same person. I walk in the park across from my home every day and I listen to your tapes on my Walkman. This is "my time," no phones, no children, no noise, only your voice in my ears and the beautiful park I have come to love so much. I wonder why I didn't hear you ten years ago, or five years ago when I was so unhappy. I realized that I wouldn't have listened then, not like I am listening now. Now is my time to hear your message. Now I am truly listening and I love what I hear. Tomorrow I will walk again and probably finish hearing *The Awakened Life*. I can just walk and walk and walk while listening to you. It's so peaceful. Thank you from the bottom of my heart. My life is now a miracle unfolding everyday. I am on purpose.

For this woman, her life is a miracle yet nothing outside has changed. The children, the chores, the job are all still there, but she feels purposeful now and is unconcerned about what the outcomes are going to be. This is the state I am hoping to help you to achieve.

Yes you can create miraculous changes in your life. Yes you have the power within you to manifest what may have seemed impossible only a short time ago. Yes you can know the meaning of real magic in your life. The setting for making this your reality is right there inside you. Get yourself aligned with your purpose. Discover the joy and peace of giving, not getting; of contributing, not acquiring; of doing, not competing or winning. Why? Because you can't really get anything. The message of your life is in what you give. You show up with nothing. You leave with nothing. All you truly can do with this life in form is to give it away. Purpose is always about giving. When you experience giving, serving, loving and promoting harmony you will feel the difference within yourself. André Gide summed it up so beautifully in his journal: "Complete possession is proved only by giving. All you are unable to give possesses you."

As you prepare for this exploration of real magic, you may be asking, "How will I do it?" "What if I need help?" These are sensible questions to which I want to help you find your answers.

WHEN THE STUDENT IS READY

The first time I read the Bhagavad Gita it was as if a lightning bolt had illuminated my life. I had a similar experience when I read St. Paul's letters in the New Testament. Both of these wise and ancient works had been part of my library for over thirty years. I must have passed by them hundreds of thousands of times and probably had glanced through them as a young boy and a college student. Yet they had no meaning for me until I was ready, when they guided me to miraculous discoveries and helped me to get my life on purpose.

An ancient Zen proverb says, "When the student is ready the teacher will appear." When you are truly determined in your own mind to experience real magic and to live each day at purpose, you will be shown how to make it happen. Let's examine the four key words in this Zen proverb.

Student. Be a student. Stay open and willing to learn from everyone and anyone. Being a student means you have room for new input. When you are green you grow, when you are ripe you rot. By staying green you will avoid the curse of being an expert. When you know in your heart that every single person you encounter in your lifetime has something to teach you, you are able to utilize their offerings in a profound way. The ability to create real magic involves first of all being a student of life.

Ready. Be a willing student. Your level of readiness to grow and become your own miracle worker is simply a state of mind. As a student you know that everyone and everything is in some way your teacher. As a student who is ready, you are eager for what it is that everyone and everything has to offer you. The "wrong turn" leading to a new and unexpected place is an opportunity to grow. When you are a student who is ready, the stranger who talks to you about how he overcame his addiction years ago becomes a guide sent to you to help you cope with your own personal addiction.

When I was ready to leave alcohol behind me, truly ready, the teacher appeared for me in a meditation with these words, "You don't have to look any further. Do it now, you'll have all the help you are ready to receive." I had heard such words thousands of times, but my lack of readiness always interfered. This time, I was ready, and I was able to walk away from alcohol and never look back. Almost every magazine article I read in the next few days seemed to describe people finding the courage to leave alcohol and drugs behind them. Perhaps those same personal stories had always been there, but it wasn't until I was truly ready that they served as powerful reminders.

Ready means willing. Genuinely, authentically willing. When you are this ready, you will discover your own personal teacher.

Teacher. The teacher is everywhere. The assistance you need will be provided by the universe as soon as you convert your readiness to willingness. Once you are willing you will find teachers in every niche of your life.

The teacher might well be an experienced soul who is ready to assist and guide you to the miracles you seek. That person showing up in your life now, at the very time you are ready, might be construed as an accident or a divine break on your part. But that wise soul, in one way or another, has always been available to you. Your willingness makes the teacher able to assist you.

Teachers appear in various forms. Your teacher might be a tape that someone "accidentally" leaves in your car and that you "accidentally" play at just the right time. Last week you might have played it for two minutes and rejected the contents; now your willingness allows your teacher to be there for you. Your teacher might be a book or an article that a friend recommends. It might be your unplanned attendance at a lecture or a church service to which someone gave you their ticket because he or she had to be out of town; the message of the speaker seems to be directed specifically at you. Your teacher might be a child who takes you by the hand and asks you a question that you hadn't considered before, and your answer to the child is your answer to yourself. Your teacher might be invisible and show up as a thought that comes over you in a quiet, contemplative moment and encourages you to go in a certain direction now.

Hundreds of times people have come up to me after speaking engagements and told me how they "accidentally" showed up at one particular event or another and heard exactly what they needed at that time. For example, one woman was listening to a tape of mine while driving home. On the tape I was talking about the subject of "when the student is ready the teacher will appear." Suddenly, as she was driving by the Unity Church where I was to speak, she saw my name on the marquee advertising my appearance there that evening at 7:00. The time was 6:45. She pulled into the parking lot, purchased a ticket and attended the event. At the conclusion of the presentation she was shaking as she approached me on stage to tell me of this incident. "I've never driven home this way before, ever. I was driving my girlfriend's car and she happened to have your tape in her tape deck, so it was playing when I started the car. I've been thinking so hard about making some domestic changes in my life and after hearing you tonight I know that you showed up here in Chicago just so that I could hear you. I was ready and I was sent directly to hear you tonight."

This kind of story has been repeated to me hundreds if not thousands of times. "I needed to hear you today, and I know you came just for me." Yet I've been giving public seminars throughout the country for twenty years in virtually every major city over and over again. These people have seen the advertisements in the past, but their lack of readiness kept the teacher from appearing even though the teacher may have appeared right next door.

When you, the student, are ready and willing, the teacher will show up. You simply have to look around, open your new eyes and silently ask yourself, "Who is my teacher?"

Appear. The teacher is making an appearance in everything and everyone you encounter. As we've discussed, there really are no accidents. The universe is on purpose. When the teacher was there and you ignored that teacher, that was part of the perfection at that particular moment. The teacher, although there before you, wasn't there *for* you. That was then and this is now. Today, as you are getting your life to purpose and gaining the ability to make miracles show up in your life, you will recognize the teacher.

When the wounded, dying insect becomes your reminder of the need to be compassionate, the teacher has appeared. When the homeless person with his soiled presence and out-stretched hand reminds you of your need to be merciful, the teacher has appeared. When the soldier loaded down with his instruments of death and ready to kill his assigned enemy reminds you of your need to send love and peace where it is most difficult, again, the teacher has appeared.

As you ask the question, "How will the teacher appear?" meditate on James Broughton's little ditty and you will have your answer:

This is It
and I am It
and you are It
And so is That
and he is It
and she is It
and it is It
and that is That

And that is that! The appearance of the teacher is everywhere, and without the teacher you will find yourself floundering.

Truly, no man is an island. We are all connected and we all learn and grow in this journey together. You will have all the help you need as you prepare yourself for miracle making and real magic.

You have now examined the idea of getting your life to

purpose and setting yourself up for the assistance you will need in this endeavor. Yet the major premise of this book is that there is a realm of human existence that transcends what we have come to view as normal or possible. I am calling this dimension *real magic*. Once you genuinely feel yourself open enough to experience your own purpose for being here, and you have opened yourself up to receiving whatever divine assistance you may require by being a willing student, you will be ready to believe in your own capacity for becoming your very own miracle worker.

BELIEVING IN MIRACLES AND REAL MAGIC

When I write about the world of real magic and miracles I am not referring to developing a talent for turning rocks into gold, raising the dead or commanding the seas to part. When I speak of miracle making I am discussing whatever you have considered beyond your ability to create for yourself because of limitations you believe you have. In later chapters I will describe the major areas of life where real magic is available. For now, I want you to cultivate the foundation for creating real magic in any area that you would like. If you have lived your life believing that certain accomplishments or levels of achievement were impossible for you, then first you must begin by examining your life focus and beliefs before attempting to implement any real magic strategies.

Getting your life to purpose and creating an openness to being assisted are crucial to becoming your own miracle worker. Beyond these qualities of purposefulness and openness there are guidelines for putting yourself in the proper mental framework. These beliefs, or "knowings," are necessary to help you go within and literally manifest what you have previously believed impossible. I will be alluding to these "knowings" throughout the pages of this book.

In my own life, I have had to travel through a sequence of steps, all within my mind, in order to be at the point where I can write that I feel confident in my ability to manifest what I can only call miracles. I call them miracles because only a short time ago, before I experienced this inner awakening, the things that I can now create and manifest seemed to be impossibilities. I offer these sequential steps believing that if it is possible for me, it is certainly possible for anyone else.

I am reminded of the words of Christ on his own miracle making: "He that believeth in me, the works that I do shall he do also; and greater works than these shall he do. . . ." Somewhere deep within you, you know that you have this kind of power. Even though you may not have an inkling of how to use it, or how to begin to tap into it, you still know that within each of us is a divine, invisible presence that has something to do with creating a state that can only be described paradoxically as real magic.

Christ went on to say, ". . . But ye shall know him; for he dwelleth with you, and shall be in you." That's correct, *in you* is that magic invisible presence that I am writing about here. It is not something outside of you requiring a lifelong search to attain. It dwells within you, in that invisible part of yourself, where the rules that pertain to the physical world simply do not apply. In your soul, your spirit or higher self, your mind or thoughts or whatever you choose to call it, lies that entryway to the world of real magic.

When you master the inner path of awareness presented in Part 1 of this book, you will not greet the application of this awareness with any skepticism, nor will you doubt that I am talking through that divine inner presence directly and unequivocally to you.

SEVEN BELIEFS FOR MANIFESTING
REAL MAGIC

I have identified seven beliefs, or knowings, that can help you tap the power of real magic. They are presented sequentially and once you find yourself with the internal knowing that comes from adopting these beliefs, you will be on your way to becoming your own miracle worker.

1. *There is an invisible but knowable life force within you.* Try cultivating an awareness of the invisible life force that suffuses all form in the universe, including your physical body. This is the same universal intelligence that directs a rose to be a rose, a beetle to be a beetle, the planets to align and move through space, and you to be you. It is without boundaries or dimensions in the same way that your thoughts, feelings, imaginings, dreams, fantasies and emotions are. This universal life force that is a part of you cannot die. Death implies an ending, and ending implies boundaries. For this first step, just know that this powerful, divine but invisible force is within you. Trust totally that it is there. It is in fact what allows you to perceive and experience your physical body and this physical world in which you find yourself temporarily housed.

2. *Your thoughts are something that you control and they originate with you.* In *You'll See It When You Believe It*, I wrote an entire section on the power of thoughts. Here I simply encourage you to realize that thinking is our way of processing and recording our human experience. Thought originates from within a nothingness inside of you and gives you your humanity. All of your past is in this realm of thought, as is your future. Your thoughts create your experience of your health, wealth and every detail of your world.

Ralph Waldo Emerson reminded us that "the ancestor to every action is a thought." You live the life you imagine you are living. When you stop imagining or imaging or thinking, you cease actively participating in your physical world. As a step toward the awakened life of real magic, you must consider how your thoughts have contributed to a nonmiraculous, limiting approach to life. Then you will know that you can also produce the opposite. If, in fact, miracles are available for anyone, you can be one of those people who experience them. But they begin in that ancestor to all of your actions, your thoughts.

3. *There are no limits.* All of the things that you have become convinced are limits are products of the way in which you have learned to think. You probably were taught that logic and scientific verification dictate what is possible and what is not. Before the invention of the microscope most people did not believe in the existence of microscopic life. People who believe only what they can see or prove scientifically are limited by the current level of sophistication of our measuring devices.

You know that at some future time we'll be flying from place to place on this planet in moments rather than in hours, and interplanetary travel will be a fact of life. The capability to do so is already here. That is, the universal force that is timeless already exists, only the technology is missing. Do you believe in this possibility now, or must you wait until the technology arrives before you can believe it? Only twenty years ago the idea of a remote control that would allow you to switch television stations was an impossibility. Renting a movie was unthinkable. Microwaving meals in a few moments at home was not at all a part of our consciousness. Although the capacity to create these miracles was available even at the time of Hannibal, the devices came along at their own pace. Be a person who accepts no limits in your mind. None!

4. *Your life has a purpose.* The entire universe is an intelligent system. The universe that is your physical body is a multitude of systems all functioning with amazing perfection, and it too is an intelligent system. The invisible parts of you, your thoughts and feelings, are also part of the system that is you. That intelligence is invisible and can be described or spelled in any way that you choose; thousands of terms have been invented to describe it. But the intelligence is not the label, just as the statue is not the saint and the menu is not the meal. You are that intelligence from which you can never separate yourself, and you have a purpose.

I have explained the necessity of getting your life to purpose and about getting yourself on that purposeful path. What I ask of you here is to simply know it. Know you have a purpose and you will be on your way to creating magical life in any and all areas of your choosing.

5. *You overcome weaknesses by leaving them behind.* You cannot outthink your weaknesses and limitations. You will not get yourself to the place of inner harmony necessary to create real magic by working hard to overcome your old self-defeating behaviors. What you can learn to do is leave that stage of your life behind you and walk through the gate into a new way of being.

This process of leaving behind old habits begins in your invisible dimension—that is, your thoughts. You see yourself truly letting go of the obstacles that you've chosen for a lifetime, you picture yourself no longer needing to rely on those self-defeating patterns. Then, the thinking part is complete. Now you move forward to a new you. When you leave behind the belief that you cannot change, or that you cannot create the miracle you want for yourself, you will leave behind the physical activity that has supported that belief. Picture it behind you, look back at it and know that you no longer live that way.

I can see myself at a distant time actually behaving in those old ways. And I smile inwardly, knowing that I have left that part of me behind. It started with a thought and then an action based on the new thought, and for me this is a miracle that I now live every day. I did it not by constantly trying to outthink the problem or by gradually sneaking up on it but by leaving it behind me. This is in fact the way all miraculous changes are made, when it gets right down to "How do I change?" or "How do I create the miracle that I want my life to be?"

After all the talking, counseling, support groups, medicines, elixirs, pep talks and proddings by others, one must ultimately leave behind that which is self-destructive or functioning as an obstacle to growth. Every single person who has ever overcome any difficulty or brought about positive change in their lives, when faced with the bottom line, has had to leave behind the old habit through their own will. Know this to be a truth and you'll soon see yourself creating real magic in your life.

6. *When you examine what you believe to be impossible, you can then change your beliefs.* Take an inventory of what it is that you believe cannot happen in your life. Whether it is related to your physical accomplishments, relationships, health or finances, vow, at the very minimum, to rid yourself of these beliefs. I am not asking that you fool yourself or engage in self-deception. I am asking you to create an openness to the possibility rather than continuing to subscribe to the impossibility. That's all. Just an openness to a new idea. And remember, you do not have to do anything

different in your life at this moment, only change around some mental images. New thoughts will ultimately lead you to new and miraculous behaviors.

If anyone has ever overcome a diagnosis of "terminal," then know that such a capacity exists within all of us. The universal force or energy that once created a miracle is still present. The force itself has not disappeared, even if the miracles themselves have. Stuart Wilde writes in *Miracles*, "Because the universal law is indestructible and therefore infinite, we can presume that whatever power was used by miracle workers in the past must still be available today." And if it is still available, I am asking you to believe that it is there for you to tap into. This universal law that created miracles has not been repealed, and never will be.

This entire book is about helping you align yourself in such a way that this universal force or energy is something that you can know intimately, and use in your life, even if no one else around you knows what you are doing or believes in what you are talking about when you speak of miracles. Once you know and choose to use this force, your life will take on the flavor of real magic. I guarantee it.

At this point I am not asking you to begin performing miracles. I am asking you to simply open yourself to a new inner belief system that says maybe, just maybe, this is a possibility for me. Everyone who has ever come from dirt-poor origins to create abundance for themselves (including myself) has had to use the universal energy within their minds before it could happen in the physical world. If that miracle-making power was available to any impoverished soul, it is available to your impoverished soul should you decide that this is your truth.

Know that if anyone has gone from sickness to health, fat to slim, addiction to choice, poor to rich, clumsy to agile, miserable to happy, or discontentment to fulfillment, then that capacity is part of the universal human condition. Even if only one person has ever accomplished it, then it is indeed possible. And, even if it has never been before— such as a cure for polio prior to 1954, or an airplane ride in 1745—the fact that one unique individual is capable of conceiving it in his or her mind is all that is required for humankind to be open to the possibility. Replace the belief that something you are capable of imagining in your mind is impossible with the belief that it is possible. Go to work on that thought right now, in this moment, which is the only physical reality you have.

7. *You can go beyond logic.* Although you may not be completely comfortable relying on something other than logic and rational thinking, try to let in the idea that there is another dimension that is very much a part of you, which has nothing to do with logic or scientific validation. You have never seen, touched, smelled or physically felt a thought or a dream or a feeling, yet you know they exist. There is no rational proof for the existence of intuition, yet you know that it exists within you. Until a few years ago there was no physical proof for the presence of microscopic life, yet it existed. And so it is with a portion of your humanity that I call your soul. While we haven't come up with a "soulscope" to rationally prove its existence, we have, nevertheless, an inkling that such a dimension persists as part of our humanness. There are some who will never believe it unless they see it. Others will see it because they believe it.

These are the seven beliefs you can use as mental steps to setting your internal gyroscope for real magic. There are some who live their entire lives content with the limitations of their five senses. Real magic and miracle making are not on their life agenda. For others, like you and me, while we know the physical part of us to be a beautiful miracle in and of itself, we also know there is a spiritual dimension, beyond the scope and boundaries of our physical universe. The differences between these two awarenesses—physical only versus spiritual *and* physical—are many. The next chapter will describe in more detail what these specific differences are and how the benefits of real magic and miracle making become available by shifting your consciousness to include your spiritual side.

2

BECOMING A SPIRITUAL BEING

We are born into the world of nature; our second
birth is into the world of spirit.

— BHAGAVAD GITA

Few of us have been trained to tap into the power of our
minds. We have been raised on a steady diet of logic,
rationality and a "believe it when you see it" mentality. In
short, we have been brought up to believe only in those
things that we can understand and verify. Miracles cannot be
understood by the rational mind. They defy logic. They cannot be "understood" in the ways we have been conditioned to
think. Therefore, in order to enter the world of real magic you
will need to learn how to go way beyond your rational mind
and enter the dimension of spirituality.

MOVING PAST SKEPTICISM

Any minimal spiritual training you have received has likely
come through the medium of some religious organization.
The wonderful gift of religion is the teaching that we are spir-

itual in nature, and that we all have a soul as part of our humanity. The major drawback of religion is that it teaches that the soul must conform to rules and regulations, and that these restrictions of the soul come directly from the dogma of a particular religion and its representatives. But the soul does not conform to any of the boundaries or laws that have been assigned to it. It is dimensionless, formless and invisible. Even writing about it is very difficult because sentences must come to an end, while the soul is endless.

Because of your formal training you have very likely adopted a skeptical attitude toward spirituality. In order to participate in the high drama of miracle making and real magic, you must believe in your spiritual self, which has absolutely nothing to do with your religious affiliation. Whatever you choose to call that higher intelligence that suffuses your form, whatever the name of your spiritual teacher, it is inconsequential to your miracle-making potential. I am simply encouraging you to develop an authentic knowing about this part of your humanity. Maurice Nicoll wrote in *Living Time* these words, which I find most appropriate on this matter:

> We do not grasp that we are invisible. . . . We do not understand that life, before all definitions of it, is a drama of the visible and invisible. We think that only the visible world has reality and structure and do not conceive the possibility that the inner world we know as thought, feeling and imagination, may have a real structure and exist in its own space, although not the space that we are in touch with through our sense organs.

To develop the knowing within you of the truth in Nicoll's words, you have much to overcome. You will be asked to believe in the unknowable, something that you've been taught not to do. But it is always there, as H. L. Mencken put it so deliciously: "Penetrating so many secrets, we cease to believe in the unknowable. But there it sits nevertheless, calmly licking its chops." Indeed, it is right there and yet you cannot put your fingers on it for even an instant. Becoming a spiritual being involves forgetting about your five senses, including that finger that you cannot place, and developing a calm sense of trust in that which you know suffuses you but which you can never prove with logic or our current measuring devices.

Once you have the experience of this invisible dimension—and you know this higher place you can go to within your mind, and receive guidance and, yes, even the help in creating real magic for yourself—you will have shifted from being an exclusively physical person, a human being having a spiritual experience, to a spiritual being having a human experience. Certainly you will not deny your physical self in any way. In fact, your shift to becoming a spiritual being will magnify and enhance your physical life in a multitude of ways. The place for creating real magic will be in your spiritual awakening, yet it will be manifested here and now in this physical world where you find yourself every day.

You want your enhanced miracle-making ability to appear in the reality that you call your physical life. When this special knowing becomes real for you and is something that you can turn to and trust within yourself, it is like being so wealthy that, regardless of what you do, you'll always have money. You will be comforted in knowing that you can never lose your spiritual contact once you have it, and know that it is always a part of you.

While I am asking you to accept this invisible world that you know exists but, as Nicoll stated, you cannot point to with your senses, there are many respected people in our scientific community hard at work attempting to prove scientifically the existence of the soul. Though it is not my purpose here to prove or disprove anything in the scientific sense, a few words about these studies will help you to get moving in the direction of becoming first a spiritual being and then a physical being that is a result of your spirituality.

In the fascinating book *Recovering the Soul*, Larry Dossey, M.D., presents a comprehensive picture of the evidence supporting a nonlocal theory of the human mind. The theory states that the human mind is not restricted to a body or a brain, but somehow exists in time and space in concert with the physical body. This nonlocal view of the mind opens up enormous possibilities. As Dr. Dossey puts it:

> Suppose for the moment that we could show that the human mind is nonlocal; that it is ultimately independent of the physical brain and body, and that as a correlate it transcends time and space. This I believe would rank in importance far beyond anything ever discovered, past or present, about the human organism. This discovery would strike a chord of hope about our inner nature that has been silenced in an age of science; it would stir a new vision of the human as triumphant over flesh and blood. It would anchor the human spirit once again on the side of God instead of randomness, chance and decay. It would spur the human will to greatness instead of expediency and self service. . . . And once again we might recover something that has been notably absent in our experience of late: the human soul.

This idea that the soul is timeless and nonlocal is indeed fascinating. It is being investigated by scientists in various specialties, and I am certain we will soon have incontrovertible evidence of this nonlocal position. Imagine the difference such a piece of evidence would provide for us as human beings. Knowing that the soul survives death of the physical body will help us to rearrange our ways of dealing with each other while we are here on earth. It will drastically affect our medical practices. As Dr. Dossey points out:

> No longer would it be the ultimate goal of the modern healer to forestall death and decay, for these would lose their absolute status if the mind were ultimately transcendent over the physical body. . . . And if humanity really believed that nonlocal mind were real, an entirely new foundation for ethical and moral behavior would enter, which would hold at least the possibility of a radical departure from the insane ways human beings and nation-states have chronically behaved toward each other, and further, the entire existential premise of human life might shift toward the moral and the ethical, toward the spiritual and the holy.

It is within this context that I ask you to look carefully at becoming your own spiritual being, for it is within this context that all miracle making and real magic will be experienced. And once you have developed the inner knowing of your spiritual, nonlocal self, all of the external scientific data becomes meaningless. But, to help you suspending your disbelief, here are a few opinions from contemporary scientific thinkers on this subject.

Robert Herrman—scientist, executive director of American Scientific Affiliation and author of *The God Who Would Be Known*—puts it this way: "Everywhere you look in science, the harder it becomes to understand the universe without God."

When pressed to define God, theologians and scientists find themselves in rare agreement. They know that in a physical world of cause and effect, somehow the whole thing had to get rolling. They also know that some kind of invisible force holds the whole thing together, including all matter. Rather than viewing God as a deity off in the sky somewhere, they see God as a presence pervading the universe. Hence the biblical notion of "in him we live and move and have our being."

For the scientific community, who live and feast on hard evidence, there is much disagreement on this entire business of the soul and God as a presence in all life. Yet scientists know that something exists in all life that defies logic. A heart begins beating within a mother's womb six or seven weeks after conception and the entire process is one gigantic mystery to even our most sophisticated scientific minds. Forty years ago the answer to the question "Do you believe in God?" was most commonly answered with, "Of course not, I'm a scientist." Today, more and more, the scientist's answer to the same question is, "Of course, I'm a scientist."

Those in the new physics of quantum mechanics are only beginning to prove what metaphysics (beyond physics) has indicated for centuries. We are all connected, there is an invisible force in the universe that pervades all life. Even more astonishing, as reported by John Gliedman in *Scientific Digest* a decade ago (July 1982), is that "several leading theorists have arrived at the same startling conclusions: their work suggests a hidden spiritual world, within all of us." Gliedman sardonically called it "the ghost in the machine." It is this apparition within all of us—this dimension of our humanity that defies measurement, rules and cause and effect—that continues to baffle scientists. Yet even many of their own are now concluding that the "soul"—that "ghost in the machine"—exists. Gliedman's article, titled "Scientists in Search of the Soul," quotes many of the most respected and distinguished scientists from all over the globe. Some conclude that our nonmaterial (invisible) self is what constitutes our human traits of conscious self-awareness, free will, personal identity, creativity and emotions. They contend that the invisible presence exerts a physical influence on us and, even more astounding, that this nonmaterial self survives the death of the physical brain.

Another intriguing notion comes from John von Neumann, a mathematician and scientist described by Nobel laureate Hans Bethe as perhaps "the smartest man who ever lived." Bethe once remarked, "I have sometimes wondered whether a brain like John von Neumann's does not indicate a species superior to that of man." And what were von Neumann's conclusions? "That physical reality was a figment of the human imagination and that the only true reality was thought." Eugene Wigner, winner of the 1963 Nobel Prize in physics who studied von Neumann's formulations, stated publicly, "Man may have a nonmaterial consciousness capable of influencing matter."

To put it in my own non-Nobel-laureate language: You have the capacity to create miracles and live a life of real magic, by using your invisible self to influence your physical reality. When you truly become a spiritual being first and a physical being second, and know how to live and breathe in this new alignment, you will become your own miracle worker.

In all fairness, Gliedman also writes at length about the many distinguished scientists who take the contrary position that we have no proof of the existence of the soul. We can recognize these people as members of the same fraternity who throughout recorded history have declared that we have no proof—and thus microscopic life does not exist, flying machines are impossible and the earth is not round. For me, the existence of the soul does not need any scientific validation. I know what I know about myself and my proof is in my own experience. The metaphysicians and the poets have expressed truth for me that is particularly relevant on this matter of the existence of the soul. Listen to William Blake's *Auguries of Innocence*:

To see a World in a grain of sand,
And a Heaven in a wild flower,
Hold Infinity in the palm of your hand,
And Eternity in an hour. . . .
We are led to believe a lie
When we see with, not thro' the eye,
Which was born in a night, to perish in a night,
When the Soul slept in beams of light.

How magnificent a vision! Holding infinity in the palm of your hand. Indeed we are led to the big lie—that we are just these aging bodies. Instead, Blake reminds us that our soul, our spiritual being, does not die nor is it born, but is eternal and formless as a beam of light.

Keep uppermost in your mind that becoming a spiritual being involves being able to touch your invisible self and know that it is the secret to your ultimate ability to become a miracle maker. That inner formless self is your imagination. Albert Einstein, who combined the qualities of both poet and scientist, summed it all up nicely: "Imagination is more important than knowledge." When you examine the lives of the most influential people who have ever walked among us, you discover one thread that winds through them all. They have been aligned first with their spiritual nature and only then with their physical selves.

OUR GREATEST TEACHERS

Without exception all of our greatest teachers, and those who have made the greatest impact on humanity, have been spiritual beings. They did not limit themselves to the five senses in any way. All of the great teachers and doctrines, including Christianity, Buddhism, Judaism, Islam, Sufism and Confucianism, have left us with a similar message. Go within, discover your invisible higher self, know God as the love that is within you.

These spiritual masters were all miracle makers. They were here to teach us about the incredible power that resides within each of us. It seems ironic that as a people we have been obsessed with what divides us, with war and the building of more and more powerful delivery systems of hatred and killing, yet the most influential and revered of the world's teachings all have a message of love. For example:

Christianity: God is love, and he who abides in love abides in God, and God abides in him.

Buddhism: He that loveth not, knoweth not God. For God is love.

Judaism: Love is the beginning and end of the Torah.

Confucianism: Love belongs to the high nobility of Heaven, and is the quiet home where man should dwell.

Sufism: Sane and insane, all are searching lovelorn For Him, in mosque, temple, church alike. For only God is the One God of Love, And Love calls from all these, each one His home.

Becoming a spiritual being is synonymous with becoming a miracle worker and knowing the bliss of real magic. The differences between people who are nonspiritual, or "physical only," beings and those whom I call spiritual beings are dramatic. Examine the following delineation of how both of these beings live with their invisible selves, their minds. Getting yourself aligned with the thinking of spiritual beings is your task, if you truly want to know this illusive thing that I keep referring to as real magic.

SPIRITUAL VERSUS NONSPIRITUAL BEINGS: THE SPIRITUAL DOZEN

I use the terms *spiritual* and *nonspiritual* in the sense that a spiritual being has a conscious awareness of both the physical and the invisible dimension, while the nonspiritual being is only aware of the physical domain. Neither category, as I use them, implies atheism or religious orientation in any way. The nonspiritual person is not incorrect or bad because he or she experiences the world only in a physical manner.

Below are listed the "spiritual dozen," twelve beliefs and practices for you to cultivate as you develop your abilities to manifest miracles in your life. Becoming a spiritual being as outlined here is an all-out necessity if real magic is your objective in this lifetime.

1. *The nonspiritual being lives exclusively within the five senses, believing that if you cannot see, touch, smell, hear or taste something, then that something simply doesn't exist. The spiritual being knows that, beyond the five physical senses, there are other senses we use to experience the world of form.*

As you work toward becoming a spiritual being as well as a physical being, you begin to live more and more consciously within the invisible realm that I have discussed in this chapter. You begin to know that there are senses beyond this physical world. Even though you cannot perceive it through one of the five senses, you know that you are a soul with a body, and that your soul is beyond limits and defies birth and death. It is not governed by any of the rules and regulations that govern the physical universe. To be a spiritual being means that you allow yourself the option of being multisensory. Hence a whole new world opens up. As Gary Zukav writes in *The Seat of the Soul*, "The experiences of the multi-sensory human are less limited than the experiences of the five-sensory human. They provide more opportunities for growth and development and more opportunities to avoid unnecessary difficulties."

2. *The nonspiritual being believes we are alone in the universe. The spiritual being knows he or she is never alone.*

A spiritual being is comfortable with the idea of having teachers, observers and divine guidance available at any time. If we believe we are souls with bodies rather than bodies with souls, then the invisible, eternal part of ourselves is always available to us for assistance. Once this belief is firm and unshakable it can never be doubted, regardless of the rational arguments of those who live exclusively in the physical world. For some this is called intense prayer, for others it is God, that universal, omnipresent intelligence or force, and for others it is spiritual guidance. It matters not what you call this higher self or how you spell it, since it is beyond definitions, labels and language itself.

For the nonspiritual being this is all hogwash. We show up on Earth, we have one life to live and no one has any ghosts around or within to help out. This is a physical-only universe to the nonspiritual being and the goal is to manipulate and control the physical world. The spiritual being sees the physical world as an arena for growth and learning with the specific purpose of serving and evolving into higher levels of love.

Nonspiritual beings accept the existence of a supreme being or God, not as a universal force that is within us but as a separate power that will someday hold us accountable. They do not see themselves as having assistance or a higher self, unless they have the kind of direct experience of divine presence recorded by St. Paul or St. Francis of Assisi.

Spiritual beings simply know, through their personal

experience of having been in contact with their own divine guidance, that they are not alone, and that they can use that guidance to become miracle makers in their lives.

3. *The nonspiritual being is focused on external power. The spiritual being is focused on personal empowerment.*

External power is located in the dominance of and control over the physical world. This is the power of war and military might, the power of laws and organization, the power of business and stock market games. This is the power of controlling all that is external to the self. The nonspiritual being is focused on this external power.

By contrast, the spiritual being is focused on empowering himself and others to higher and higher levels of consciousness and achievement. The use of force over another is not a possibility for the spiritual being. He or she is not interested in collecting power, but rather in helping others to live in harmony and to experience real magic. This is a power of love that does not judge others. There is no hostility or anger in this kind of power. It is true empowerment to know that one can live in the world with others who have differing points of view and have no need to control or vanquish them as victims. A spiritual being knows the enormous power that comes with the ability to manipulate the physical world with one's mind. A mind at peace, a mind centered and not focused on harming others, is stronger than any physical force in the universe. The entire philosophy of aikido and the Oriental martial arts is based not on external power over the opponent, but on becoming at one with that external energy to remove the threat. Empowerment is the inner joy of knowing that external force is not necessary to be at harmony with oneself.

To the nonspiritual being, no other way is known. One must constantly be ready for war. Even though the spiritual masters to whom they often pledge allegiance speak against such use of power, the nonspiritual being simply cannot see any other alternative.

Authentic empowerment is surrendering to that which is loving, harmonious and good in ourselves, and not allowing for enemies in our consciousness. It is an alignment with the soul that is our very purpose for being here.

Once you no longer need to dominate others, to acquire more possessions or to control the environment around you, you will have shifted your focus from external power to personal empowerment. You will find that being personally empowered does not reduce you to wimphood and being the victim of others in any way. Quite the opposite is true. You will find that you do not even perceive others to be potential victimizers. You will be a defuser of such threats, and in fact will not even encounter such proddings. Moreover, the absence of a need on your part to prove how powerful you are will give you the opportunity to empower others.

When you get to the giving stage, you will be aligned with your purpose and then you will be at the place where you can be a miracle maker. You will ask nothing of others, not because you are proud or omnipotent, but because you are a light unto yourself. This is the way of the spiritual being, and only when you abandon the need for external power and align yourself with your soul's purpose, will you be ready for real magic.

4. *The nonspiritual being feels separated and distinct from all others, a being unto himself. The spiritual being knows that he is connected to all others and lives his life as if each person he meets shares being human with him.*

When a person feels separate from all others he becomes more self-centered and much less concerned about the problems of others. He may feel some sympathy for people starving in another part of the world, but that person's daily approach is, "It's not my problem." The splintered personality, the nonspiritual being, is focused more on his own problems, and often feels that other human beings are either in his way or trying to get what he wants and so he must "do in" the other guy, before he gets done in himself.

The spiritual being knows that we are all connected, and he is able to see the fullness of God in each person with whom he makes contact. This sense of connection eliminates much of the inner conflict that the nonspiritual being experiences as he constantly judges others, categorizes them according to physical appearances and behaviors and then proceeds to find ways to either ignore or take advantage of them for his own benefit. Being connected means that the need for conflict and confrontation is eliminated. Knowing that the same invisible force that flows through himself flows through all others allows the spiritual being to truly live the golden rule. The spiritual being thinks, "How I am treating others is essentially how I am treating myself, and vice versa." The meaning of "love thy neighbor as thyself" is clear to the spiritual being, while it is considered nonsense by the nonspiritual being. Negative judgment is not possible when one feels connected to all others. The spiritual being knows that he cannot define another by his judgments, that he only defines himself as a judgmental person.

Research at the subatomic quantum level reveals an invisible connection between all particles and all members of a given species. This oneness is being demonstrated in remarkable scientific discoveries. The findings show that physical distance, what we think of as empty space, does not preclude a connection by invisible forces. Obviously there exist invisible connections between our thoughts and our actions. We do not deny this, even though the connection is impervious to our senses. The nonspiritual being cannot make such a leap, but the spiritual being *knows* that this invisible force connects him to all others, and therefore treats all others as if they were a part of himself. It is all a question of knowing. The nonspiritual being knows and acts as if he were an island, separate and distinct from others, unconnected. The spiritual being knows the truth of John Donne's famous lines:

> No man is an island, entire of itself; every man is a piece of the continent, a part of the main; if a clod be washed away by the sea, Europe is the less, as well as if a promontory were, as well as if a manor of thy friends or of thine own were; any man's death diminishes me, because I am involved in mankind; and therefore never send to know for whom the bell tolls; it tolls for thee.

There can be no finer description of the spiritual being. He is indeed involved in mankind and lives his life each day in this fashion. Plainly stated, miracles and real magic are simply unavailable to those who believe themselves to be islands in the sea of humanity.

5. *The nonspiritual being believes exclusively in a cause/effect interpretation of life. The spiritual being knows that there is a higher power working in the universe beyond mere cause and effect.*

The nonspiritual being lives exclusively in the physical world, where cause and effect rule. If one plants a seed (cause) he will see the result (effect). If one is hungry, he will seek food. If one is angry he will vent that anger. This is indeed a rational and logical way to think and behave, since the third law of motion—for every action there is an equal and opposite reaction—is always operating in the physical universe.

The spiritual being goes beyond Newton's physics and lives in an entirely different realm. The spiritual being knows that thoughts come out of nothingness, and that in our dream state (one-third of our entire physical lives), where we are in pure thought, cause and effect play no role whatsoever. In the dream state you can be age forty in one moment and age twelve in the next, you can climb into a car and fly over your childhood home. Thoreau summed all of this up nicely with his provocative observation, "I do not know how to distinguish between our waking life and a dream. Are we not always living the life that we imagine we are?"

Thus the spiritual being knows that thoughts are not subject to the laws of classical physics, and that it is with our thoughts that we create our reality. When one lives purely by the laws of cause and effect, one can never expect to create miracles, because miracles and real magic are beyond the logic of physics. It is with the power of our minds that miracles originate, and therefore cause and effect are replaced by a belief in the effects that come out of what we call nothingness or emptiness.

Our thoughts and beliefs are miracles unto themselves, and they are our only tools for processing this physical world. They defy cause/effect logic, since our thoughts come from seemingly nowhere; therefore our miracle-making ability also stems from that divine place of no thing. If you need a cause/effect explanation, then you are unable to enter the world of real magic. Just as all sounds that we make stem from silent emptiness, so too do our thoughts, and our capacity for miracles is thus also a power that comes from within the silent empty space of our true being.

6. *The nonspiritual being is motivated by achievement, performance and acquisitions. The spiritual being is motivated by ethics, serenity and quality of life.*

For the nonspiritual person, the focus is on learning for the purpose of high grades, getting ahead and acquiring possessions. The purpose of athletics is competition. Success is measured in external labels such as position, rank, bank accounts and awards. While these are all very much a part of our culture, and certainly not objects to be scorned, they simply are not the focus of the spiritual being's life.

For the spiritual being, success is achieved by aligning oneself with one's purpose, which is not measured by performance or acquisitions. The spiritual being knows that these external things flow into one's life in sufficient amounts and that they arrive as a result of living purposefully. The spiritual being knows that living purposefully involves serving in a loving fashion. Mother Teresa, who has spent many years of her life caring for the most downtrodden among us in the slums of Calcutta, defined purpose this way in *For the Love of God:*

> The fruit of love is service, which is compassion in action. Religion has nothing to do with compassion, it is our love for God that is the main thing because we have all been created for the sole purpose to love and be loved.

It is in ways such as this that the spiritual being's inner and outer reality is experienced. It is not necessary to become a saint ministering to the impoverished to become a spiritual being. One simply must know that there is much more to life than achievement, performance and acquisitions and that the measure of a life is not in what is accumulated, but rather in what is given to others. The spiritual being knows that he showed up here with nothing material and leaves the same way. All he can do therefore is give of what he has in this metaphysical instant called his life, his parenthesis in eternity. While the spiritual being will achieve and perform at high levels and even acquire

many possessions, the motivation to do so is not the orga-
nizational principle that guides his life. Living ethically,
morally and serenely while being aligned with a spiritual
purpose is at the core of his being. Real magic cannot be
experienced when your focus is on getting more for yourself, particularly if it is at the expense of others. When you
experience a sense of serenity and quality about your life,
knowing your mind is what creates such a state, you will
also know that from such a state of mind flows miracle-
making magic.

7. *The nonspiritual being has no place within his awareness for
the practice of meditation. The spiritual being cannot imagine life
without it.*

For the nonspiritual being the idea of looking quietly
within oneself and sitting alone for any period of time—
repeating a mantra, emptying one's mind and seeking
answers by aligning oneself with one's higher self—borders
on lunacy. For this person, answers are sought by working
hard, struggling, persevering, setting goals, reaching those
goals and setting new ones and competing in a dog-eat-dog
world.

The spiritual being knows about the enormous power of
the practice of meditation. He knows meditation makes
him more alert and able to think more clearly. He knows
the very special effect meditation has in relieving stress and
tension. Spiritual people know, by virtue of having been
there and experienced it firsthand, that one can get divine
guidance by becoming peaceful and quiet and asking for
answers. They know they are multidimensional and that
the invisible mind can be tapped at higher and higher levels through meditation, or whatever you want to call the
practice of being alone and emptying your mind of the fre-
netic thoughts that occupy so much of daily life. They

know that in deep meditation one can leave the body and enter a sphere of magic that is as blissful a state as any drug could temporarily provide.

The great French scientist Blaise Pascal provided us with this insight: "All man's miseries derive from not being able to sit quietly in a room alone." One of the greatest joys of becoming a spiritual being is learning about this whole new phenomenal world. You will actually feel lighter, more blissful and, ironically, more productive than you ever felt before. For the nonspiritual being this is perceived as an escape from reality, but for the spiritual being it is an introduction to a whole new reality, a reality that includes an opening in life that will lead to miracle making. (More on how to meditate and some useful techniques will be found in chapter 3.)

8. *For the nonspiritual being, the concept of intuition can be reduced to a hunch or a haphazard thought that accidentally pops into one's head on occasion. For the spiritual being, intuition is far more than a hunch. It is viewed as guidance or as God talking, and this inner insight is never taken lightly or ignored.*

You know from your own experience that when you ignore your intuitive proddings you end up regretting it or having to learn the hard way. To the nonspiritual person, intuition is completely unpredictable and occurs in random happenstances. It is often ignored or shunned in favor of behaving in habitual ways. The spiritual being strives to increase consciousness concerning his intuition. He pays attention to invisible messages and knows deep within that there is something working that is much more than a coincidence.

Spiritual beings have an awareness of the nonphysical world and are not stuck exclusively in a universe restricted to the functioning of their five senses. Hence all thoughts, invisible though they may be, are something to pay attention to. But intuition is much more than a thought about something, it is almost as if one is receiving a gentle prod to behave in a certain way or to avoid something that might be dangerous or unhealthy. Although inexplicable, our intuition is truly a factor of our lives.

For the nonspiritual person, this seems to be merely a hunch and nothing to study or become more attuned to. The nonspiritual person thinks, "It will pass. It is just my mind at work in its disorderly way." For the spiritual person, these inner intuitive expressions are almost like having a dialogue with God.

I view my intuition about everything and anything as God talking to me. I pay attention when I "feel something" strongly and I always go with that inner inclination. At one time in my life I ignored it, but now I know better and these intuitive feelings always—and I mean always—guide me in a direction of growth and purposefulness. Sometimes my intuition tells me where to go to write, and I follow, and the writing is always smooth and flowing. When I have ignored this intuition, I have struggled tremendously and blamed "writer's block." I have come to not only trust that guidance in my writing, but to rely on it in virtually all areas of my life. I have developed a private relationship with my intuition—from what to eat and what to write about to how to relate to my wife and other family members. I meditate on it, trust it, study it and seek to become more aware of it. When I do ignore it, I pay a price, and then remind myself of the lesson to trust that inner voice the next time.

I figure if I can talk to God and call it prayer, believing in such a universal divine presence, then there is nothing loony about having God talk to me. All the spiritual people I've read about share a similar feeling. Intuition is loving guidance and they know enough not to ignore it.

9. *The nonspiritual being hates evil, and is determined to eradicate that which he believes to be evil. The spiritual being knows that everything that he hates and fights weakens him, and all that he is for, all that he supports, empowers him.*

The nonspiritual being is involved in a lot of fighting; he is aligned with the tools of power in a war against that which he believes to be evil. This person knows what he hates, and experiences a great deal of inner turmoil over perceived wrongs. Much of his energy, both mental and physical, is devoted to what he perceives to be bad or evil.

Spiritual beings do not order their lives to be against anything. They are not against starvation, they are for feeding people and seeing that everyone in the world is nutritionally satisfied. They work on what they are for, rather than fighting what they are against. Fighting starvation only weakens the fighter and makes him angry and frustrated, while working for a well-fed populace is empowering. Spiritual beings are not against war, they are for peace and spend their energy on working for peace. They do not join a war on drugs or poverty, because wars need warriors and fighters, and this will not make the problems go away. Spiritual beings are for a well-educated youth, who can be euphoric, giddy and high without the need for external substances. They work toward this end, helping young people to know the power of their own minds and bodies. They fight nothing.

When you fight evil by employing the methods of hatred and violence, you are part of the hatred and violence of evil itself, despite the rightness of your position in your own mind. If all the people in the world who are against terrorism and war were to shift their perspective to supporting and working for peace, terrorism and war would be eliminated. For every dollar we spend on peace, we spend two thousand on war. On the entire planet we spend approximately $25 million every minute on the business of war and upgrading our capacity for killing each other, while in the same minute (and every minute of every day) approximately forty children die of starvation. It is as if every ten minutes a Boeing 747 loaded with children were to crash, killing all of the passengers. How much does it cost to feed forty children? Who is going to reverse these telling statistics? The spiritual residents of our planet? Or the non-spiritual? No matter how much you may think these things are irreversible, you are part of the problem as long as you opt to be a fighter, rather than a person who knows what you are for, understands your purpose here on earth for this short period of time and works toward empowerment in spite of what you may see so many others doing.

Somehow our priorities are turned inside out. Spiritual beings do not get tied up with hatred. They are focused thoughtfully on what they are for and they translate that into action. Spiritual beings keep their thoughts on love and harmony, in the face of things they would love to see changed. All that you fight weakens you. All that you are for empowers you. In order to manifest miracles you must be totally focused on what you are for. Real magic occurs in your life when you have eliminated the hatred that is in your life, even the hatred that you have against hatred.

10. *The nonspiritual person feels no sense of responsibility to the universe, therefore he has not developed a reverence for life. The spiritual being has a reverence for life that goes to the essence of all beings.*

The nonspiritual being believes, as Zukav has said, "that we are conscious and that the universe is not." He thinks that his existence will end with this lifetime and that he is not responsible to the universe. The nonspiritual being has become arrogant.

The spiritual being behaves as if the God in all life matters, and he feels a sense of responsibility to the universe. He is in awe of this life, and that he has a mind with which to process the physical universe. That awe leads him to look outward at all life and the environment with a sense of appreciation and reverence, to engage with life itself at a deeper level than merely the material world. To the spiritual being the cycles of life are approached as representatives of infinity, with reverence that is truly an honoring of life. It is a gentle and kind approach toward all that is in our world, a recognition that the earth itself and the universe beyond has a consciousness and that our life is connected in some unseen way to all life now and in the past. The invisible intelligence that suffuses all form is a part of ourselves, thus a reverence for all life is knowing that there is a soul in everything. That soul is worthy of being honored.

The spiritual person is conscious of the need not to take more from the earth than is needed and to give back to the universe in some fashion for those who will habitate the planet after himself. Miracle-making capability comes out of a strong reverence for all life, including your own, and therefore in order to know real magic you must learn to think and act in ways consistent with being a reverent spiritual being.

11. *The nonspiritual being is laden with grudges, hostility and the need for revenge. The spiritual being has no room in his heart for these impediments to miracle making and real magic.*

The spiritual being knows that all spiritual masters have talked about the importance of forgiveness. Here are a few examples from our major religious teachings:

Judaism: The most beautiful thing a man can do is to forgive wrong.

Christianity: Then Peter came up and said to him, "Lord, how often shall my brother sin against me, and I forgive him? As many as seven times?" Jesus said to him, "I do not say to you seven times, but seventy times seven."

Islam: Forgive thy servant seventy times a day.

Sikhism: Where there is forgiveness there is God himself.

Taoism: Recompense injury with kindness.

Buddhism: Never is hate diminished by hatred: It is only diminished by love—This is an eternal law.

For the spiritual being it is crucial to be able to "walk the talk." One cannot profess to be a practicing member of a given faith, and then behave in ways inconsistent with the teachings. Forgiveness is an act of the heart. (An entire chapter of *You'll See It When You Believe It* is devoted to this matter.)

If you fill your inner invisible self with bitterness and revenge toward others, you will leave no room for the harmony and love that are necessary to experience real magic in your life. From a position of hatred toward others will come more hatred and disharmony for yourself. It should be obvious that you simply cannot manifest miracles in any area of your life when you are tangled up with such negativity as hatred and vengeance toward anyone or anything. Forgiving others is the essential component of one of the most oft-quoted prayers in Christianity: "Forgive them their trespasses as we forgive those who trespass against us." The spiritual being knows that these are not simply empty words to recite in a ritual before bedtime. They are in fact a necessary ingredient for becoming a spiritual being.

12. *The nonspiritual being believes that there are real-world limitations and that although there may be some evidence for the existence of miracles, they are viewed as random happenings for a few fortunate others. The spiritual being believes in miracles and his own unique ability to receive loving guidance and to experience a world of real magic.*

The spiritual being knows that miracles are very real. He believes the forces that have created miracles for others are still present in the universe and can be tapped into. The nonspiritual being sees miracles in a totally different light. He knows them to be accidents, and therefore has no faith in his own ability to participate in the miracle-making process.

The spiritual dozen require very little of you. They are not difficult to understand nor do they require any long training or indoctrination on your part. They can be accomplished in this very instant in which you are reading.

Becoming a spiritual being takes place within that invisible self I have been writing about. Regardless of how you have chosen to be up until now, working toward becoming a spiritual being can be your choice today. You do not have to adopt any specific religious tenets or undergo a religious transformation, you simply have to decide that this is the way you would like to live out the remainder of your life. With this kind of inner commitment you are on your way.

It is important to recognize that real magic is unavailable to those who choose the nonspiritual life. Being able to make

miracles happen is fundamentally a result of how you choose
to align yourself, how you choose to use your mind and how
much faith you have in being able to use it to affect your
physical world.

A SUMMARY OF THE SPIRITUAL DOZEN

Following is a brief summary of the spiritual dozen. Refer to
it often and know that the difference between being spiritual
and being nonspiritual is not located in your physical form or
in the physical circumstances of your life. It is located within
the invisible dimension of your being.

SPIRITUAL BEING	NONSPIRITUAL BEING
1. *Utilizes multi-dimensional thinking.*	Limited to five senses in beliefs and thoughts.
2. *Believes loving guidance is available.*	Believes we are always alone.
3. *Focuses on authentic personal empowerment.*	Focuses on demanding external power.
4. *Feels connected to all of humanity.*	Feels separate from all others.
5. *Knows a dimension beyond cause and effect.*	Believes excessively in cause and effect.
6. *Motivated by ethics, serenity and quality of life.*	Motivated by achievement, performance and acquisitions.
7. *Practices meditation.*	Rejects meditation.

SPIRITUAL BEING	NONSPIRITUAL BEING
8. *Understands intuition as God talking.*	Views intuition as unpredictable hunches.
9. *Knows a violent response to evil as participating in evil. Focuses on what he is for.*	Hates evil and fights against it. Focuses on what he is against.
10. *Feels a sense of responsibility and belonging to the universe. In awe of being here.*	Feels no sense of responsibility or belonging to the universe.
11. *Lives a life of forgiveness.*	Holds grudges and seeks revenge for perceived wrongdoing.
12. *Believes in being able to manifest miracles.*	Believes in limitations. Miracles are unpredictable, lucky occurrences.

SOME SUGGESTIONS FOR BECOMING A SPIRITUAL BEING

Remember, the ancestor to every action is a thought! Here are some practical suggestions for getting in touch with yourself as a spiritual being.

- *To prove to yourself that you are more than a five-sensory being*, write down all of the things that you experience within yourself that are beyond your sense of taste, sight, hearing, smell and touch. Keep a thought journal for one day and record the insights of your inner world. Note any intuitive hunches and record them for your own satisfaction. By keeping track of your actions in the physical world you learn that you are a physical being, but by keeping track of what created that action, you gain the insight that your actions are coming from something that isn't physical at all.

- *To help you experience yourself as a multisensory being*, test the power of your mind on something that you perceive to be difficult. Visualize yourself doing something such as improving a golf swing, not having a drink at a cocktail party, jogging one mile, baking a cake for the first time or spending a Saturday afternoon at a movie theater with your five-year-old. Picture anything that seems tough or unusual for you to accomplish. Create a mental image of yourself performing this difficult task. Describe it in detail in writing or record it on tape. Do this several times and see if you can then manifest the vision in your physical world. When you do you will have broken through the limit of your five senses. Since the image is beyond your senses and is invisible to them, then the action came from that invisible part of you. Get to know this higher part of yourself that truly wants to transcend the many limits that you believe in by functioning exclusively as a five-sensory being.

- *To get acquainted with the reality of your invisible world*, question the pure physical evidence reported by your five senses. Your senses tell you that the world is flat, which is a delusion. Your senses tell you that the world is standing still and you are moving upon it. But you know that the world is traveling at dizzying speeds, spinning on its axis and hurtling thousands of miles through space each hour. Your senses tell you that objects are solid, but one look through a powerful microscope and you see that those objects are empty space, and a dance of activity. Trusting the limitations of your senses is to be living a delusion. Get acquainted with the reality of your invisible world by beginning to question the pure physical evidence reported by your five senses. Assess how much your five senses delude you about your own reality, and then ask yourself why you put so much faith in those senses.

- *To make contact with divine or spiritual guidance*, just for a day suspend your skepticism. Give yourself a gift of a quiet place and a quiet hour all to yourself. Start this experiment with an absence of skepticism and doubt. Ask for assistance in an area that is troubling you, and make every attempt to empty your mind of any and all distracting thoughts. See if you can create an image of receiving help from a guide that cares about you and wants to extend love toward you. In this state of quietness, with your mind empty of distractions, know within that the answer you seek is forthcoming and that you are not alone. Just know it, and feel yourself receiving that help. I am not asking you to listen for voices or to see apparitions, but rather to feel exquisitely peaceful. Keep a record of what you feel at the end of this hour, and what hunches or assistance you have received. I guarantee if you make this a regular habit, you will begin to go to this magical inner place regularly, and you will receive the guidance that has previously been so elusive. Go ahead, give it a try. You don't have to tell anyone else what you are attempting. You will be making direct contact with your higher self, with the divine intelligence that is always with you, no matter how much it is resisted.

- *To connect with the invisible dimension we call death*, keep track of your dreams for a short time, particularly those dreams in which you were in the presence of someone who was in your life but has now passed on. As you go to sleep and enter the invisible world of thought, wherein you create with your mind all of your characters for your dream, remind yourself that no one dies, only form changes. Then be aware of the guidance that apparition in your dream provides for you. Be prepared to talk with that soul in your formless dream state. Ask questions of him or her and verify for yourself that you have the ability to do this. If in fact we are souls with bodies, rather than bodies with souls, then all souls live on after what we call death, in an invisible dimension. Those souls will appear as very real and very much alive while you are in your own formless invisible dimension of pure thought.

When you are able to make contact with those souls in your dream, and experience how real they still are, you will see that aging and death are only realities for the five-sensory world. Once you know this, and have made that contact, you will have an awareness of your own immortality, and you will have a completely new vision of death. You will know in your heart that those whom you've loved and who have passed on are not truly gone from your life. They are there and available for you. Open yourself up to making this contact, and you will experience it and all the guidance that it can bring you.

• *To extend the sense of loving guidance in your life*, begin to know that you do not have to sleep to make contact with a soul. If you can connect with the invisible dimension in your sleep, work at believing that the same connection, the same loving guidance, is available to you whenever you choose to recognize it. You will begin to look for this guidance more frequently and less dubiously. Prayer will take on new meaning. It will not be a ritual of silent, one-way communication. It will become a virtual transformation in which you put your brain into a higher state and *literally* participate with God in the ebb and flow of your life. Silently listen and be willing to hear communications that will come to you in the form of overwhelming feelings. Be thankful and appreciative for whatever assistance you may receive. Always ask the question, "How may I serve you and others in resolving this issue that I am facing?" When you keep your inner communications focused on assisting others and staying purposeful, you truly will receive the answers you seek.

- *To find models and companions for your journey*, read about the personal experiences of people you admire. As you do, look for the spiritual dimension in their personal journeys. You will invariably find that the people you most admire often go within in times of difficulty, and have received the guidance and assistance they sought at the time. Great scientists often report that they feel a special spiritual connection to inner guides as they proceed through their careers. Most autobiographies show that those who are highly successful attribute their success to establishing a connection to a higher part of themselves, and to feeling the presence of divine assistance at highly charged moments in their lives. Whether your heroes be athletes, writers, clergymen, astronauts, musicians, artists, businessmen or anyone else, virtually all of the truly inspired leaders in their fields reached a point in their lives where they felt they were being guided. They knew that they were not alone, and they began to trust divine guidance in reaching levels they believed could not have been achieved otherwise.

Once you know that most people who reach the higher levels of achievement in their areas of expertise have felt the same way, you will not be so squeamish about admitting it to yourself, and even seeking it out. Soon you, like me, will be "going public." For those who think this is absurd and "off the deep end," send them love and stay focused on your purpose. Their skepticism is their current path, as it once was mine and yours. Be at peace with it.

- *To learn new ways of relating to others*, examine your behavior toward those people in your life whom you feel a need to dominate or control. Be it a spouse, children, coworkers, employees, clerks, service people, whoever, take some time to relate to them differently by seeing beyond their physical form to the fullness of God in them. This is a great exercise for shifting to a spiritual consciousness, because you will not be coming from the need to control, judge or dominate. Instead you will be attempting to empower those whom you may have previously viewed as subservient to you. Once you begin to see past the physical bodies of those around you, you will begin to relate to the very same invisible force that flows through you and them.

  I started doing this with my children many years ago. I try to look at the loving thoughts that are behind their actions, to see past their faces, and their tiny selves, to the souls they house within their little bodies. When I lose the need to be powerful and controlling, I empower my children to be in control of their own lives, and I see them for what they genuinely are—little souls with bodies, who also have a purpose for being here. When I lose my need to dominate anyone, I help that person get on with his or her purposeful life, and I stay locked on my purpose as well.

- *To practice a life without a focus on control*, attempt to help someone do something for themselves where previously you would have instructed them how to do it. Rather than giving an order, try asking the question, "What would it take for you to prove that you can do this yourself?" Then say, "Let's work together to make it happen." A simple offer of assistance rather than taking over or giving an order will infuse you with authentic power instead of provoking you to rely on external power methods. This is particularly useful if you can help empower someone with whom you are in conflict.

  Most conflicts arise from a need to control someone or to prove that you are right and the other person is wrong. If you can give up the need to control as well as the need to be right just once in your own private practice session, then you will be able to empower another person in a unique way. Giving up the need to dominate is at the core of being a spiritual person. Replace the search for external power with genuine authentic power, which is the ability to empower others to take control in their own lives.

- *To demonstrate to yourself that you are not alone*, picture yourself connected by invisible strings to everyone that you encounter. In this vision, as you move to the right, those to whom you are connected also move to the right. As you push, they go tumbling. Now when you encounter another person, imagine that connection. In this way you will begin to treat others as if they were truly a part of you. You will have a tendency to extend love and help rather than feel enmity and competition.

  I have always loved the story of the man who was given a tour of heaven and hell. In hell he saw a large kettle of soup. The only utensils were a series of very large spoons. However, the handles were all longer than the arms of people, making it impossible to feed themselves. Everyone was in various stages of starvation, since they could not bend their arms. In heaven the man saw the identical scene. However, the people were all healthy and smiling and obviously well fed. When the man inquired about this he was told by his guide, "Oh, in heaven the people have learned to feed each other." Your purpose is always found in giving to others. This is heaven on earth.

- *To recognize how you've been taught to hate*, begin to rethink the concept of enemies and hatred. Make a mental note of all the people you regard as enemies. Realize that you have been taught whom to hate and that these lessons are only a result of the geographic accident of your birth.

  In recent years, Westerners were told to hate the Iranians; then they became our official friends. Then the Iraqis, who were previously our friends, became our enemies.

  This goes on and on, with few people ever understanding the simple message: *The enemy is hate itself.* Rid yourself of this hatred and the list of people whom you are told to hate, and fill yourself with harmony. Once you know yourself and feel love within, you will extend harmony outward to all people, regardless of whom you have been taught to hate. In fact, you will never be a part of that large mass of people who are so willing to hate and kill based upon what they are told is appropriate by their government leaders.

  Try to imagine that everyone—yes, all people on all sides of an issue—knows that one cannot choose up sides when living on a round planet. Imagine all people refusing to hate or have so-called enemies. You can help the world get to a peaceful place by refusing to have your own hate list, and by seeing all members of all conflicts as victims. This does not imply that you should be victimized by the ugly actions of others. It means you do not have to have hatred and killing in your heart. Reflect your understanding that we are all connected. When you reach outward in anger and hatred, you are in fact hurting not only your supposed enemy, but yourself and all humanity as well. If this message troubles you, remind yourself that it is at the core of all religions and has been encouraged by all spiritual masters since the beginning of recorded history.

• *To put yourself in touch with the nonphysical universe*, become comfortable with the concept of *nothingness*. Your thoughts come out of the silent empty space of your mind. From nothingness to a thought. From silence, you suddenly make a noise. Effect without cause, in the purely physical sense. Give yourself time to be in touch with this phenomenon of nothingness. Try emptying your mind of thought and then observe as thoughts emerge. Once you know that there is a dimension beyond the world of form that does not obey the laws of motion, you can accept the nonphysical world. You must somehow demonstrate to yourself that anything can be created out of nothing, and in fact it is happening all the time. Miracles do not need a physical cause, but you must get comfortable with the notion by allowing yourself to experience the "something out of nothing" phenomenon. You can accomplish this by realizing that you are almost totally empty space yourself. An examination of your body with a high-powered microscope shows that the physical you is nothing more than particles separated by empty space. With even stronger microscopes, you discover that those particles are also subdivided into more dancing particles separated by space. Most of what you think of as your physical body, when viewed from a different perspective, is empty space. So too is your mind a large lesson in what we have come to call nothingness.

Become familiar with this concept of nothingness and you will be in a place where you can create miracles. Keep track of your thoughts for a portion of a day, and remind yourself that they have nothing to do with what you call cause and effect. Where do they come from? Once you are comfortable with this, you will be able to see miracles coming from that same "place."

• *To put yourself in touch with your nonphysical self*, remove yourself from the physical world for a brief period of time. If you can, immerse yourself in a sensory-deprivation tank, in which you lose all contact with your senses and experience only the nothingness of your mind. If you do not have access to such a setup, then quietly, within your mind, let go of each of your senses in this exercise. No touch, no taste, no hearing, no sight, no smell. As you let these senses go (as you do every night while sleeping), observe what is happening to your body. The more you are able to let go of your attachment to your body through your all-knowing, all-powerful mind, the less you will use your physical state as a way of assessing your life. This is called getting in touch with your true self, your invisible self, and it is the key to becoming a spiritual being.

• *To keep your focus on purpose rather than outcome*, keep your mind, body and soul totally in the moment of your activity. Six million people play tennis every single day in America; three million of these people do not win. Does this mean there are three million losers every day? In all of *your* activities, stop and ask yourself, "Truly, why am I doing this?" You will find that the outcome (the win, the reward) is just as fleeting as the moments you participate in the activity. Stay on purpose in your activities, rather than focusing on the ultimate reward. The wins and losses will still arrive, yet you will find yourself on automatic pilot. Though you may plateau for a while, ultimately you will automatically move to a higher level. Become detached from the outcome of your actions and paradoxically your level of performance will climb.

- *To rid yourself of a preoccupation with valueless things*, rethink your attitude about your possessions. Make an inventory of everything you own. Is there anything in that inventory that you would die for? Now think about your values, your ideals, your loved ones, and ask yourself the very same question. You know what your priorities are, and they all have to do with what you think and believe, not with what you own. Detach yourself from those possessions, and get your life on purpose, which is to say, make the daily thoughts and actions of your life work toward that which matters to you in the truest sense. You are here for a reason, and it is not to hoard a lot of physical stuff. You came here without that stuff and you will leave without any of it. What will linger is how you served your ideals and those with whom you came in contact. Stay on purpose and you will find yourself automatically shifting to a spiritual focus in your life.

- *To conduct yourself on a spiritual plane*, begin living one day at a time emphasizing ethics rather than rules. Inventory all the rules that you follow so emphatically.

Rather than conducting your life according to someone else's rules, try having an "ethics day" for yourself. Base all of your behavior—including your eating, dressing, working, home life, everything that you do on that day—on ethics rather than rules. Ask yourself what is the moral, purposeful, loving thing to do, not what the rules are. In this way you will shift your consciousness away from outcome and toward purpose. Keep in mind that some of the most despicable human behavior has been conducted in the name of "I'm only following the laws." The laws told black people to sit in the back of the bus, the laws said women could not vote, the laws said owning a submachine gun was fine. People who live by ethics have moved away from arcane victimizing rules. Be that kind of person. For a day. Get yourself away from the rules and live ethically, regardless of what the rules have to say.

• *To become more peaceful with yourself and the world*, give yourself a quiet time alone daily for one week. This is extremely important and something that you will quite likely resist. I encourage you to give yourself this wonderful present and a ticket to real magic at the same time. The best time is early in the morning after a brisk shower and before anyone else arises. Set aside thirty minutes to be alone and peacefully go within and quiet your mind. Sit in a comfortable position, close your eyes and simply focus on emptying your mind and becoming intensely aware of your breathing. You will soon note that you are becoming more peaceful, and even if you get nothing more out of it, you will find that this is an enormous aid in reducing stress and tension in your life. If you stay with it and follow some of the tips I write about in the next chapter, I absolutely, emphatically guarantee that you will discover a part of yourself that will provide you with all of the loving guidance you need in every single area of your life. More than anything else, meditation will shatter the illusion of your separateness.

• *To befriend and cultivate your intuition*, treat those inner proddings that crop up in your mind as welcome guests instead of labeling them nothing but random hunches. Try stopping yourself during your next intuitive episode, whatever it is about, and make a mental note of what is taking place. Now, instead of ignoring it, or pushing it out, ask that intuitive part of yourself, "Why am I being pushed by my mind in this direction?" Develop a dialogue with that intuitive voice and simply note what you learn or what happens in the next few days as a result. By learning to have internal dialogues you will begin trusting your intuition and ultimately discover its loving presence and valuable contribution to your mind. Consider this ancient story:

> Two monks were arguing about the temple flag. One said the flag moved, the other said the wind moved. Master Eno . . . overheard them and said, "It is neither the wind nor the flag, but your mind that moves." The monks were speechless.

The next time you have an intuitive notion that you are tempted to ignore, choose to follow its lead. You must learn to cultivate the habit of trusting your intuition. Notice the outcome of that intuitive action. Begin to notice all the beneficial results that flow into your life when you follow your intuitive voice. Those inner conversations that you have, those debates about what to do and which course to take, can best be resolved by simply

asking, "What is the choice that will keep me on purpose?" Then go in that direction one step at a time.
Before long, your intuition will become your most
trusted companion, one that you will value and celebrate
as it surfaces within your mind.

- *To stay focused on what you are for in life rather than what
  you are against*, inventory everything in your life that you
  are opposed to and then reword your list to reflect what
  you are for. Rather than being against evil, be for love.
  Replace being against your child's bad study habits with
  being for a self-disciplined young person. As you shift
  your thoughts away from what you oppose, you will
  shift your inclination away from fighting those things
  and to supporting that which is on your "for" list. This
  is an excellent method for eliminating much of the inner
  turmoil and stress that surfaces from your fight list.
  Remember, all that you fight weakens you, all that you
  support empowers you.

- *To develop a loving, empowering attitude toward yourself*,
  restate everything that you dislike about who you are in
  positive, affirmative ways. Instead of being against your
  laziness, be for having more energy. By being for your
  energy, you will take actions correcting your laziness. By
  being against your laziness, you will stay angry and
  upset with yourself and thus weaken your resolve to
  change. This is true of your weight, your addictions,
  your entire physiology and all of your "bad habits."
  Restate them in terms of what you are for and what you
  are capable of, and you will automatically empower
  yourself to correct them.

- *To enter a state of enlightenment*, spend some time every day
  in awe. Yes—in total, complete awe. Be thankful for

your liver, your hands, your brain and your invisible, incomprehensively awesome mind. Be in awe of the very fact that you showed up here, particularly when you consider the mathematical odds. Observe the functions of your body and the trillions of cells that all work together to make you function. This sense of awe is something to practice daily. The air you breathe, the water you take for granted, the food that grows from infinitesimal seeds to nourish you. The atmosphere, the ozone, all of it. Be thankful and appreciative and also feel a sense of responsibility to your universe. Treat all life with reverence and awe, and know that it is all working purposefully. A few minutes a day in total awe will contribute to your spiritual awakening faster than any metaphysics course. Enlightenment is simply the silent acceptance and appreciation for what is. In this very moment you can get into that state of mind, by being thankful for the mind and the tools to read these words, and realizing how magnificently they are working. Be in awe and be enlightened. Be enlightened and miracles will be your way of life.

• *To move past anger and bitterness*, in your mind isolate one person such as you feel has wronged you at some time in your life, someone who has not repaid a long overdue debt. Perhaps an ex-spouse who left or abused you in some way, a parent or a long-lost love who jilted you. Isolate this one person in your thoughts. Now, just for a few moments, instead of feeling hate and bitterness, try to imagine yourself sending them love. Try to grasp the idea that they came into your life to help you learn a lesson, and no matter how painful the lesson, they showed up in your life for a purpose. When you are able to send them love instead of hate, you will not only be healing yourself, you will be on your way to becoming a spiritual person.

Think of a wrong that was done to you as being like a snake bite. When you are bitten by a snake there are two sources of pain. One is the bite itself, which cannot be unbitten. It happened, it hurt and you have the mark to prove it. You then go on from there and learn how to avoid snakes in your life. The second source of pain is the venom that is now circulating through you. This is the killer. No one has ever died from a snake bite—it is the aftershock of the venom circulating in the body that is fatal. So it is with hatred and forgiveness. The event happened. It cannot unhappen in your physical world. But the killer is the hatred and anger that continue to circulate in your system like venom, long after the bite wound has healed and disappeared. You, and only you, have the power to send that killer venom out of you; that it is still present within you is your choice. Remember the sage words of Buddha, "You will not be punished for your anger, you will be punished by your anger." Miracle making is impossible to experience when your insides are poisoned by bitterness toward others.

Begin today affirming, "I know I have the power within me to create a life of fulfillment and joy. I am a miracle and therefore I am a creator of miracles." One primary message in this chapter explains how to become a spiritual being having a human experience, rather than a human being having a spiritual experience. This chapter can also be summarized in the words of a simple man, who traveled the country in the early twentieth century speaking folk wisdom. Will Rogers reminded us all: "So live that you wouldn't be ashamed to sell the family parrot to the town gossip." Good spiritual advice indeed!

3

CREATING A
MIRACLE MIND-SET

As our case is new, we must think and act anew.
— ABRAHAM LINCOLN

The final task on the journey to real magic is to set your mind, your invisible self, on the path of miraculous living. In the previous chapter you examined the idea of a purposeful universe and of you as a purposeful entity within that universe. You examined how to align your thoughts and actions with the divine purpose that brought you from a formless state in eternity into this world of form. Your awareness should now also acknowledge the existence of an available loving guidance that you need only learn how to use wisely. You may feel what Hazrat Inayat Khan meant when he said: "The mystic does more than quote scriptures, he not only says 'seek ye first the kingdom of God,' his whole life is absorbed in that seeking."

It is a whole life absorption, which does not, however, demand withdrawing from the world nor changing your living or working situation. What you *will* change is the invisible reality that is uniquely yours.

What follows in this chapter is a guide for shifting your mind-set to experiencing a world where real magic is not only possible, but your birthright. With this shift, miracle making will become something that you not only believe in, but that you manifest in your everyday life. I have studied and spent time with those whom I consider miracle workers, and I know from their experiences and my own that this is the paradigm of the mind that consistently succeeds in creating that miracle mind-set.

FOURTEEN KEYS FOR CREATING A MIRACLE MIND-SET

Here are fourteen keys for creating an environment in which miracle making and real magic can flourish. Although these are all intentions for your mind, that invisible part of your humanity, there are specific, real-world things you can practice as well. After each key, I've listed suggestions for implementing this miracle mind-set in the physical, visible world.

1. *Reserve your judgment and disbelief.* Like most of us, you have very likely been taught to be skeptical about anything other than what you can see and touch. You need to suspend that disbelief, just like you do while watching a movie or reading a novel.

When you are watching a movie or reading a novel you willingly suspend disbelief. In this way you allow yourself to enjoy the story without constantly reminding yourself that you are the reader or observer. And so it is with the world of real magic. You willingly suspend your disbelief and temporarily enter a world of ultimate possibilities. If you do not like it, at any point you can discontinue the activity and rejoin the world of skepticism and disbelief. Let me share with you an experience I had recently.

In Shirley MacLaine's book *Going Within* there is a description of a gentleman from Brazil named Mauricio Panisset. She describes him as possessing miraculous powers, unlike anything I had ever witnessed in my life at the time of reading her book. All of my training had, in fact, led me to consider such claims with doubt and skepticism. Here is an excerpt:

> Mauricio Panisset was born March 6, 1930, in Minas Gerais, Brazil. He was the third child born into a family in which the father, a Methodist minister, was also interested in metaphysics. But shortly Mauricio's mother claimed she couldn't handle her son's uncontrollable rebelliousness. Out of desperation, when he was nine years old, his parents sent him to live with his grandmother on a farm. . . . He often walked to the forest where he (later) claimed that "lights" followed him. The lights appeared as shimmering balls and "talked" to him whenever they appeared. . . . When he reached puberty the lights disappeared. In 1949, at age nineteen, he joined the army and one night while he was on watch the lights reappeared. . . . In 1969 the lights became so strong that they again began to "speak." On April 19, 1969, one of the lights spoke so strongly that Mauricio could not ignore it. It said, "You must use your own light to heal the sick. You must go to the hospital and begin."

I was intrigued with Mauricio but I also have to admit I wondered whether Shirley had been tricked in some clever way, or even perhaps had "gone over the edge." After all, we all *know* that lights do not speak and act in the way she describes in her book. My opportunity to suspend my disbelief was to arrive the following summer.

Toward the end of our annual summer stay on Maui I was

the guest speaker at the Unity Church of Maui in Hawaii. This is something that I do each year before departing, as my way of returning something to that beautiful, spiritual, Pacific Ocean paradise where I have received so much inspiration and divine guidance.

After my talk, a woman came up to me and invited my wife, Marcie, and me to join her and her husband and a small group of friends at their home in the city of Lahaina. The woman, Gail Longhi, and her husband, Bob, own one of the most famous and successful restaurants in Hawaii. Gail explained that she had a very special guest, named Mauricio, whom Shirley MacLaine had written about in *Going Within*. Based upon what she heard me speaking about at the church, she thought we would enjoy a private meeting with this remarkable man. I immediately recalled the reaction I had had while reading about Mauricio's talents and I happily accepted the invitation. Marcie and I agreed that this was an opportunity to experience firsthand the magic of this master and, equally important, to willingly suspend our disbeliefs and judgments.

When we arrived we were told that Mauricio would see us in about forty-five minutes. He was having a session with Gail's mother in a bedroom that had a window overlooking the patio. Suddenly, while we were outside on the patio, we saw what appeared to be lightning bolts in that bedroom—it seemed to be exploding with enormous blasts of white light— a literal light show! Gail's mother descended the stairs soon after. She walked past us with a vacant, peaceful look and disappeared into another part of the house. Mauricio followed down the stairs a few minutes later in a sleeveless T-shirt that was drenched with perspiration. We met him in the kitchen where he was consuming large amounts of water. He appeared to be in his late fifties, was short, with magnificent white hair and a stocky build, and was gloriously serene and humble.

Apologetic, he explained he would need another fifteen or twenty minutes before seeing us. We thanked him and he replied in broken English, "No, no, no thank me. God's work, not mine."

About twenty minutes passed, during which Bob assured everyone that there was no possibility of fraud. He explained that the light show had taken place in his own bedroom and that he had escorted Mauricio personally into the room and had had the first session with him. He even discussed how he had searched the room. I was simply waiting with my open mind, my willing suspension of disbelief.

Mauricio asked us to follow him upstairs. Marcie and I had decided to do this together so we could corroborate each other's experience and share what we had witnessed together.

We lay on the bed diagonally with our heads side by side and held hands the entire time. Mauricio started a cassette player and the room was filled with low-volume meditation music from a flute. He came up behind our heads and placed his fingers on Marcie's forehead. He then spoke loudly the words "energia, energia, energia" and some words in Portuguese that we could not understand. He removed his fingers from Marcie's forehead and snapped his fingers loudly, repeating "energia, energia," again and again. Suddenly, miraculously, the room was literally lit up. Light emanated from his hands and it was as if lightning had struck right in the room. Marcie had her eyes closed but could still see the light through her eyelids. I never once closed my eyes and I was transfixed.

Then Mauricio touched my forehead with his fingers. His hand was actually very hot. Again, "energia, energia, energia," followed by some Portuguese words. I felt as if I'd temporarily gone to another dimension. The light and energy were electrical. My entire body convulsed with enormous shock. The room was aglow. From total darkness to a bright light from this man's hands!

We stayed in the bedroom for over twenty minutes. During this time he put his hands on the knee and the ankle of my leg, which I had injured in a bad fall on some slippery rocks the previous week. I felt enormous heat, and the light again emanated from Mauricio and lit up the room. He did this twelve to fifteen times during our session. Then he left the room and walked downstairs drenched with perspiration. Before he left he asked us to stay on the bed for a few moments and let the experience sink in, explaining that we might experience some dizziness.

We remained on the bed holding hands in silence for several minutes, feeling as close as we'd ever felt in our lives together. We didn't need to speak. Slowly we walked down the stairs together, looking past the other seven or eight people gathered in the room.

My wife is extremely close to our children. She totally devotes herself to her babies, and seems to become more and more intensely bonded with each of the seven she has given birth to. On the night of our meeting with Mauricio, our teenage daughter Stephanie was babysitting our daughter Saje Eykis, who was nine months old and nursing full-time. Marcie came downstairs after our session almost trancelike, with a totally different, peaceful look on her face. A few moments later the phone rang and it was Stephanie, telling us that she was having difficulty with the baby, who wouldn't stop crying and fussing. At all other times, a phone call like this would have caused us to leave immediately so that Marcie could nurse the baby and give her the comfort that only she could provide. But Marcie was in another world after the experience with the lights. Her response to Stephanie shocked me out of my own trancelike state.

"I'm sorry, Stephanie," she said, "you will just have to take care of it. We'll be home shortly, but in the meantime you do whatever you have to do to make her stop crying." This was a different Marcie than I had ever experienced before or since. As we drove home we both agreed that we had just had an experience that was very special and beyond description.

The next day I noticed that a bothersome growth on the skin of my collarbone, which had been there for several years, was completely gone, and the leg I had injured was no longer sore. In fact, the scabs were almost totally healed over and there was hardly any evidence of the injury.

I had been meditating on writing this book for several weeks before this event took place. I kept hearing reassurances in my meditation that I would receive all of the proof that I required in order to write a book about manifesting miracles. I repeatedly was assured that the doubt would be gone and I would know. The presence of Mauricio and the actual experience of seeing the lights felt like convincing evidence that real magic is indeed real.

I believe that I experienced real magic because I had willingly suspended my disbelief. I am convinced that suspending disbelief is the first step in setting one's mind for miracle making. I encourage you to cultivate a new, self-declared openness to anything and everything being a possibility for you.

The following riddle from the mathematician Douglas Hofstadter is a quick test of how open your mind is:

A father and his son are driving to a football game. They begin to cross a railroad crossing and, when they are halfway across, the car stalls. Hearing a train coming in the distance the father desperately tries to get the engine started again. He is unsuccessful and the train hits the car. The father is killed instantly, but the son survives and is rushed to the hospital for brain surgery. The surgeon, on entering the operating theater, turns white and says, "I cannot operate on this boy. He is my son." The question is, what is the relation between the boy and the surgeon? Take a few minutes to ponder this one before looking at the answer, which I will write in reverse: eht noegrus saw eht s'yob rehtom.

Having an open mind and suspending our disbelief allows us to experience new vistas, while our closed mind and unwillingness to shed our disbeliefs keeps us trapped in our old ways of thinking and seeing. Real magic is available only to those who can imagine any and all possibilities, while letting the how-it-will-happen take care of itself. What I am asking of you here is simply to do that. Nothing more. Just open your mind and suspend your disbelief. This is the beginning of miracle making.

Suggestions for Implementing This Mind-set:

- *Practice inner affirmations giving yourself permission to adopt new ideas.* Say to yourself, "I will keep an open mind." "I refuse to judge anyone or any idea." "I am open to an infinite number of possibilities that are presently available to me." "Just because I can't see it, or don't fully understand it, does not mean it is nonexistent." "Today, for this one day, I will suspend my disbelief and be open to anything being possible for me." "I will act on my new openness, rather than my old skepticism."

- *Keep one little corner of your mind open to miracle making.* Investigate the lives of others who have experienced miracles. Know this is possible for you too. Talk to your friends and new acquaintances and ask them if they have ever experienced that which you would consider a miracle. Read books and articles about people who have had these kinds of experiences. By allowing yourself to be receptive to these stories and genuine experiences, you will open up your mind to these very possibilities for yourself.

2. *Create a real-magic zone in your mind.* Once you begin to suspend your disbelief and skepticism, you can begin setting your mind on miracle working. Make this a very private part of your life. Reserve a small piece of your consciousness exclusively for the purpose of testing yourself in this area. I have been able to manifest what constitute miracles for myself by having this very private zone.

It was while taking a shower and quietly meditating that I considered being completely alcohol-free. Drinking wasn't a major problem, but it was something I did each day—only a few beers after running, but still something I intuitively felt was not in my best interest. I asked myself (or my guide, Eykis), "Can I give up alcohol beginning January first of next year?" A simple pondering question in my mind. The answer was crystal clear: "Just don't drink today, and ask again tomorrow. Just today. Now! You don't have to look any further."

My private magic zone is reserved for questions like this alcohol-free query about what direction to take in my life. It never fails me. I recommend that you reserve your own invisible and formless zone in your mind. Treat it as your corner of freedom. Retreat there often to ask for the loving assistance and guidance that is there for you.

Suggestion for Implementing This Mind-set:

- *Affirm to yourself out loud each day that you are a spiritual being having a human experience, and that in this spiritual realm there are no limitations.* Affirm aloud that the universal intelligence that flows through all form in the universe flows through you, and that the universal law that has permitted any miracle to occur at any time in the history of this planet has not been rescinded. It is still operating and working today and is available to you. This affirmation will help you open yourself up to tapping into the universal forces, rather than continue being a skeptic and never allowing them to work in your life. Affirm it first, and then begin to act on that affirmation.

3. *Affirm yourself as a no-limit person.* When you have developed this real-magic zone in your mind and trust that you can go there at will, begin to affirm to yourself privately that there are literally no limits to the powers that you possess. A great rule of thumb is this: If you can conceive it in your mind, then it can be brought into the physical world.

At one time I believed I could not hit a backhand shot in tennis, and as long as I believed it, I saw that result. Today it is my steadiest shot. I changed my belief and my form followed that belief. Believe me, when I hit a winning backhand shot in a tennis match, for me that is a miracle. For you, the belief in any limitation, and I emphasize *any*, is a strike against you in your desire to experience real magic.

The point is that you and only you have the ability to create magic in your mind. The choice is always with you. It has nothing to do with luck, but with believing in yourself as a part of the divine force that suffuses all form in the universe.

As a child you most likely were on friendly terms with the invisible magic within you. You created what amounted to fantasies that you would crawl, you would walk, you would climb a tree. You would swim, no matter how difficult that may have seemed. You knew you would do it, and it started in your mind. Invisible thoughts followed by whatever was necessary in the material world. You would learn to ride that bike, even if you did wobble all over the place and fall down repeatedly. In your mind there were no limitations. All of your accomplishments began with a belief. You weren't physically different the moment you let go of the side of the dock and swam by yourself. Your physical self was precisely the same as a "swimmer" as it was as a "nonswimmer." The difference was a belief. The same was true for you as a walker and a nonwalker. A climber and a nonclimber. You didn't stop to say, "Nope, I'll never be able to stand up, I'll just sit here forever. I guess I failed to inherit the necessary standing genes." There was no room in your mind for doubt about your own greatness in those areas. You conceived the impossible idea first in your mind and then you acted upon it.

Somewhere along the way you began to doubt your ability to create magic for yourself. Never doubt that being able to walk from the perspective of a crawler is truly a miracle. You lost the ability to extend that belief to new and more "impossible" miracles. You began to buy into the misbeliefs of those around you who were "many limits" people, who said, "You must learn your limitations." Or, "You can't do that." Or, "You are just like your father, and he couldn't do those things either." The list was endless, and so too became the limitations.

To recapture that childhood magic and become your own miracle worker, you will have to change the thoughts that created your world of limits and boundaries. That takes place in your mind first, and since thoughts originate with you, you have the ability to re-create your own image of what your life is going to be from now on. Why not include the presence of real magic in your life as well?

Suggestion for Implementing This Mind-set

- *Make a list of those self-perceived limits that you have convinced yourself are true for you.* Then examine each one in light of how others have transcended them. Once you realize you have the inner power to go beyond those self-definitions, you will be on your way to creating the real magic I write about throughout this book.

4. *Develop a new mind-set toward the concept of intuition.* You must become comfortable with the idea that strong "inner pleadings" and "sudden hunches" are truly inner voices offering you guidance. As I said in chapter 2, think of your intuitive self as God talking privately to you, just as you talk privately to God and call it prayer. A return call is not that farfetched, particularly if you believe that there is some universal intelligence out there that you are addressing. Remember, it is not *what* you call this universal intelligence that matters. I'll use *God* here, but if you want to use something else, do. It is not the label that matters. What's important is knowing that the intelligence is there and that it is a part of you and all life.

Become comfortable with your intuitive voices and hear them as loving guides from the nonphysical, spiritual world. My own personal formula is this: If I feel it, it is real; because it is real I refuse to ignore it. Here are two examples.

On a vacation trip to Panama City, Florida, my wife was driving the car while my daughter Tracy and her cousin were asleep in the back seat. I was napping after six hours of driving. Suddenly an overwhelming insistence made me sit up and I could see that the car in front of us was about to have a head-on collision with the car in front of it. My wife could not see over the car ahead of us and was unaware of what we were heading for when the car in front of ours swerved toward the gravel alongside the road to avoid the collision. At the same instant that that car swerved, I grabbed the wheel of our car and moved us onto the gravel and the errant driver suddenly became alert. Another horrible head-on crash was avoided.

What was that intuitive feeling that righted me at that instant? You call it what you want; I know it as God speaking to me. I am convinced that God, in some incomprehensible way, nudged me awake that summer day in the 1970s. Why? I am inclined to believe that I still had much to accomplish here—my yet-to-be-born children, my writing, and all of my life activities since that time were my reason for continuing. How can we argue with the perfection of the universe? Close calls are just that. And when it is our turn, nothing will stop that either.

Our friend Larry, who helped decorate our home several years back, told us how he was once approaching a green light at forty-five miles per hour when suddenly a strong inner voice implored him to slam on his brakes for no apparent reason. As he obeyed his intuition, his car stopped inches short of a car speeding through a red light.

I am absolutely certain that you too have numerous stories of times that an inner voice prompted you to behave in what seemed an irrational way and turned out instead to be life-saving. It happens to everyone. Anything that happens to everyone cannot be attributed only to coincidence or simple luck. There must be more to it than that. Most of us get these intuitive signals on a regular basis.

Know in your invisible mind that hunches are not accidents. Respond in ways that allow you to benefit from the guidance. You are being guided. As you learn to trust these guides you will begin to recognize the lessons offered, even if they are not immediately discernible.

Miracle making and real magic are unavailable to many of us in the Western world largely because we are taught by those who have no faith in their own intuition. We are presented a life curriculum that places almost all of the emphasis on logical, rational thinking and problem solving. Our schools focus on the acquisition of knowledge, while virtually ignoring the feeling aspects of students' lives. Intuition, the how-I-feel part of life, is treated as infantile and inferior and unworthy of attention. In fact, your intuition, that fuzzy inner voice that you hear so often, is really as much a part of your life as is your ability to solve quadratic equations, read a poem or eliminate your bodily wastes. It is there, it is real. Pay attention! For only when you transcend the belief that cognitive knowledge is superior to intuition and feelings will real magic become a way of life for you.

Suggestion for Implementing This Mind-set:

- *Practice listening to and following your intuition once a day.* Have conversations with yourself affirming the power of your invisible hunches. Try following one of those hunches in a new way just once today. Forget about the outcome and remind yourself that by listening to those intuitive proddings, you overcome an inner mental inclination to ignore them. Beginning to be attentive is a big step toward understanding the vocabulary of those intuitive thoughts. All of your thoughts originate in that loving intuitive guidance that you are always receiving. Begin to fine-tune your intuitive antennae so that you know when to pay attention. You can only get good at receiving those intuitive signals when you tune in consciously.

5. *Discover the secret that sits in the center and knows.* Become familiar and comfortable with the notion that nothingness has something to offer you on your path to real magic. Ponder Robert Frost's tantalizing words that inspired this idea: "We dance round in a ring and suppose,/But the secret sits in the middle, and knows."

What does Robert Frost mean by this secret in the center? When you have the answer to this question you will have unlatched the most difficult door blocking your entrance to real magic.

Consider that it's the space between the notes that makes the music. Music (sound in form) is not a note or even a series of notes. What is required in order to have music is silent empty space between the notes. A note without space is one long sound. Music comes from the silence between the notes. Nothingness? Yes, but also absolutely necessary in order to create sound in the world of form. No nothingness, no music.

Consider that it's the space within the vase that allows a vase to be a vase. The vase is not simply clay or crystal, or whatever material is used. What you must have in order to have a vase is silent empty invisible space surrounded by material. Take a hammer to the vase and you still have all of the material, but no vase. You absolutely must have the nothingness of silent empty invisible space in order to have a vase. No nothingness, no vase.

Consider that a room is not a room without silent empty space within, surrounded by the shape of material form. The room is not the mortar, wood, or beams that make up the material part of the room. Put it all in a heap and you have no room. You must have the silent empty invisible space surrounded by all that form in order to have a room. No nothingness, no room.

This silent empty invisible space that is within *all* form is called the Tao. It is written that the Tao that can be described is not the Tao. It is beyond description, beyond language, beyond symbols. Paradoxically, it is a part of everything. Shen-hsui said it this way: "Seeing into nothingness—that is the true seeing, the eternal seeing." The vase, the room, the music, all make sense to us as we attempt to understand nothingness with our rational mind. Without the empty space they simply cannot exist. And so is this true for all things made of matter. They must have the silent nothingness in order to exist. "Therefore just as we take advantage of what is, we should recognize the usefulness of what is not," said Lao-tzu.

You too are material form (skin, bones, blood, gristle) surrounding the invisible silent emptiness that is also you. Without that nothingness inside, there can be no you. No nothingness, no you. Every cell of your body is composed of particles circling a void of nothingness. Every molecule is similarly fashioned of particles circling nothingness. It is the very story of life. When life leaves your body it will not weigh any less. Therefore your very life, your very existence, is weightless and invisible. Nothingness!

The secret that sits in the center and knows, is the emptiness that is externally silent yet always there. And it is also out of that secret in the center that you will be able to create miracles for yourself.

As so often is true, the poets are in touch with these nonmaterial concepts. Here is Wordsworth on this subject.

And I have felt . . . a sense sublime
Of something far more deeply interfused,
Whose dwelling is the light of setting suns,
And the round ocean and the living air,
And the blue sky, and in the mind of man;
A motion and a spirit, that impels
All thinking things, all objects of all thought,
And rolls through all things.

Suggestion for Implementing This Mind-set:

- *Remind yourself that the world of form surrounds invisible emptiness.* Remind yourself you are form surrounding the invisible life energy. Keep this in mind and make every effort to discover "the secret that sits in the center and knows." Since it is invisible, you need to go there mentally. Ask yourself, "Why am I here? Who am I?" Your deeply sought answers will astound you.

    Spend time in that inner space befriending the invisible director that guides your life. Trust it today. Allow it to function in the loving way that it wants to. Go with what it directs you to do, trusting and surrendering, and you will discover you can rely on the secret that sits in the center and knows. Make contact with that inner director often, and don't be embarrassed about it. The more you trust that your life is on purpose and that you will not be misguided, the more you will commune in the peaceful, harmonious world of real magic.

6. *Learn to learn through knowing and trusting rather than doubting and fearing.* There are two primary ways of acquiring new understanding. You can choose either the path of fear and doubt or the path of trusting and knowing. When you choose the latter path, you truly open yourself to your magical potential. Much of your learning has likely involved questioning your ability to gain a particular skill. At one time you were full of doubt about most of the things that you know to be true today.

For me, at one time in my life I was doubtful about my ability to speak to an audience extemporaneously for several minutes, let alone several hours. My doubt led to fear and all sorts of behaviors dedicated to overcoming the fear. Learning through the process of fear and doubt was a long, painful experience. Whether it was for a school group or business meeting, I would literally make myself sick whenever I had to get up in front of an audience.

Learning to speak to an audience through the path of knowing and trusting was a much more rewarding experience. I began to see myself as capable of delivering a speech, knowing within that I could do it, and trusting that I would be taken care of if I abandoned my doubts. I learned that an audience would not mind if I made a few errors or got temporarily lost, provided I was speaking from my heart and conveyed a sense of excitement about my topic. The day I received the Golden Gavel Award from Toastmasters International for outstanding speaker of the year, I knew that the shift from fear and doubt to knowing and trusting had led to a true miracle for me.

You can look at much of your own experiences in a similar way. You have been taught to doubt in a culture that stresses: you can't, it's wrong, you're too little, too big, too young, too old, a girl, a boy, you don't have the right background, credentials, training, experience. Out of doubt came a fear of your greatness, a fear of disapproval, failure, intimacy, and even success.

Doubt and fear do provide you with learning experiences, but the negative payoffs are obvious. It is easy to see that this is not the path to becoming a happy, fulfilled, fully functioning person. If you want to become acquainted with real magic, fear and doubt as your primary method for learning must be replaced with trust and a strong reliance on internal knowing.

In order to shift from fear and doubt to trust and knowing, you must develop a different mind-set. Your new thinking might go something like this:

I am going to learn what I have to learn regardless. So instead of taking the limiting path of fear and doubt, I am going to work at learning my life lessons by trusting and knowing. I'll trust in my own unique ability to create in my mind anything that I choose. It is my mind and these are my thoughts and I can choose doubt or I can choose trust. I am selecting trust. I can either doubt that I am capable of performing miracles or I can trust in my ability to do so. I will act upon whichever I choose. I believe that the saying, "As you think, so shall you be," is an accurate description of the human condition.

When my daughter Serena was five years old we encouraged her to utilize this type of thinking when she wanted to learn how to ride a two-wheeler bicycle. For eight months she had avoided having the training wheels removed, saying that she just wasn't ready. Now she was ready, and she practiced trusting and knowing for three days before she even got on the two-wheeler. She practiced out loud her personal affirmations: "I see myself riding a bicycle. I can ride a two-wheeler. I have the ability to balance myself. I trust myself as a person who can learn anything, including how to ride a bike."

When it was time to get on the bike, she was so pumped up to do it that fear was impossible. I've rarely seen such confidence and determination in anyone undertaking a new task. Her mind-set created her miracle. She was literally riding by herself within a matter of minutes. A few falls, some shaky beginnings, but off she went down the sidewalk all by herself proudly exclaiming aloud, "I can ride a two-wheeler, I can ride a two-wheeler!"

After hitting a sprinkler head and tumbling onto the grass, she changed her mind for a split second, lying on the ground muttering, "I can't ride a two-wheeler." But her positive affirmations and her inner trust and knowing immediately won over her temporary doubt, and she jumped up, balanced herself, asked me for another fast push, and was soon shouting, "I can do it!"

Serena's mind-set created her miracle. And don't doubt for a second that this wasn't a miracle for her. When her time came and she felt ready, it was what she worked out in her mind in the way of trust and inner knowing that allowed her to go out into the material world and bring about her miracle. The miracle started in her formless, dimensionless mind, and was played out in the physical world as a result of her inner trust and knowing.

Whatever it is that constitutes your miracles, a shift to an attitude of trusting and knowing is mandatory. Keep in mind as you shift to this new consciousness that behind fear is powerlessness. That which you fear, you are fighting, and fighting always weakens you. Fear makes you impotent and makes higher levels inaccessible. But behind trust is empowerment and love. No judgment, no anger, no hatred, no fear and no need to fight. Love empowers you to higher levels. It is your choice always, and the choice begins in that amorphous inner world of the mind.

Suggestions for Implementing This Mind-set:

- *For a few moments, in your encounters with strangers today, shift to knowing and trusting as your way of interacting.* Let go of doubt and treat that clerk or telephone contact with trust and confidence. Just try it. Say to yourself, "I trust this person. I will not doubt him, and I know that things will work out in a positive way." This business of learning through knowing and trusting serves you in millions of ways! Suspend your doubt and fear and trust that things will work out.

7. *Affirm that your intention creates your reality.* Memorize and continually remind yourself, "My intention creates my reality." Experience with intention as a way of creating miracles is probably an unfamiliar concept to you. Most of us have been raised to think of our desires, wishes, hopes and fantasies as the seeds to our personal fulfillment. However, desires are stagnant, they do not set energy into motion, they do not create for you. Intention is the energy of your soul coming into contact with your physical reality. What you see around you, whom you associate with, how you function daily, what your relationships are like, how much money you make, how you get along with others, the shape of your physical body, and

virtually everything about the physical you, is a result of your intention, or how your thoughts become energized into action.

Becoming aware of your intentions will lead you to an awareness of your spiritual nature. Your intention may be synchronized with what you know to be your purpose, or it may be otherwise aligned. If you know your purpose is about giving, loving and serving, whether in the field of education, parenting, law or cab driving, then your intention will indeed follow. You very likely often find yourself surrounded by others with similar values. Your values and higher spiritual self reflect your intentions. You view the world as a giving place; you are probably optimistic about man's abilities to become less militant; you probably see the goodness in others; and you likely see a lot of people who want to be giving back to you. You experience much gratitude and are teaching others to be loving.

The reverse is also true. If your intention is to get all that you can, you most likely encounter lots of greedy, power-hungry people. Your associates have a similar mind-set, and you repeatedly convince yourself of the greed and shallowness of the world. Can you see how your own invisible intentions can create your reality?

The secret to changing your life is in your intentions. Wishing, hoping and goal setting cannot accomplish change without intention. What is needed is a shift from the inert energy of wanting to the active energy of doing and intention. Realize that all of your accomplishments, even those of which you are not so proud, have come about as a result of your intentions. Your relationships are a reflection of what you have created with your intentions. Your financial picture is the result of your intentions. When you know that you are in charge of your intentions, that they originate with you, then you will also come to know that you are in charge of your entire world and always have been.

As you work toward a mind-set of real magic, please keep this notion uppermost in your mind. Creating miracles in your life comes from your intention to do so, not from your wish or desire or goal. You must move from an inert to an active mode within your mind to establish an inner environment of real magic potential. Then, and only then, you will turn that same potential into your reality in the material world.

Suggestion for Implementing This Mind-set:

- *Rather than simply laying out goals or wishes for how you want your life to go, try shifting to the active language of intention.* If you are ill, for example, try saying to yourself, "I intend to heal myself of this illness" rather than, "I wish it would go away" or, "I have set a goal to be free of this disease." The concept of intention, of applying action to your inner pleadings, will allow you to activate what needs to be done in order to complete the thought and make it a physical reality. Make a sharp distinction between what constitutes for you mere wishes and hoping, and what you are now in the process of intending to make happen. When I intend to be healthier, and I know this is the case in my mind, I usually get right up and do some exercise, even if it means simply walking around the block. The intention can literally put the thought into action. That is the very stuff which constitutes miracles.

8. *Experience surrender and satori.* Surrendering is an act of the heart, an acceptance of what you have always vaguely sensed:

- This is an intelligent system I am a part of.

- This intelligence is invisible.

- This intelligence is also a part of me.

- I decide to trust in this intelligence.

Surrendering is the equivalent of putting inspiration into your life. When you are inspired you feel purposeful. When you trust in the invisible intelligence of the universe, you feel guided. This process is not something that involves a difficult mastery of an esoteric curriculum. It can happen in a moment and it often occurs just that quickly. In Zen, this process is called *satori*, which translates roughly to *instant awakening*. Alan Watts describes it this way:

Essentially Satori is a sudden experience, and it is often described as a "turning over" of the mind, just as a pair of scales will suddenly turn over when a sufficient amount of material has been poured into one pan to overbalance the weight in the other.

I call this process of satori "going through the gate." You may spend decades of your life wondering, struggling, worrying, slipping and falling in a slow process of approaching the gate that seems so far away. Then inexplicably, the instant arrives when you go through the gate. You may then look back at those times when you were approaching the gate, and wonder, really wonder, "How could I have been so blind for so many years?" What seemed so difficult and so impossible for you at one time is now your way of being. It is so effortless that you realize that the "big lie" involves the notion that it is only through struggle and effort that you achieve anything. This feeling of satori, or going through the gate, is a result of an inner decision to be at harmony with yourself and your physical world. It is a decision of surrender.

I've had many satori experiences in different areas of my

life. One had to do with my growing up with a poverty consciousness. As a child I learned that everything had to be purchased on sale or at a bargain price and I believed there was never enough of anything. I deduced that I would never have enough money, should never overspend and the best I could hope for in life was a middle-class designation on the national census. I acted on this inner picture of my mind-set for the first thirty or so years of my life. I thought about scarcity a great deal, and not having enough of anything was the way I looked at my life. I was extremely cautious about any money that was spent and monitored expenditures very carefully. In short, while not starving, I was a victim of a scarcity consciousness, and inner invisible beliefs ruled my actions and pretty much dictated what my world was like.

Then I went through the gate in this area. Boom! Satori! It happened in a meditation when I heard, "You are it all already." Five simple words that kicked me in the rear end and gave me a whole new perspective on wealth. At that time I was waging an inner battle about whether I should leave my safe teaching position, with a guaranteed income, or go to work for myself and *know* that it would work out. When the words "You are it all already" came to me, I knew in that instant, while meditating, that I didn't *need* anymore. I already was what I needed. I could stop chasing, stop struggling, and know that I was here, I had arrived. I had to get on purpose and stop worrying about what I didn't have. I surrendered right then and there. I had a new knowing. A shift occurred from knowing that I would never have enough to one that said, "You will be taken care of. You don't need to spend your life energy on worrying about it anymore." And I haven't!

The result is I have been taken care of in ways that are too spectacular to even describe. I have become a much more focused person. I have given away more than I could have imagined having. It was the act of surrender that took place in a moment of awakening. That is satori.

You too can very likely look back to some significant positive shifts in your own life and realize you experienced a moment of awakening. A woman who lost 160 pounds in a five-month period told me that she could recall the instant in which she looked in the mirror and an overwhelming thought infused her: "Now is the time. I will help you. You don't have to poison yourself any longer with overeating."

A certain client told me how he changed from one occupation to another:

After years of knowing that I was doing the wrong thing and that I was off of my purpose, one morning on the way to work my mind suddenly knew that I could no longer continue to deceive myself. In that overpowering instant I surrendered. I knew I would be taken care of. That was it. I quit that same day and I have never looked back. I used to sell insurance and made a good living. Now I work as a camp counselor with underprivileged children. I feel fulfilled and I have never been concerned about my income. The moment I quit was so intense, all I can say is that I felt totally confident for the first time that all would be fine, and that I could make this shift without any anxiety or stress. I had an inner knowing, and all I can say is that I surrendered.

Satori is available to you at any moment of your life. But it can only come if you have an openness to it and if you are willing to surrender. All the spiritual masters tell us that the reality of life speaks to us in silence. Your noisy waking consciousness may not let you hear that silent pleading. What you must do to move yourself into the mental framework for living miracles is to just let go. Just know. Just simply trust.

Become still and then listen to your own mind. Be guided by an awakened attitude of surrender. Being free from a perpetual inner quarrel with life is a pleasant preliminary to satori.

Surely you have experienced quiet, contemplative moments when you've had a sudden insight and an internal knowing that you can and should do something. You can attract such moments to you through the practice of surrender. Surrender to the knowing that you are powerful and capable of being purposeful in your life. The rest will happen as you "see the light" or experience the glorious feeling of satori.

Suggestion for Implementing This Mind-set:

- *Think of the habits that have long plagued you.* They can be addictions, laziness, short-temperedness, phobias, fatigue, relationship-sabotaging or anything that does not produce the results you seek. Determine to go through the gate and change unwanted habits one day at a time. Recall the wisdom of satori. Surrender to this radical notion that is required for you to awaken to the awareness that all habits begin with thoughts. Surrender to a new consciousness, a thought that whispers, "I can do this thing in this moment. I will receive all the help that I need as long as I stay with this intention and go within for assistance." Now announce to yourself that you are no longer that old habitual person, for just this moment. Satori is your experience. You have awakened for a moment. Now go to the next moment with this same surrender, not thinking about tomorrow or anything in the future. Simply be in the now; in this moment you have the answer. This is how you go about making those seemingly difficult changes—one step at a time with an inner grace that allows you to surrender and stop fighting.

9. *Learn to act as if the life you visualize were already here*. Act as if that which you perceive in your mind were already here in the physical world. Begin treating your thoughts and visions as much more than simple amorphous meanderings of your mind. You create your thoughts, your thoughts create your intentions, your intentions create your reality. Consequently, you must begin the practice of ignoring your own doubt about the importance of your inner world and start the practice of acting as if the images you desire were already your reality. This may sound like self-deception, but it is the only way I know for you to get past the limitations you believe you have.

If you want to be energetic and you act fatigued, you are sabotaging your own vision. Even if you look into the mirror and see wrinkles and other evidence for your fatigue, you must begin to act as if your vision of being energetic were already here. Don't let a tired person move into your body under any circumstances. Affirm that the energetic person you want to be, the vision you have in your mind, is already here and put it into practice by pursuing some activity of your choice. It is no longer just a wish or a desire, that person has arrived. This may start out as a self-deception, but in one instant of acting as if your miracle were here, you have created it for yourself. If you think it is foolish to act abundantly when the evidence for scarcity is all around you, do it anyway. Act as if you were in possession of all that you need just for a moment and then the next moment, which is all that any of us truly have.

This same principle applies to how you can treat others and assist them in entering the realm of real magic. Treat them as if all that they wish they could be or have, you see them as being or having. A child that hears you say, "You already are brilliant and talented; you already know how to do it, and I know how great you are; regardless of anything you say to the contrary, in my heart I know you are capable of anything you decide to achieve," is way ahead of the game. When my children express self-doubt, I acknowledge their feelings, but I always act toward them as if they were capable of everything. "I know you don't believe it yet, but I know differently. To me, you are already ready and able but have decided to mask it by doubting yourself. You might fool others, and you might even fool yourself once in a while, but you'll never fool me. I know better."

When you begin to get the hang of this, you soon start treating everyone as if they were already experiencing their own miracles. Your aging parents who want to complain are seen by you as able to overcome their self-imposed limits. You treat them as capable. The person who is sick is treated by you with actions of wellness. "You are too strong and healthy to even think sick thoughts, you are already healing yourself." Similarly, you take the same approach to your own health, treating yourself as a well person and not allowing your mind to sabotage your body with the expectation of illness and incapacitation. Although a broken leg is a broken leg, it is a liability in your life only if that is how you choose to see it. If you decide that you are not going to be immobilized by the break, that you are not going to think about how unfortunate you are and that you will do all that you possibly could do if your leg were not broken, then that will be your reality.

I have watched my wife, Marcie, through many pregnancies, acting each day as if there were absolutely no impediment to her doing all that she does, pregnant or not. She thinks thoughts of being active, healthy, fully alive and in awe of the human life growing within her body. She then experiences this reality, and she has given birth to seven children all with the same approach to the miracle she is creating. I have also seen many of our friends go through pregnancies constantly complaining and predicting how terrible it all is going to be, and they too create their own reality. Learning to act as if the miracle you seek in your mind is already here gives you a big head start on this phenomenal world of real magic.

In 1965 I was teaching at a public high school in Detroit, Michigan, and going to graduate school in the evenings. While standing in the school office one day after classes were completed, I heard the principal ask a secretary if there were any staff members who knew anything about federal grants. He was looking for someone to head up a special program that would require federal funding, but he knew of no one who had the qualifications for such a ponderous undertaking. At that time I was not making much money, and the idea of additional income plus heading up a special tutoring program for underprivileged students sounded great. I immediately told the principal that I was an expert on federal funding programs and that I could write up a proposal and get it funded. I could hardly believe what I was hearing myself say. I was announcing my expertise in something with which I had only a slight familiarity.

He gave me the OK and that evening I spent six hours in the university library becoming an expert on federal funding on tutoring programs for disadvantaged youth. The very next day I wrote out the proposal using the guidelines I had discovered in the library. I appointed myself the director of the program, detailed the funding required, including my own salary, and, using a prototype that was in a federal publication, I sent it off to Washington.

Within three weeks we had a federal grant, and I was the resident expert on federal funding for special projects. Two additional schools sought my consulting services and offered to pay me to conduct federal funding workshops with their staffs. I had a well-paying second job, I was helping young underachievers and my principal was thanking his lucky stars that he had been fortunate enough to have a resident "expert" on his staff when he needed one.

When you have a vision and you act as if that vision were already here, you create not only the necessary expertise, but you literally become your own miracle worker. If you believe that you could never head up such an undertaking because you "don't have the necessary training, credentials, experience," or whatever, then that is what you will act upon. Begin to act as if you were that expert, even if you have to fool yourself in the beginning. If you have enough belief in yourself, and you are ready, the teacher will appear and you will plunge right in and create the credential that you need to get the job completed.

This process begins with your mind. It allows you to see beyond the physical evidence and into another dimension, a dimension where all things are possible and all learning is available. When I announced my expertise to my principal, I wasn't deceiving him or myself. I saw beyond the physical to the invisible region, where I know I can do anything that I make up my mind to do. In my mind I was an expert, and all I had to do was convert my expertise from the realm of thought to the material world. As it turned out, and as it almost always turns out, an expert is someone who believes in his own expertise and isn't afraid to act on those beliefs. While I would not perform brain surgery, I have no doubt that if I visualized myself to be a surgeon, I could get the necessary training. Obviously, it would take much longer than one evening in the library.

For most of the things that you want to accomplish, all the expertise you need you can gain quite readily, but you must begin with a belief and then act as if that which you believe or visualize were already your reality. I have never visualized myself as a brain surgeon, but I can visualize myself as capable of performing many different jobs. In fact, there are very few jobs that I cannot see myself being able to accomplish, including all political, administrative, managerial and even technical areas, with only a minimum of actual physical training. The fact is, for myself, I know that if I believe it strongly enough, and have enough confidence in myself to learn what I need, then there are very few things that I could not accomplish in a rather short period of time. Once you know you can do it, and act that way, the means will be obvious. Acting as if you were what you want to become and know you can become is the way to remove self-doubt and enter your real-magic kingdom.

Suggestion for Implementing This Mind-set:

- *If you want to achieve something that has always eluded you, for this day act as if it were already here.* For example, if you have always wanted to be in excellent physical shape, but have never achieved it, act as if today you are a perfect physical specimen. Ask yourself, "What would I do if I were in perfect condition?" Then be that person today. Walk instead of driving to the store. Swim fifty laps. Eat properly. Exercise. Read a book on nutrition. In other words, live in the physical world as if that which you want in your mind were here already. This is the avenue of miracle making. If you want to be confident but don't normally act that way, today, just this once, act in the physical world the way that you believe a confident person would.

10. *Live according to your spiritual self first and your physical self second.* In developing your mind-set for real magic, you must begin the process of living primarily according to your spiritual self. This is an alignment that I presented in depth in chapter 2. Within the grand scope of your higher conscious-

ness is your ability to create miracles for yourself and your world. Those miracles will occur only if the choices you are making are in concert with your spiritual self. This means making daily choices that are based upon the qualities of the spiritual dozen (see summary on pages 56 and 57). The entry point for the world of miracle making is the ability to *make choices based exclusively on the part of you that is spiritual and knows how to guide you in the physical world.*

For instance, deceiving another person is clearly not in alignment with your spiritual self. However, for some reason, you may have chosen to make your deception personally valid. This is an example of alignment with your physical self first. Your soul, or your invisible self, is aligned with love, harmony, giving, truth, sharing, peace and forgiveness. Any choices you make that are inconsistent or in opposition to those qualities shield you from access to real magic.

Within your mind you can begin to realign yourself and practice new choices that will lead you away from being a splintered person, and into the experience of wholeness and oneness with yourself and the world. You will experience authentic power for miracle making when you are aligned with your spiritual side first and your physical side second.

If you are deceiving others and know it is inconsistent with your spiritual self or your life purpose, then in your own mind, for this one day, start to choose an authentic, truthful way to relate to the people you are deceiving. This does not require a noble statement or confession, it just gives you an opportunity to get realigned. Once you begin to experience nondeception it will become habitual, just as deception did. The benefit to you will be that you will be able to create miracles, which eluded you while you practiced deception. You cannot escape from your soul. Like your shadow, it is there even when it seems not to be! When you are aligned primarily with your physical self and are seemingly benefiting from some sort of lie, your invisible self is patiently there and aware. Your invisible self, your soul, will simply not permit the physical you to go beyond the limitations inherent in being a self-deceptive person.

This realignment to the spiritual part of you first, and the physical part second, is necessary in all areas of your life. Your thoughts are much more important than you may have realized. Love is a virtue of the soul. It is an alignment with your spiritual self first. When you are so aligned, you act on that principle of love. If you are aligned with your physical side first, you probably find yourself behaving toward others in nonloving ways, and regretting it in your thoughts. The person who is physically or verbally abusive to others and knows inner remorse is misaligned, just as is, more obviously, the remorseless person.

Your first responsibility is to your spiritual side. Consult your mind before acting, and therefore become authentic to yourself. Create an inner harmony where your loving soul guides your physical behavior, rather than having your soul always coming in second place, following physical outbursts.

True joy and the exhilarating feeling of being at peace with yourself and your world come to the person who lets his or her physical world flow from the pleadings of the soul. This is the atmosphere of miracles and real magic. This is when you are inspired, when you know that all that you desire, all that you do, comes from what you think in that quiet empty space within that can be called your soul. It is nothing more than an internal shift. There is no need to rid yourself of physical habits, nor pretend that your physical longings do not exist. Instead, you rearrange your priorities, making contact first with that inner invisible world called your soul, paying attention to it first, and allowing your behaviors in the physical world to flow from those thoughts. Instead of making your physical urgings the paramount focus of your life, the engine that is pulling the entire train, so to speak, you make a shift. Those physical behaviors become the cabin cars and the caboose, being pulled by the engine that is your invisible soul. Both are forever omnipresent. It is just a matter of which is in charge and which is following. When you understand this, you will know what is meant by the statement "As you think so shall you be," and you will realize how dramatically different that is than "As you be so shall you think."

Paramahansa Yogananda described this realignment in these poignantly beautiful words in *Metaphysical Meditations*. I recommend that you reread them often.

The joyous rays of the soul may be perceived if you interiorize your attention. These perceptions may be had by training your mind to enjoy the beautiful scenery of thoughts in the invisible, intangible kingdom within you. Do not search for happiness only in beautiful clothes, clean houses, delicious dinners, soft cushions and luxuries. These will imprison your happiness behind the bars of externality, of outwardness. Rather, in the airplane of your visualization, glide over the limitless empire of thoughts. There, behold the mountain ranges of unbroken, lofty, spiritual aspirations for improving yourself and others.

When you behold these spiritual aspirations not only will you improve yourself and others, you will be in a position to know the meaning of real magic. It is accomplished with the inner click of your mind that connects you to the source of your soul in the same way a wall switch connects to an electrical source. The right way to guide your physical life becomes clearly illuminated, rather than your physical life determining how you are feeling and thinking. Your soul, that inner quiet empty space, is yours to consult. It will always guide you in your right direction. It will provide all the tools that you need to produce magical results in your life, but only if you let it take priority and truly guide your material life. The choice is yours to make. Realignment is an act of the heart that connects you to your soul. Look within and listen, and your priorities will be clearly seen and heard by your physical self.

Suggestion for Implementing This Mind-set

- *Rearrange your priorities for a day.* Make your mental images the most important part of your life and live according to them for this day. See yourself having a pleasant, loving evening with your spouse or loved one. Get the picture in your mind and see it working out exactly in the way that would be most pleasant for both of you. Don't let this picture go. This is an alignment with your spiritual self first. It is all still an invisible thought. Now act that thought out exactly in the manner you first created in your mind. This is how you shift your alignment to consider first your spiritual side, and then allow your physical world to flow from that new alignment.

  You can do this with a business encounter, a vacation or anything that occupies your daily life. First align yourself with the loving presence that is there with you in your mind, get the picture firmly and intend that you are going to act on that picture. Spiritual beings do not allow their thoughts and feelings to flow from their actions, they understand that their thoughts create their physical world. By aligning yourself here first and keeping that priority uppermost in your mind, you will soon see how easy it is to keep that alignment operating throughout your daily life.

11. *Study the paradox, "You can never get enough of what you don't want."* Keep this paradoxical statement uppermost in your mind as you prepare yourself to experience the miracles of real magic. Consider all of the things that people do not want. The alcoholic despises the alcohol that consumes his life, yet he can never seem to get enough of it. So too the drug addict. The person who is argumentative and full of rage despises the anger in him, yet never seems able to resist the invitation to argue. The overweight person hates the food that he craves and yet never has enough. So many of us disdain the money that seems to run our lives and the need to chase it, yet we never seem to get enough of it.

The answer to the riddle of getting to the point of not craving what is poison to us is to understand what we mean by a want. There is an ancient Zen saying that goes like this: "When you seek it, you cannot find it." That which you crave sends an unwritten, unspoken, but nevertheless real message to you, something like: "I am incomplete without that which I crave. If I get it, I will be more whole, more complete." But this incompleteness is an illusion. Since you already are it all, you truly do not need anything else to complete yourself. When you truly know this, your wants disappear and you are able to do nicely without that which you don't want but mysteriously keep craving. This is not to say that you will simply be like a mindless feather blowing haphazardly in the wind without any direction. However, you will be free from the insanity of vigorously pursuing that which you don't want and which is, in some way, damaging you.

When I gave up the pursuit of money, more of it flowed into my life than I had ever known before. Why? Because I was living my purpose and surrendering to the universe to provide for my needs. When I gave up the pursuit of feeling high or relaxed or euphoric from alcohol, I became more of what I had been seeking with external substances. Why?

Because I aligned myself first with my spiritual side. When I knew that my mind was capable of creating the level of euphoria, giddiness or relaxation that I wanted—and when I wanted—and my purpose was to give, love and serve others from this "high" state, I no longer needed the poisons that till then I had been unable to get enough of. I hated the hostile environment I often created, and yet I seemed hellbent on creating more of what I disdained. When I gave up needing to be right, I gave up the anger and grief that accompanied that need. I truly believe that one cannot enter the realm of real magic by diligently pursuing undesirable inner thoughts.

St. John of the Cross told us that if a man wishes to be sure of the road he treads on, he must close his eyes and walk in the dark. I interpret that as a direction for us to trust in the guidance we receive from our invisible self. The following poem, also by St. John of the Cross, elaborates on this theme.

If you would come to taste all things,
  then do not seek to taste anything.
If you would come to possess all things,
  then do not seek to possess anything.
If you would come to be everything,
  then do not seek to be anything.
To reach that which you do not know, you have
  to go by the way where you know nothing.
To come to possess what you do not possess, you have
  to go by the way in which you have no possessions.
To reach what you are not, you have
  to go by the way in which you are nothing.

As paradoxical as it sounds, it is the mind-set for the miracle worker. Surrender, trust, turn away from outer accumulation and achievement and allow yourself to be purposeful and guided. You will find a peaceful place in your mind when you achieve this blissful state, and you will find yourself more active, more fulfilled, and the riches you used to crave will arrive in your life in amounts more than sufficient to meet your wants and needs. The essence is knowing that you are already complete, already whole, and that nothing external to yourself in the physical world can make you any more complete.

Knowing this, the pursuit of things that you truly do not need or want diminishes, and your life takes on a new flavor, the delicious flavor of purpose. Then the irony comes full circle. The things that you used to crave and desire arrive in your life without you chasing them, and you, from this glorious new position of feeling whole and complete without them, pass them along and keep them circulating. Give up the want, know in your heart that you do not need one more thing to make yourself complete, and then watch as those external things become less and less significant in your life.

Suggestion for Implementing This Mind-set:

- *Create an inventory of those things that you continue to pursue but truly do not want in your life. Then create an inventory of what you would like.* You might substitute truth for deception in your relationships. For booze, you might substitute eight glasses of water a day. For anger, you might substitute love and harmony.

  By becoming aware of the poisons in your life, and using your invisible miracle-making mind to create what you truly want and know you deserve, you will find yourself living in harmony. You will experience in your physical world precisely what it is that you think you are entitled to create. Inventory your life and get it on purpose.

12. *Ask nothing of anyone and practice unconditional acceptance.* Your miracle mind-set requires what may seem like an alien

stance at first reading: "Ask nothing of anyone." All your demands of others create an environment where miracles are impossible to manifest. The place you are attempting to reach within your mind is one of complete unconditional acceptance of others. That is, you must be empty of judgment and demand in order to experience real magic in your life.

At first this might appear to be an impossible task, but before rejecting it, remember at this stage you are only working on a mind-set. So, since your mind is your own private territory, you can simply give this unconditional acceptance a private audition for a few days and see if you don't soon begin to experience a new kind of serenity.

Asking nothing of anyone gives you a true sense of freedom. Whenever you are about to be upset or angry at someone, stop yourself with the statement, "They owe me nothing. I expect nothing of them. I'll just accept them where they are right now." You will find that two days of practicing this attitude will convert you quite nicely, particularly if you practice this with the person to whom you are the closest.

For me, this person is my wife. When I remind myself that she owes me nothing, that she is a loving presence in my life with no obligations to me, I then have to be accepting of her unconditionally. Notice I did not say that I had to agree with her 100 percent of the time. I simply remind myself to demand nothing. Her presence is a gift to me, and her beautiful soul and body are wondrous gifts offered to share with me. But they are not obligations or debts. She is not mine to own in any way, nor likewise am I owned by her or anyone else. We are totally responsible exclusively for our own souls. When I remember that, my wife and I have a beautiful, spiritual, joyous partnership. When I forget that, as I do occasionally, we have stress and unpleasantness, and real magic is impossible.

This principle frees you up immensely in all areas of your life. You look upon others as gifts of which you ask nothing, while simultaneously you are engaged in your worldly roles. Even those who are paid to serve you, such as waitresses, clerks, salespeople, attendants, employees and the like, need to have this kind of attention from you. I have expectations and am grateful for whatever they bring into my life in exchange for the salary or fees I pay, but I am not better than they are in any way simply because I have chosen to be the payer and they have chosen to be the payee. These are chosen roles. Nothing more, nothing less. The amazing thing about developing such an attitude is that the less you expect or demand, the more that seems to come your way, and the better the service as well.

Seeing the fullness of God in service people, and treating them with respect rather than demanding their attention, creates a magical response most of the time. But you do not treat people that way because of what you will get, you do so because that is how you are aligned in the world. Love and harmony are your purpose. Send that out everywhere and you will discover amazing results.

This business of not demanding anything of anyone is also appropriate in your relationship to God, or the universe, or spirit, or whatever you choose to call the invisible intelligence that suffuses all form. That invisible intelligence is a part of you as well. "The kingdom of heaven is within you" is not an empty cliché, it is a reality. God will work with you, not for you. Know that your life is a gift and that the universe owes you nothing and is not beholden to you in any way.

To get to a position of being able to create miracles, you must understand the difference between willing something extraordinary to happen, and being willing for it to happen. Demanding a miracle in order to prove God's existence is an exercise in futility. Miracles do not, and will not, occur in your life or anyone's life because of some demand. You must be willing to allow miracles to transpire.

This point was clearly brought home to me as I was doing some research for this book. I spent every morning meditating for about an hour under a particular Hawaiian flowering tree. Each morning I would look up at the same branch of this tree and think: "If there is anything to this spiritual stuff that I am experiencing now, and if I truly do have the power in my mind to affect the world around me, and if miracles truly are within our grasp, then just let that flower above me drop onto the ground next to my outstretched hand. Let me be able to will it just with my mind and then I will be convinced." So went the internal dialogue between my mind and the physical world. But the flower never wavered. Each morning I'd think, *this* is the morning. I will make it fall today, just with the power of my mind.

Then one day I was invited to give a talk for a local church. At 5:30 the morning of the talk I was meditating under "my tree" asking the internal loving guidance I have written so much about, "How may I serve? Who am I to be giving spiritual messages to people who have come near and far just to hear me? Is there really any substance to this growing knowing within me that miracles are a possibility for all of us? Am I to write and speak about this subject in greater depth than I have ever before considered?"

It was as still and windless a morning as I had ever experienced. The branch above me was stationary as I contemplated what I would say to the people who would be gathering in a few hours. I had only a twinge of doubt, but nevertheless it was there. At the very moment in which I was asking about the authenticity of all of this, and asking whether I was really to play a role in talking about miracles, that flower dropped from the branch and landed in my outstretched hand—at the very moment when I was *not* concentrating on my wish. Out of a windless morning that branch was the only thing moving. It was shaking above my head so noticeably that it was as if an invisible force were present in it and only it.

The strangest calm came over me at that moment. It was crystal clear, and all doubt was removed and has remained absent from my consciousness since that morning. "You cannot will miracles, Wayne, instead, *be willing* to allow them to come to and through you." I stopped meditating that instant, took the flower with me, and went to the church knowing what I would be talking about that morning. It was at that service that I met Gail Longhi and our meeting with Mauricio came about.

I knew I had been sent a very special message that morning. Nothing could ever persuade me that that flower—which dislodged itself on a windless morning and landed in my hand when I was asking nothing of it, and yet had been attempting to will it down magically just with my thoughts—was all a gigantic coincidence. When I let go of my demand, I was given the answer I needed. The teacher, so to speak, appeared at just the right moment, and I began to see miracles showing up in my life in new and exciting ways. When that flower fell into my hand, I also knew that I had the ability and would be given the tools that I needed to speak and write about the world of real magic. That simple little event that morning on Maui just before I gave my first speech on this subject was to transform my life in ways I had not even considered, and this was just a few short years ago.

Life is what it is. No more, no less. Ask nothing of it, as Emerson reminds us: "These roses under my window make no reference to former roses or to better ones; they are for what they are; they exist with God today." As do you and I. Come alive in your mind to the point of demanding nothing of anyone or even of life itself. See the divineness in all of the people you encounter. Accept that and you will be in the inner frame of mind for creating real magic.

Rather than asking something of others, try giving instead. Become the giver, even if what you give is simply the radiance of love and unconditional acceptance that you are feeling within. It is the giver, not the taker, who is the true miracle worker and, ironically, it is the one who is focused on giving as his or her purpose in life who seems to receive so much more than those who are always looking for more. It is all in your mind-set!

Suggestion for Implementing This Mind-set:

- *Give yourself a day to ask nothing of anyone.* For your spouse, your children, your co-workers, everyone that you encounter today, decide to give to instead of taking from. What a pleasant surprise awaits you as you simply extend yourself to others and expect nothing in return. As you will see, the less you expect from others and the less demanding you are that they serve you, the more will come your way.

Just give love and unconditional acceptance to those you encounter and notice what happens. How can you be angry or hurt when you have no expectations? This is a wonderful exercise to implement when you find yourself feeling victimized or underappreciated. Expect no appreciation and allow those you meet to be what they need to be. Then you will see that the appreciation that you think you need is unnecessary. In fact, being upset because it is lacking is just another way of allowing someone else to control you with their actions or lack of actions. When you relinquish that and simply give to others because that is your purpose, and for no other reasons, then you will find yourself receiving the very appreciation that you coveted so desperately. Now you will not need it. You'll acknowledge it, and then get back on purpose.

13. *Begin to develop authentic power for yourself.* As you proceed in developing your miracle mind-set, think about what it is that will make you an authentically powerful human being. This concept of personal power is often tossed around without stopping to consider what it takes to be personally powerful.

By authentically powerful I do not mean the ability to dominate or control others. If power is measured in such terms, then where is your power when those people, whom you control, leave? To be authentically powerful, your power must not reside in how others react to you, nor exclusively in your physical strength or appearance. If power is dependent on your physical beauty, where is your power when it is gone? Authentic power is not located in the physical body— inevitable changes transpire in the material world. Exclusive alignment with the physical side of your humanity is a movement away from true empowerment because it is transitory and dependent on how others react. And anything that is dependent upon the physical, material world to be authentic always slips away as that material world changes and becomes less of what has been called attractive or strong.

Authentic empowerment is a different kind of journey. It is found on the path of alignment with your soul's purpose. With each step that you take to align yourself with your soul's purpose, you further empower yourself. You must remember, however, that you are in a culture that places primary emphasis on the physical side and minimal emphasis on the spiritual, or invisible, side. You are constantly encouraged to align yourself exclusively on the physical side of your humanity. So, as you read these pages, remind yourself that your objective is personal empowerment—to literally become your own miracle maker.

Transforming your body into as healthy a specimen as possible will probably require a complete about-face in your nutritional and exercise habits. These habits have developed in a culture that has daily tempted you to align yourself with your physical self exclusively. Your spiritual side, as you become realigned, will implore you to eliminate poisonous items. Yet your physical side will tempt you with toxic allure. Your physical alignment can literally disempower you and make the transformative miracle you imagine for yourself an impossibility. Yet the light that is within you, invisible though it may be to your five senses, knows precisely what you require in the way of nutrition and active exercise.

When you become realigned you will follow your inner signals almost effortlessly. You will see and feel yourself changing. That shift will signal a movement away from inauthentic power, to personal empowerment. The physical temptations will remain, and occasionally you will allow them to win, but your new spiritual alignment will dominate your life, and a periodic slip will not dislodge your authentic self. This realignment will show up in virtually all areas of your life.

Alignment with the physical realm will cause you to be tempted to cheat, steal, cut corners, deceive, bully, angrily lash out, or give in to an addiction. If you stay with this alignment, you will witness the disintegration of your power. You will have made the irresponsible choice to disempower yourself. The immediate rewards may make you look more powerful, especially to others, but you will know inside yourself that you are weaker. You will know that you once again succumbed to the weakness of temptation and ignored your inner urgings.

Authentic power, the ability to create what seems impossible when totally aligned with your five senses, is accomplished step by magic step. These steps are inner thoughts that guide you to pay attention to something you already know but have ignored in favor of the immediate gratification of your physical-world sensations. Just one little victory at a time is the way to experiencing authentic empowerment, perhaps for the very first time in your life.

Authentic empowerment is the knowing within that you are on purpose, doing God's work, peacefully and harmoniously. It is knowing that you can create whatever you need to further that work, without resorting to manipulating or harming another. It is a new way of being, and it can show up in thousands of tiny ways.

For example, in the seventeen miles I drive between my office and my home there are numerous traffic lights, often heavy traffic, and a multitude of construction delays. When I was more physically aligned I was always in a hurry, and angry over every little delay or slow driver, rushing through yellow caution lights and generally in a state of upset for about ninety minutes each day. I was allowing myself to become inwardly upset as a result of the physical-world realities that were a part of the life I had chosen for myself.

When I realigned myself, I began to experience authentic power in that same situation. Now, before leaving on that seventeen-mile excursion through those real-world conditions, I play it all out in my mind first, before even getting into my automobile. I see it going the way I would like it to go. I picture myself peaceful throughout the trip, stopping at caution lights, staying in one lane, and even blessing those who drive at a pace that requires me to slow down. This is my mental picture as I enter my automobile for the trip to the office. I am calm, relaxed, and ready to enjoy the next forty-five minutes of my life.

I am empowered authentically! I am no longer victimized emotionally by how others choose to drive, or how the traffic lights perform. I do not need any specific external conditions for me to feel loving and purposeful and to enjoy the present moments of my life in traffic. I have shifted my alignment primarily to the spiritual, invisible domain, and only secondarily to the physical.

Whereas previously my thoughts and feelings in the invisible domain of my life flowed from whatever was happening in the physical world, now it is reversed. My thoughts and feelings—my invisible, spiritual self—dictate how my physical world is going to be experienced. This is authentic empowerment—to have control over one's environment— and it is possible in virtually all areas of your life, if you choose to be empowered with the miracle that is your spiritual, invisible soul first and foremost in all of your physical-world undertakings.

Being personally powerful in any life situation becomes easy and natural when you realign yourself in this fashion. This is empowerment, and it works in everything you do and with everyone you meet. Align yourself to your soul, listen to those inner pleadings to be at ease and on purpose, and you will shift your life over to being an authentically powerful person. It is with this mind-set that real magic will become available to you as a life choice.

Suggestion for Implementing This Mind-set:

• *Detach yourself for a brief period from the behavior of controlling others through your size, authority position, physical prowess, physical appearance, age, wealth or anything external to yourself.* Imagine yourself as just a soul interacting with other souls. Truly treat others as if the fullness of God resided within them. Imagine that all manner of physical-world attributes are nonexistent. Give this a try for a day or two. See how much authentic power you truly possess.

I often do this with my little children. I imagine myself without my adult-size body and all of the power that goes with being grown up. I try to relate to them for a period of time, say, on the way to school, as if we were all without bodies and only our thoughts and souls were present in the car. I see how empowering this is to them and to me. I listen to them, rather than giving them orders. I send them love rather than directions. They see me as a loving guide, rather than a big-person father who can make them do what I want them to do.

Give up your need to control, and substitute a kind of unconditional acceptance of those you meet as soul mates, all equal in the eyes of God. Convert your marriage or primary relationship into a spiritual partnership. No authority. No one in charge. Simply two mates connected by an invisible bond, without one needing to dominate the other. You will be surprised at how you will empower others as well as yourself when you shift your inner world away from domination and control, to one of unconditional respect and loving harmony. While this world is of course invisible, it nevertheless is much more powerful and authentic than that which resides exclusively in the visible, material world.

14. *Practice daily meditation.* Learn how to meditate, and make meditation an integral part of your daily life. This final step in creating your miracle mind-set is, for me, the most significant.

Five years ago, I could not imagine myself meditating on a regular basis. Today, I cannot imagine my life without it. It is the vehicle I use to create the state of mind I have been writing about in this chapter. I cannot imagine myself going on stage to speak, without first meditating. Similarly, every single writing session is preceded by a meditation. My life is primarily about meditation, or quietly going within to discover the invisible intelligence and loving guidance that is always available to me.

The process of meditation is nothing more than quietly going within and discovering that higher component of yourself. After a while, you come into direct contact with what has always been a mystery in your life. You will discover God, that infinite invisible intelligence that is always a part of you and your daily life. Here is how Richard D. Mann describes it in *The Light of Consciousness:*

> The body seems to be moved, purified; the imagery has an unfamiliar and awesome clarity; the spontaneous registry of what one's life and current experiences all imply at their core may take the form of searing insights. Even the stillness comes as a blessing and a discovery. Whatever happens, it continues to suggest a shift in the inner structure of one's consciousness. . . .

Learning to meditate begins, like all learning, with a belief, a thought that must originate with you. The thought is simple: "I believe there is something to this experience of meditation and I am willing to invest the energy to discover it." That's it! A simple acknowledgment that meditation, though you may know nothing about it, has some inherent value, and a decision to approach it with an open mind.

In order to create that open mind, contemplate for a moment on the greatest thinkers you have admired. Consider the lives and the advice of these spiritual masters who have been more influential than the billions of other people who have lived on this planet. They all encourage us to meditate, to go within, to seek guidance in the silent invisible empty space that resides in all of us. Meditation gives you an opportunity to come to know your invisible self. It allows you to empty yourself of the endless hyperactivity of your mind, and to attain a calmness. It teaches you to be peaceful, to remove stress, to receive answers where confusion previously reigned, to slow yourself down and, ultimately, when you adopt meditation as a way of life, to be able to go to that peaceful place anytime. I do mean anytime. In the middle of a business meeting, in the midst of a tragedy, during an athletic competition—anytime! Meditation can and will help you become your own miracle worker and come to know the meaning of real magic.

I want to remind you again what the brilliant French philosopher and scientist Blaise Pascal said about the benefits of meditation: "All man's miseries derive from not being able to sit quietly in a room alone." I find this fascinating, and wonder why we don't include meditation in our education programs at all levels. In my experience with meditation, I have never felt anything but more peaceful, loving and confident after meditating. Here is something so simple, available to all of us whenever we choose to use it, that contributes enormously to our well-being.

And how do you do it? It's simple! You just make up your mind to do it. Listen to the literary genius Franz Kafka:

> You do not need to leave your room. Remain sitting at your table and listen. Do not even listen, simply wait. Do not even wait, be quiet, still and solitary. The world will freely offer itself to you to be unmasked, it has no choice, it will roll in ecstasy at your feet.

There is no right or wrong way to meditate. There is no specific strategy to follow. It truly is just allowing yourself to go into another dimension that is free of the limitations you experience in your physical world. In your meditative state, you can play out a difficulty or problem, in your mind. See it, experience it first within your invisible self and then play out how you want it to go in your physical world. You can also ask for divine guidance by silently asking questions like, "How may I act lovingly and serve you while participating in this upcoming event?" "What can I think to replace the self-destructive thoughts that are now in my mind and destroying my happiness?" Remember the key: "As you think so shall you be."

Meditation is your opportunity to create what you will be, by entering the invisible world of thought and playing it out there first, almost like a divine rehearsal for your life. Yes, you will receive the answers you seek. Yes, you will be able to manifest miracles that were all but impossible previously. Yes, you will be able to leave your physical body and enter the kingdom of heaven that is within you and come back to truly experience real magic.

In *The Three Pillars of Zen*, Philip Kapleau summarized what you can receive from the commitment to the exercise of meditation.

> For the ordinary man, whose mind is a checkerboard of crisscrossing reflections, opinions, and prejudices, bare attention is virtually impossible; his life is thus centered not in reality itself but in his ideas of it. By focusing the mind wholly on each object and every action, zazen [meditation] strips it of extraneous thoughts and allows us to enter into a full rapport with life.

Yes, you will truly move from ideas about your life to experiencing your purpose here, your heroic life mission. Another way of saying this was offered by Taisen Deshimaru: "If you have a glass full of liquid you can discourse forever on its qualities, discuss whether it is cold, warm, whether it is really and truly composed of H-2-O, or even mineral water, or saki. Meditation is Drinking it!"

Beautiful! Learning to meditate is learning how to live rather than talking about it. It is a true alignment with your purpose as a spiritual being having a human experience.

There are many wonderful books and guides on the subject of meditation, by people far more qualified than I may ever be. I will describe how meditation works, but I want to emphasize that this is what works for *me*. I would be most pleased if my description encourages you to begin the practice of meditation; however, you will only know what it is, and what benefits it offers you, when you experience it directly.

I have found that my most valuable meditation time is early in the morning. You might want to take that last hour in the morning before you normally would have awakened and devote it to meditation. Don't worry about being fatigued—it seems that one hour of meditation can be equivalent to a night's sleep. When I finish meditation I feel more rested than after awakening from a full night's rest. I take a long, hot shower or bath, then sit on the floor, legs crossed and eyes closed.

My first objective in meditating is to get myself to an alpha state. It is the equivalent, for me, of how I'd feel if hypnotized. The brain waves are altered. They are actually slowed down. I know when I'm there because I begin to feel light and euphoric. My arms feel lighter, almost like feathers, and will rise with a minimum of effort, seemingly assisted by an invisible force that is part of me. It is like a tipsy, light-headed, overall good feeling without chemicals or alcohol. After several years of meditation, I can get to this alpha state in a matter of seconds.

Burt Goldman, writing in *How to Better Your Life with Mind Control*, has a superb chapter called "Getting to Alpha," which describes in specific detail how to get there. What works for me is taking deep breaths and concentrating totally on the longest intake and outtake I can manage without having any intervening thoughts. I avoid the temptation of end-less thoughts bombarding my consciousness by repeating "Ey-Kiss" as an inner mantra, very slowly to match my breath-ing pattern. I can actually feel the chemistry of my brain altering as I sit concentrating on my breathing and repeating "Ey-Kiss" slowly over and over.

I have also used what I call the twenty-four-second-clock approach to getting to alpha. I visualize a clock made of numerous lights outlining the number 24. Then I shift it down to "23." My own personal rule at the beginning is to get the clock in my mind to go from "24" down to "0," *seeing* each number light up. If at anytime in that interval I become distracted, or a thought pops into my mind for even a fleeting microsecond, I start the clock over again at "24" and work it back to "0" without any intervening thoughts or mental dis-tractions. This is a way of learning to discipline yourself to concentrate on one thing and to empty your mind of all other thoughts. Getting all the way to "0" from "24" is a monu-mental accomplishment! I am at alpha when I succeed.

The alpha state is an incredible lightness of being. I feel lighter, and a wonderful, joyous feeling of inner goose bumps overwhelms me. As I stated earlier, at this stage for me my arms are like feathers and my head feels weightless. I then concentrate more fully on my inner vision and may elect to create a pastel-colored or pure-white screen. I feel alone, peaceful, blissful and ready to use this meditation time in any way I desire.

WHAT TO DO WHILE MEDITATING

Each session offers numerous opportunities to use the time in valuable ways. Your options are unlimited. You are entering the spiritual world as you elect to go within your self and dis-cover God. This is the avenue through which miracles will begin to manifest in your physical world. I welcome this time and suggest it be treated as divine and special. Don't let anyone degrade it or impinge upon it.

The practice of active meditation includes presenting problems or questions for consideration. About a current life problem I often ask, "What is the lesson here?" or "How can I benefit from this situation?" For example, at one time I was experiencing some difficulties with my fourteen-year-old daughter. At issue was a boy she wanted to date, and it felt impossible to talk to her without our communication becoming mired in upset and obstinate behavior. In a meditation I asked, "What is the lesson here? How can I be of service to my daughter?" Suddenly I saw her on my inner screen. She was crying and I asked her, "What's the matter? Let's talk about it."

She responded, "I can't talk to you about it, you're my father, you're from a different generation. You really don't understand."

I visualized what I call my *circle of truth*, which is my meditation technique wherein whoever goes into the circle can speak only the truth. I placed my daughter in the circle and she told me that it was impossible for her to share with me, her father, what she was feeling. I joined her in the circle, held her hand and said, "I agree with you. You are troubled and you can't share it with me because I am prejudiced and overly protective as your father. I am so preoccupied with you not getting hurt and getting in above your head, that I can't truly hear what you are saying or feeling. But I do know someone you can talk to."

Then, in my mind, I transformed myself back closer to her age. There I was, fifteen years old, holding my daughter's hands. I could experience in my mind everything I wore then, including the cheap after-shave lotion, the moccasins, and the

Brylcreem in my hair. As a teenager I asked her to tell me what was bothering her.

Standing in the circle of truth, she opened up, telling me, teenager to teenager, all that bothered her about her father. She related, among other things, how I couldn't be objective and didn't trust her to have good judgment.

When I came out of the meditation I was crying, but felt as if I had made a breakthrough. While it was "merely" a ritual of the mind, it was truly a miracle in the making.

Later that morning I had perhaps the most meaningful conversation with my daughter of our entire lives. I related what had taken place in my meditation. We sat holding hands, explaining to each other how we felt and vowing to share more openly what was troubling us. The situation was resolved. We hugged each other and both said the magic words, "I love you. I will try harder to hear your concerns." I've included this story as an example of one of the many things you can do while meditating.

The vehicle of meditation offers innumerable opportunities to resolve conflicts. The guidance is there within yourself. While meditating you can ask questions and receive answers. You also can go backward in your life and relive experiences and be able to see the lesson that each of those life experiences provided. You can commune with those who were once in your life and now are either in a different part of the physical world or have left this physical world. You can make contact with the divine intelligence within you and use it in dramatic new ways. You can learn to get to the heart of any illness that may be a part of your life, blessing the discomfort or disease and seeking the meaning of the illness. You also may come into contact with your healing capacity. You can discover that your mind is capable of creating chemicals that will reduce your discomfort and aid your healing. You can learn to ask for and receive the courage to make significant changes away from addictive poisons and unhealthy life-styles.

Ultimately you will get to the point of going beyond thoughts and the activity of the mind. You will "transcend" to that unified field of consciousness where you have no mantra and no thought—this is bliss. And the glimpses of this state simply cannot be explained. They will be experienced and treasured—I promise.

After meditating I enjoy a continuation of the experience of that incredible lightness of being. I feel centered and focused and relate to others seeing that fullness of God in them. It seems that I automatically eat better, make healthier choices, drink more water, exercise more, and feel more generous, more forgiving, less stressful and less fatigued. I really cannot emphasize enough how valuable the practice of meditation is for me.

Recently I was asked to contribute, along with the Dalai Lama, Mother Teresa and almost thirty others, a personal experience of God for a book titled *For the Love of God*. Because meditation presently feels like my most meaningful experience of God, that is what I wrote about. Here's a portion of what I said:

> I find God by giving myself time every day—through prayer, or meditation, or whatever you want to call it— to go into another level of consciousness. I close my eyes and breathe. I center myself and empty my mind and begin to feel the love that is there when I quiet down enough to feel. As I do this I transcend time and space, and I am in the very presence of God, and it puts me into a state of harmony and bliss that transcends anything I've ever known. . . .
>
> How you do it doesn't matter. It doesn't come about

in some linear fashion or by studying somebody else's ways. The secret is in giving yourself permission to experience it first-hand, and then living whatever messages you're getting. When you experience this, you connect in a loving way to everything in the universe.

My technique is my own. It is not a part of any formal meditation training. It works for me and it has evolved, as will yours, from having the intention to make contact with this higher part of yourself. When you believe it is there, you will discover how. It will not match mine nor anyone else's. It will be your very own, very personal, very effective means of going within. There are many wonderful books and guides available to assist you in the how. But at this point, you need the intention to discover it yourself.

A SUMMARY OF THE FOURTEEN KEYS TO A MIRACLE MIND-SET

When you have committed yourself to achieving your miracle mind-set you may find the following checklist helpful. These fourteen suggestions, which have no preferential order, are only a beginning. All of them originate with your invisible mind. They are the keys that can unlock the door to real-magic thinking in your daily life.

1. Reserve your judgment and disbelief.

2. Create a real-magic zone in your mind.

3. Affirm yourself as a no-limit person.

4. Develop a new mind-set toward the concept of intuition.

5. Discover the secret that sits in the center and knows.

6. Learn to learn through knowing and trusting rather than doubting and fearing.

7. Affirm that your intention creates your reality.

8. Experience surrender and satori.

9. Learn to act as if the life you visualize were already here.

10. Live according to your spiritual self first and your physical self second.

11. Study the paradox, "You can never get enough of what you don't want."

12. Ask nothing of anyone and practice unconditional acceptance.

13. Begin to develop authentic power for yourself.

14. Practice daily meditation.

Once you have the inner way, the outer way will follow. The next chapters are devoted to helping you with that outer way. As you move on to the implementation of this miracle mind-set in all areas of your physical world, let the words of *Lao-tzu* in the *Tao-te Ching* echo in your mind:

When you find the way
    others will find you.
Passing by on the road
    they will be drawn to your door.
The way that cannot be heard
    will be echoed in your voice.
The way that cannot be seen
    will be reflected in your eyes.

PART II

APPLYING REAL-
MAGIC AWARENESS
IN YOUR
EVERYDAY LIFE

4

REAL MAGIC AND
YOUR RELATIONSHIPS

> . . . all you behold; tho' it appears Without, it is
> Within; In your Imagination; of which this World
> of Mortality is but a Shadow.
>
> — WILLIAM BLAKE

Although I have been talking at length about the inner journey and enormous joy that comes to you when you discover and retreat often to that inner quiet place of emptiness, where divine guidance is a part of your being, the journey still gets played out in your relationships to others who share this world with you. The true measure of how your life is going is in how you function with other people. When you are inspired in your relationships and have mastered how to live peacefully and joyfully with others, your life will be on the path that I have called purpose. In short, you will be experiencing real magic throughout your life, when your relationships are in order.

Imagine what would be the ideal state for you in terms of how you relate to others. Do not let anything get in the way of this vision. This is your fantasy. How would you like your love relationships to be each and every day? How would you like to relate to your children? Would you like to feel loved and important, and know that those you associate with in the most important roles in your life truly feel loving toward you? Would you like to feel sexually satisfied and blissful? How about your relationships to friends and acquaintances? Would you like to see a perfect kind of give and take, mutual respect and caring? How about your relationships at work and in the business community? Would you like to see those you work for have a great trust in your abilities, and be able to garner the respect and love of those you are responsible for guiding in an employment role? And what about your relationships to everyone else in your world? The strangers you pass each day, the clerks who wait on you in a multitude of roles, the people you sit next to on airplanes and buses. What would you like all of these relationships to be like if you could wave a magic wand and decree that it would be so?

The ability to create magical relationships in your life begins and ends with you. If you want to create miracles for yourself and truly live a fulfilled, self-actualized life, you need only accept complete responsibility for how you choose to go about relating to all of the other people with whom you share this divinely perfect planet. This, like the other areas of real magic, may require a great deal of unlearning, and a willingness to think in new and magical ways. You can have perfectly loving and fulfilling relationships with everyone in your life.

Now here is the hard part. It has absolutely nothing to do with anyone else having to change in order for this miraculous state of affairs to materialize. Just allow this "radical" notion into your consciousness for a few moments and prepare yourself for some real magic in all of your personal relationships.

THE MIND AS THE KEY TO YOUR RELATIONSHIPS

In order to manifest miracles in your relationships in *all* areas of your life, you must redefine who you are. As you know, I'm asking you to define yourself as a spiritual being having a human experience, rather than the other way around. When you emphasize the spiritual being that you are, you know that the invisible part of your humanity, your mind, is where you process all of your experiences. How you choose to process your world determines the nature and quality of your physical world, including your relationships to all others.

You obviously cannot become one with another human being in the physical sense. You cannot become the organism that another person is. Thus, really the only way you can have another person in your life in a relationship is in the invisible part of you that we'll call your thoughts or your mind. Yes, your mind is where you experience others. Even though you may touch, kiss, hold and caress others in a physical way, it is your thoughts and only your thoughts about those physical activities that determine the quality of your relationships. Your mind is all you have for relating—even your physical touchings are experienced in the mind.

Now mentally review and remind yourself of the key phrase, AS YOU THINK SO SHALL YOU BE! Since you cannot physically experience another person, you can only experience them in your mind. Conclusion: All of the other people in your life are simply thoughts in your mind. Not physical beings to you, but thoughts. Your relationships are all in how you think about the other people of your life. Your experience of all of those people is *only* in your mind. Your feelings about your lovers come from your thoughts. For example, they may in fact behave in ways that you find offensive. However, your relationship to them when they behave offensively is not determined by their behavior, it is determined only by how you choose to relate to that behavior. Their actions are theirs, you cannot own them, you cannot be them, you can only process them with your mind. Your partners in life, your children, your family, your business associates, strangers and even those who live elsewhere on this planet who are your brothers and sisters in a metaphysical sense, are all thoughts. When a hijacking occurs on the other side of the world, you feel something for those who are victimized. That something you feel connects you to those people—they are thoughts. But they are also in your thoughts as well. You are connected by invisible thoughts.

The reverse is even more difficult to process. You are a physical being *and* an invisible being to yourself, but only a thought to everyone else you encounter in your life. Just as they are thoughts to you, you are thought to them. Your relationships are located in your invisible self, which has no boundaries, no limits, nothing to keep you from experiencing bliss in your relationships to others, other than how you use your thoughts.

USING YOUR THOUGHTS TO CREATE YOUR RELATIONSHIPS

So now it is time for you to ask yourself the all-important question. What do you think about those people with whom you are in a relationship? Remember, what you think about is what expands, and your thoughts originate with you. If you are thinking about what is missing in the person you love, that will be your experience of that person, and will define your relationship. You will get stuck in a mode of dislike and unpleasantness.

When someone else behaves in a certain way, do you process that behavior negatively, saying to yourself, "I hate it when she does that," "I wish he would take better care of himself" or "I hate when he acts dumb like that in public"? A negative response results in more unpleasantness and negativity, because you can only act upon what you think about. In this scenario negativity is all that you have available to act upon.

Rather than processing another person's behavior in the judgmental way I have just described, you have the option to process the behavior in other ways. Remember, he or she is not creating the bad relationship; you are, by the way you choose to think. You could say, "She is on her own path and right now that is how she must react, but there are so many other outstanding qualities I love about her. Those are the things I am going to focus on. I want this relationship to be great, and if it is great in my thoughts, that will be my total experience of it." Or, "He can only take care of himself in the way that he knows how to now. I know it is destructive to him, but I'm not going to stay centered on what I dislike. I am going to send him love in spite of his actions."

This may seem like a Pollyanna method for relating to others, and it may even appear to be dishonest at first, since these do not reflect your true feelings. But keep in mind, your true feelings come from your thoughts, and if you are interested in manifesting miracles for yourself, you will want to think in miraculous ways.

Real magic in relationships means an absence of judgment of others. You really do not define others with your judgments. What you are doing is defining yourself as someone who needs to judge. Others are defined by their own thoughts and subsequent actions. So what you want to do is work hard at creating the exact thoughts in your mind toward others that will match up with the kind of relationship you wish to have. Just as you become what you think about all day long, so too do your relationships become what you think about.

Argue for your limitations in your relationships, and you

will produce a limited relationship. Your objective in creating miracles in all of your relationships is to get much better at seeing the people in your life in ways that reflect the miracle you want to have happen. There is no other way.

Remember that a central theme of this book is that the universe and all that is in it is on purpose. Your life has one big divine mission, and getting your life to purpose is crucial, because it is the only place where you can begin to manifest miracles. You must know and act as if you are fulfilling that divine necessity. And the most important message in this chapter is that so too are the relationships themselves some part of a divine necessity. Every relationship that you have.

Before taking a look at how to create miracles in all of your various kinds of relationships, you must get the divine necessity notion firmly planted in your mind, so you can begin to act upon it habitually, and unlearn old habits that work against miracles. Your life and all the relationships within it are purposeful.

GETTING YOUR RELATIONSHIPS
TO PURPOSE

Generally speaking, the quality of our lives is directly connected to the quality of our relationships to the people in our lives. And, to add to the equation, our relationships reflect how we relate to ourselves. That's right, to ourselves. Let me explain by way of a brief review of what I have already written in this book.

You have a constant, ongoing relationship with your mind and your body. When you say the words, "I said to myself," you are referring to two beings: The "I" refers to your invisible self (the thought); "myself" refers to your physical being that has a name, address and Social Security number. When "you" call "yourself" a jerk, that is your invisible "you" judging your visible "self." This is the ongoing relationship you have throughout all of your days here on earth.

Your objective is to see yourself as a spiritual being having a human experience and to develop a mind-set that creates real magic in your life. You want to attempt to eliminate the dichotomy between your invisible self and your physical self, between the "I" and the "self" in "I said to myself." If you think of yourself as a jerk, you must act in jerky ways. There is no other way. If you think of yourself as powerful, loving, sensitive, divine, and capable of making mistakes, you will act in those ways.

When you cultivate the awareness of your body, mind and soul as one, and experience unity within yourself, you are then ready to share this sense of wholeness and holiness with others, and this is where your relationships come in. When you have love for yourself, that is what you have to give away. Regardless of how another person interacts with you, you can give away only what you have inside to give. Just like the proverbial orange, when you squeeze it, you get what is inside—it has nothing to do with who does the squeezing, or the circumstances surrounding the squeeze. What comes out is what is inside.

What is inside you gets there by way of your thoughts; there simply is no other entry mechanism. If you harbor hate, hate is what you give away. If you harbor self-contempt, contempt is what you give away. If you harbor love and compassion, love and compassion are what you give away.

Your relationships travel the same course that you travel. If your way is through suffering and questioning why things are not working out, as I discussed in chapter 1, then your relationships also suffer. If you follow the path of outcome and begin to see that there are lessons to learn in life, then your relationships also reflect this pattern. And, if you go to purpose, and have your life on purpose, your relationships also reflect this position in your life. Remember, purpose is about giving. You acquire and keep nothing for your whole life. All you can do with your life is to give it away in the service of others. It is in this domain of purpose that miracles begin to occur in relationships.

When you are past the need to suffer and dominate others, when you are past a what's-in-it-for-me attitude toward relationships, and when you are focused on giving, serving and being nonjudgmental, then real magic begins to manifest itself in your life every day. George Washington Carver describes what I am writing about: "How far you go in life depends on your being tender with the young, compassionate with the aged, sympathetic with the striving and tolerant of the weak and the strong. Because someday in life you will have been all of these."

This is the definition of purpose in your relationships: treating others in the various stages of their lives as you would like to be treated in those stages of life yourself. These are all words about giving. Purpose is giving yourself away and refusing to ask, "What's in it for me?" Purpose is about relating with love rather than judgment. Purpose is all about giving yourself to others unconditionally and accepting what comes back with love, even if what comes back is not what you anticipated.

If you respond to hate with hate, or anger with anger, it is not because of what was directed your way, it is because that's what's inside you. You can't get prune juice from an orange no matter how hard you squeeze it. You can't give hate if you have only love inside, no matter how much squeezing comes your way.

Once you are on purpose, you will see yourself acting toward others in totally new ways—ways, incidentally, that will bring others closer to you than you ever experienced before when you were trying so hard to have them behave the way you wanted them to. It is such a paradox. The more you give away, the more you get; the more you try to force something for your own benefit, the less you seem to enjoy what you seek so desperately.

Let's take a look at the core ingredient of a relationship that is on purpose, and then examine some specific methods for getting there.

LOVE: THE CENTRAL INGREDIENT OF A RELATIONSHIP AT PURPOSE

At the center of purposeful relationships is love. But it is more than simply being able to say the words "I love you," for these words are used by people who also berate and harm each other on a daily basis. Love is giving and it has nothing to do with what you receive. Love is an inner process that you bring to a relationship. A relationship that is at purpose has love in the giving sense as its cornerstone. The best discussion I have ever read of this kind of spiritual love is expressed by J. Krishnamurti in *Think on These Things*:

> To love is the most important thing in life. But what do we mean by love? When you love someone because that person loves you in return, surely that is not love. To love is to have that extraordinary feeling of affection without asking anything in return. You may be very clever, you may pass all your examinations, get a doctorate and achieve a high position, but if you have not this sensitivity, this feeling of simple love, your heart will be empty and you will be miserable for the rest of your life.

This ingredient of love at the level of giving is how purpose is defined, and it is the ultimate in creating miraculous relationships. Even in the act of sex, the most exciting and fulfilling sexual encounters are those in which you know you are giving and asking for nothing in return. To know you are satisfying your partner truly and authentically is all it takes to have a perfect sexual encounter. When you begin to think only of yourself and how good a lover you are or how excited you feel, you have shifted off of purpose and retreated back to outcome in your sexual activity. It is perfect when you are giving; it lacks something magical when your mind is on receiving.

This ingredient of giving extends way beyond the sexual part of your relationships. It goes to all levels, and even to those relationships in which sex plays no role whatsoever. Like getting only what's inside the orange when you squeeze it, if you have love inside of you that is all you will have available to give away. And when you are giving away love, you have a different kind of sensitivity, one that allows you to see all people not in terms of their form, but in terms of the soul that is in back of the form. You begin to see the fullness of God in everyone you encounter, and the level of your relationships to others takes on the glow of real magic.

You see your children and all children not in terms of what they are doing, or how they are behaving or misbehaving, but beyond to the invisible part of them, the soul that is in that young body. If you meet that soul with love and radiate it outward to them, they will in turn respond with love. You have loving relationships with others because you bring love, rather than because you seek it from others.

Members of your family with whom you may have had a difficult time relating are no longer the source of your disdain. Your anger and negativity is gone, replaced by nonjudgmental love. This does not require long years of therapy or the assistance of support groups, drugs or special herbs. It requires only that you shift to being a spiritual being first, and a physical being second. This can be an experience of satori, an instant awakening to fill yourself with love, to ask nothing of anyone you encounter in all of your relationships, and to give that love away without asking what is in it for you.

Ironically, once you are on purpose in this manner, you will receive a great deal that has largely been missing from your life. Parents that seemed so impossible only yesterday, suddenly are no longer judged by you. Satori. You send them love, forgiving them for all that you have harbored in your invisible memory, reminding yourself that they did only what they knew how to do given the conditions of their lives at the time, and no one can ask any more of anyone than that. You send them love, looking past that which you once judged, and miraculously, your relationship with your parents is transformed. You have created a miracle!

Your friendships and business relationships can also improve dramatically with this new giving approach. When a conflict arises you suspend your negative thoughts and instead send out love. In so doing you change the actual environment from hostility to serenity. This is how conflicts begin to disappear and solutions begin to surface. A conscious loving person who refuses to use his mind to have negative hateful thoughts can literally affect his physical environment. When you respond in an unthreatened manner, and instead communicate an inner knowing in a peaceful loving way, you are incapable of being rattled by challenges. You have created a miracle in that relationship.

I can remember having some gigantic disagreements with my colleagues when I was a college professor. These colleagues often were involved in ongoing disagreeable relationships with other faculty members. There was an unwillingness to compromise and a stronger unwillingness to even discuss their differences. They were "difficult" or "impossible to get along with" unless you shared their point of view, which few did.

Yet I discovered I was always able to get my way with these "impossible" colleagues. I was experiencing real magic where others were experiencing exasperation. The secret? I sent them love and asked nothing of them. Just have love in your heart, even though you disagree, and let everything else take care of itself. The colleagues always came around, and found it impossible to be nasty or confrontational with me. I never made a big deal about it, nor did I brag to others about how I was able to have my way with these difficult people. I simply sent them the love that I had inside and then surrendered.

This approach to relationships is basically my approach to life. Stay on purpose. Know that you are here to serve. If you get off course, simply ask, "How may I serve in this situation?" and listen quietly for the solution. Get off of having to prove yourself, remove your ego from the encounter and send out love.

Many times I have stood in line at an airport counter watching an irate customer berating a clerk, and I've said to myself, "If only he could send them love he would probably get his way." The irate customer invariably leaves the encounter angry and unsatisfied, having gotten only an increase in his blood pressure. I generally say something nice to the airline representative. I give him or her a loving look and say, "Whatever you have will be fine." I get treated nicely, and more than once I've been bumped up to first class.

This is such a basic thing that I am surprised that more people don't catch on. It is the golden rule in action. Send out love, even to the stranger you pass while out for a walk. Surely it is how you would want to be treated.

FOUR ADDITIONAL INGREDIENTS OF RELATIONSHIPS AT PURPOSE

Giving love with no expectations is the cornerstone of your relationships when you are on purpose. There really is very little else that you need to know. Practice this giving of love, without conditions, and you will find yourself feeling full rather than empty, and blissful rather than miserable. Here are the four ancillary qualities that go into this real magic in your relationships.

1. *Relinquish your need to be right.* This is the single greatest cause of difficulties and deterioration in relationships—the need to make the other person wrong, or to make yourself right. To *win* the argument. To *prove* they don't know what they are talking about. To *show* that you are superior. The spiritual partnership is a relationship of equals. No one needs to be proven wrong. There is no "right" way or "winning" argument. Each person has the right to his or her own point of view. If you want to see miracles begin to take place in your life, simply let go of the need to make anyone else wrong for a few days and watch how differently things go for you.

You are capable of having a conversation with yourself before you open your mouth to make someone else wrong. A simple reminder to yourself that goes like this: "I know how I feel about this and I know that it doesn't match how she feels, but so what. It is enough that I know it in my mind, I have no need to make her feel wrong." Then stifle yourself and you have created a miracle right there. You have replaced a potential conflict with a loving response. Remember, no one, including yourself, wants to be proven wrong. You know you dislike it, so honor that place in others as well, and give up the need to take the credit or to show how superior you are. In a spiritual partnership there is no superior or inferior, both are equal and this equality is respected. Practice this and you will see love replacing anger between you.

This is also true in your relationships with all others. Your children need to be guided, not to be made wrong. There is always a way to teach young people without making them feel wrong. The embarrassment that goes with being proved "stupid" leads to a self-image of stupidity. You can replace those statements designed to prove how superior you are with loving responses designed to help your children and others examine their own point of view. Or you can quietly respond with, "I see it differently. I wonder how you came up with that conclusion?" The key is not to memorize statements to say at the right time, but to keep in mind that no one likes to be proved wrong, particularly publicly.

When you have that spiritual knowing within, that is enough, and your goal is to help others to have it as well. This can be applied in business, with strangers that you meet, in disputes with your neighbors, in virtually all human relationships. Confident people have no need to make others look bad. They know inside how they feel, they trust their own mind, and they allow others to interact with them in dignity rather than embarrassment.

2. *Allow space.* Let there be space in your togetherness. Again, it is back to loving unconditionally and giving rather than taking. When you love someone for what they are, rather than what you think they should be, or for how they please you, then allowing for privacy and space comes automatically. The loving thing to do is to allow everyone the option of being themselves. If being themselves involves time away from you, then that is not only allowed, it is lovingly facilitated on your part. The clinging relationships racked with jealousy and fear come from individuals who believe they have a right to dictate what the other person ought to be. Remember Robert Frost's line: "We love the things we love for what they are." So simple, yet so difficult for so many people to follow on a daily basis.

All of us need some time for quiet meditation, contemplation, making contact with our higher selves, self-examination, reading, listening, thinking, walking and so on. Solitude can become your most meaningful companion and it can assist you in being a more giving person in your spiritual partnerships. Rather than regarding your partner's need for time alone as a threat, see it as a time for renewal that you celebrate. Make every effort to help each other have that space. Treat that space as sacred. Keep in mind that your relationship to all others is in *your* own mind, not in what *they* think or do. Your need for privacy will be nonthreatening and loving when you become a spiritual being. You will treasure your time alone and be thankful for being with someone who encourages you in this regard, and you will do all that you can to ensure that your partner has plenty of that same space, without any judgment or threat from you.

Privacy and space are things you can give as wonderful gifts to your partner. If you refuse to give them, you will find your relationship deteriorating and all of your efforts to maintain it will be frustrated. The irony is, the more space you allow and encourage within the relationship, the more the relationship will flourish. The more you try to limit someone's space by keeping track of them or by insisting all their time be spent with you, the more you are contributing to the end of that loving relationship.

3. *Eliminate the idea of ownership.* Seek to enjoy each other, not to possess each other. You can never experience the miraculousness of a magical relationship if you feel you own the other person or in any way have a right to dominate or control them. No one wants to feel owned. No one wants to feel like a possession. No one wants to be dominated or controlled. We all show up here with a purpose, and that purpose gets thwarted when any other human being attempts to interfere with our heroic mission. Your relationship can either be the vehicle allowing your purpose to flourish, or it can inhibit

your feeling purposeful. Ownership is the greatest inhibitor to feeling a sense of purpose and mission in one's life.

You do not have the right to tell the people with whom you are in a relationship what they ought to be doing while they are here on earth. That is only between each person and their soul. You may succeed in imprisoning another, and you may have a marriage that lasts for sixty years, but you do not have a loving relationship if either partner feels owned or like a possession.

This is a lesson I had to learn the hard way. At one time I felt I could dictate how my partner should think and behave. It cost me dearly—a painful divorce, many unpleasant hours in hostile conflict and so much frustration and stress because of my unrealistic demands. Today, I have learned the lesson. I can't even conceive of the idea that I could own my wife. She is her own person and my relationship to her is based upon acknowledging that in her. It is indeed reciprocal. She encourages me to have the space and privacy that I need in order to write and speak and fulfill my own purpose. I in turn feel that she too must have the same privilege. Although it is tougher on her since we have so many small children, I am working each and every day on helping her to be able to have the same thing for herself. But both of us know within our hearts that we do not own each other. That is impossible. Our mutual love and respect for each other allows us to experience miracles in our relationship, whereas at one time they simply didn't exist. When we tried to own each other or dictate to each other even in small ways, we were driven apart. Now, each moment together is a treasure and we seem to be closer than ever, along with actually having more intimate, loving moments now that we grant each other unconditional space, love and respect. This is a miracle for us. At one time it appeared to be impossible. It came about through giving, not demanding. Through respect, not criticism.

4. *Know that you do not have to understand.* What a great lesson this is in learning how to make all relationships work at a magical level. You simply do not have to understand why someone else would want to do and think the way they do. The fact that you are willing to say, "I do not understand, and it is fine," is the greatest understanding you could exhibit.

Each of my seven children has a totally unique and separate personality and set of interests. Moreover, what interests them often holds no interest for me at all, and vice versa. I have learned to get past the belief that they should think like I do, and go through this world as I have, and instead I stand back and say to myself, "This is their journey, they have come through me, not for me. Keep them safe, guide them away from destructive self-defeating behaviors, and allow them to travel their own path." I rarely understand why they like the things they do, but I have gone past needing to understand it, and this is what makes our relationships magical.

In your love relationship relinquish your need to understand why your partner likes the television programs he watches, goes to bed at the time he does, eats the things he eats, reads the things he reads, enjoys the company of the people he is with, likes the movies he likes, and everything else. You are together not to understand each other, but to aid each other in living a life at purpose. Gary Zukav in *The Seat of the Soul* sums it up beautifully:

> The underlying premise of a spiritual partnership is a sacred commitment between the partners to assist each other's spiritual growth. Spiritual partners recognize their equality. Spiritual partners are able to distinguish personality from soul . . . because spiritual partners are able to see clearly that there is indeed a deeper reason why they are together, and that that reason has a great deal to do with the evolution of their souls.

This definition implies that one need not understand the other. Loving sacredly means loving what is, even if you don't comprehend the deeper meaning behind it. When you give up the need to understand everything about each other, you open up the gate to a garden of delights in your relationship. You can accept that person and say to yourself, "I don't think that way, but she does, and I can honor that. It is why I love her so much, not because she is like me, but because she provides me with what I am not. If she were just like me so that I could understand her, then why would I need her? It would be redundant to have someone with me who is just like me. I honor that part of her that is incomprehensible to me. I love her not for what I understand but for that invisible soul that is in back of that body and all those actions."

These are the qualities that make for a purposeful relationship. They all orbit around the planet of unconditional love. Get to this place and you will begin to see results in all of your relationships. You will begin to see the miracle of living your life on purpose.

HOW MAGICAL RELATIONSHIPS WORK

The miracle that you envision for yourself in all of your relationships very likely centers around being blissfully happy and content with all of the people in your life without any painful conflict. And maybe you even wish for the wonderful feeling of bliss that you experienced when you fell in love for the first time early in your life.

It is in your mind that you must go to work to create real magic for yourself in all of your dealings with all other people. To reach the stage of real magic, you must decide to go beyond suffering and outcome and literally live your life on purpose. When you do, your relationships will of course reflect this shift.

Furthermore, as you work on creating spiritual partnerships with all others, you will see the beginnings of miracles in other areas of your life. You will discover that you have miraculous abilities that you once ascribed only to coincidence or lucky breaks. You will begin to reach into the thoughts of others and connect with them in ways that are inaccessible when you live with doubt and fear. You will begin to know what the other person is thinking, and find yourself saying these kinds of things aloud with regularity: "I was thinking the exact same thing." "I was just going to suggest the same thing to you." "You must be able to read my thoughts, that is exactly what I was centered on in my mind." These kinds of sentiments are not haphazard or weird, they are the result of living at a higher level of consciousness.

This higher state of consciousness that begins to develop between you and others is the full-scale use of that intuition I have been writing about. You develop a sense of knowing through your connectedness to others and you relate to them on a completely different level than the mere physical one. You begin to recognize that the same infinite invisible intelligence that runs through you, runs through others as well. There is only one infinite intelligence. It is in every one of us. You now can literally connect to it in those you love deeply and experience a new connection, a new relationship.

This new way of relating does not require your physical presence with each other. You will learn to know what the other person needs and is thinking when you are miles apart. This is a connection of the spirit; you truly are one. You will telephone someone who is in a spiritual partnership with you, and they will know before picking up the telephone that it is you calling. You will find yourselves having more and more of these kinds of encounters. This kind of miraculous awareness with others will originate within you. In your mind. In your meditations you will receive guidance on what to give others, and when you go out into the "real world" and provide that which you recognized in a moment of spiritual enlightenment, the recipients may in fact be surprised at your knowing. But it won't surprise you any longer. You will begin to see this as normal. You are connecting on a higher level, a new level of awareness that you will come to call real magic.

You will find yourself capable of new and exciting feats with your mind, and you won't be dissuaded by the doubts of others. The anecdote that follows is one example of such knowing. At one time I wouldn't have written it because of a concern about how others might perceive it. No longer do I feel that way. I know it, and I share it with you. If you are a knower, then it will not surprise you. If you are not a knower or are a person who lives with doubt, you will reject it. So be it.

One morning during a powerful meditation I was able to see my wife in bed even though she was several miles away. I had left her side and gone for an early, long walk and decided to meditate before returning to our rented condominium on Maui. I felt I was with her that morning, hovering above her body in my meditation, and then suddenly I could feel her thoughts. To me it seemed I was actually able to enter her dream and experience with her what she was dreaming about.

I was absolutely certain of this, since in my meditation I could see her physical body there on the bed, and then I could feel her thoughts and images. It was a spectacular moment of connectedness at a level I had never experienced before.

When I returned to our summer home she was just getting out of bed and I began to tell her about the dream she was having a few moments before. She was flabbergasted. It was precisely what she had experienced in her mind. (Richard Bach wrote a novel based upon this idea called *The Bridge Across Forever*, in which he discussed having such an experience with his wife.) This happened two years ago, and this kind of thing has become much more commonplace for us. In fact, as I write these words I do not feel as incredulous as I did when it occurred.

Why is it so difficult for so many of us to accept such things as possible? We know there is an invisible connection between all members of the human species. We know there is only one source or one energy that flows through us all. There are not millions of Gods, only one and it is in all living things, and the source of all. We call it God, yet it is called by many names. The Tao is another name given to this oneness that is in each of us. As Lao-tzu said:

There is something obscure which is complete
before heaven and earth arose;
tranquil, quiet,
standing alone without change,
moving around without peril.
It could be the mother of everything.
I don't know its name,
and call it Tao.

It's in every one of us, and yet we still hold fast to our belief in our separateness. We think the invisible force that runs through our partners is somehow distinct from that which runs through us. The ability to wiggle your finger as a result of an invisible thought is a connection that mystifies us in the physical world. Something allows that thought to get to the finger. And the same invisible force that allows me to wiggle my finger allows my wife to wiggle hers. So why can't I wiggle her finger? Here is Einstein on this subject: "He [human beings] experiences himself, his thoughts and feelings, as something separated from the rest, a kind of optical delusion of his consciousness. . . . Our task must be to free ourselves from this prison. . . ."

As you reach higher and higher levels of spiritual awareness, you will discover what once was viewed as a miracle in your relationships is now your way of relating to all others. You reach a place within yourself where you truly know there are no limits. You truly do free yourself from the prison of your body and those delusions Einstein mentions, and you enter the world of real magic.

This new way of being in relationships extends up and down the spectrum of your contacts with all others. It even extends to your relationship to animals and all life on the planet and in the universe. With friends and acquaintances you begin to connect to their thoughts and have a knowing about what to give and what they need. With business associates you begin to trust your intuition. Instead of focusing on your own quotas and what others can do for you, you shift to a new position that puts their needs first. You become a giver, a person on purpose, and you focus on their quotas first, and trust the universe to provide for you. You have surrendered in those relationships and you see each person as a soul with a body and you reach out to that soul.

Miracles flow from this approach to business and you feel peaceful, purposeful and serene knowing that you are reaching others on a new level. Paradoxically, more flows back to you than ever before. But you are not centered on what flows back to you, and you give even more away, and so it goes. You have created miraculous relationships by connecting to all others through the Tao, or the God that suffuses their physical form. You are provided for and able to see the thoughts and visions of others. You have shattered the illusion of your separateness, and created a way to be connected instead.

This new approach to relationships incorporates a sacredness toward all living things. Animals that bark furiously at others are peaceful toward you when you do not feel fear or hostility. You sense some kind of invisible presence in all living beings. You begin to develop a tenderness toward everything and everyone and you see that wasteful, senseless destruction is impossible for you. Krishnamurti, talking about the simplicity of love, observed:

> Another day I watched some young boys picking flowers. They were not going to offer the flowers to any god, they were talking and thoughtlessly tearing off the flowers, and throwing them away. The grown up people do it too, they have their own way of expressing their inner brutality, this appalling disrespect for living things. . . . One can understand your picking a flower or two to put in your hair, or to give to somebody with love; but do you just tear at the flowers?

At a recent speaking engagement, I was invited to a luncheon reception. A young girl who was the aunt of the baby she was holding was having a bit of trouble with the child. I had been away from my babies for a week and ached to hold a beautiful baby girl. When I saw that beautiful little soul, I reached out to her and held her throughout the luncheon. She was peaceful and loving. I took her to the fish pond in the lobby and we talked to the "little fishies," making fishlike sounds. It was a special encounter. A mutual loving and giving relationship, although it only lasted for an hour or so.

Later that evening, after my presentation, I met the mother of that child and she told me something that I have become accustomed to hearing. "You are the very first person that my daughter has ever gone to outside the immediate family. She is so fearful of strangers, and has never, but never, let anyone else hold her. I was shocked that she stayed with you, and I am still in shock."

Babies know! Animals know! Strangers know! Young children know! That invisible intelligence, the Tao, flows through all of us.

When you come to another with love in your heart, asking nothing, only offering that love, you create miraculous relationships. And when you come to someone wanting something from them, not trusting them, doubting them, exploiting them, the level of your invisibleness is apparent, and the opportunity for miracles and real magic is decimated. Creating miracles in all of your relationships can be accomplished, but it is not done by memorizing techniques. It is accomplished by reorienting what is inside, which is where all your relationships are located.

APPLYING THE MIRACLE MIND-SET IN ALL YOUR RELATIONSHIPS

It is important for you to know that the willingness to encounter miracles must be located within you. You cannot wait for others to change in order for you to discover the real magic of purposeful relationships. The power, and joy, of purposeful relationships begin and end with your own mind-set.

As you read through the guidelines on the following pages, do not be full of doubt about what may seem to be impossible given the specific people in your own personal life drama. It is an inner game. Those around you do not have to understand or even agree, and it may very well be that specific persons (who are on their *own* path) may soon be out of your life on a physical level. What I am writing about here are your relationships with everyone in your life, more so than specific individuals. If you know within, after acquainting yourself with your own spiritual journey and finding your purpose, that certain people are no longer going to be sharing your physical space, then you can just as purposefully and just as lovingly make that choice. The relationship is not located in them, it is yours in your own invisible self to experience. Ending any relationship on the physical level is not a failing, any more than someone dying represents a failure, although it certainly ends the physical relationship.

This is you I am talking about here. A you who deserves to be treated with dignity and respect because that is what you are made of, and is what you are giving away. Those who do not yet understand this will move away from your physical life, and you will find it easy to allow that if it is necessary. The duration of material relationships is not on my agenda in this book. That is for each soul to determine, and I make no judgment about choosing to move on when it is time. There will be many you will leave behind in the physical sense. That does not make you or them failures; it is the relationship itself that has ended, not the person. In fact, in one grand divine way, you will ultimately leave all physical relationships behind.

But the soul never leaves. The soul is not in the material dimension. There will be many with whom you will stay in close physical contact and with whom you will choose to create spiritual relationships. So be it. Individuals will enter and exit your life much like the characters in a play. Some will have minor roles to play, and others will have starring roles for a while, and still others will help you to codirect and coproduce your life. Always they will be important to the overall play itself. Always they deserve your inner love. You will learn not to judge those who move in and out of your play, only to honor their appearance, even if they play their roles badly.

Ultimately you will get to the place where you can look back at all of the people who have been in your life, and realize you encountered them because they all had something to teach you. You will learn to love all of them, even those whom you cannot yet understand what it was they had to teach you.

With this in mind, free yourself of any nagging doubt about the specifics of your relationships. Move ahead, beyond the names and faces, to that place of real magic that has no name, no face, and no Social Security number.

- *Affirm your ability to create happy, fulfilling relationships.* This is the most important thing you can do. Know within that if anyone else is capable of being happy and fulfilled in their relationships, that capacity is available to you as well. Send away the doubt that you cannot do this thing because of others. It has nothing to do with others. It is all located within you. Removal of doubt is an exercise you can practice each and every day. Affirm aloud that you are entitled to be happy with everyone in your life. When doubt creeps in, as it will, remind yourself you have been hypnotized to believe this is impossible. Send the doubt away with mental images indicating your readiness to create fulfilling, magical relationships.

- *Once you have removed the doubt, enter your real-magic zone.* Within your mind, and your mind only, is your corner of freedom to think as you like. Think about images of happiness and fulfillment with others. See yourself sending out love, even in the face of anger, envy or dislike. Practice visualization and positive imagery, hourly at first. Think of the person who is the most difficult for you to relate to. Perhaps it is an aging, inconsiderate parent, or a co-worker who is absolutely impossible, or a tyrannical spouse. Now, in your mind only, overcome your inclination to respond with anger and hostility. Visualize yourself sending out love and paying no attention to how the person responds. Remember, you are not doing this for what you will receive. In a magical relationship, each person suspends their wants and gives of themselves from a sense of purpose. This mental practice will ultimately become your reality in the physical world. But it all begins with a disciplined effort to think magically. The universe will provide everything else that you need.

- *Accept the limitless possibilities of your relationships.* Your thoughts, your soul, have no limits. Your relationships exist in that sphere without boundaries. Now you must stop looking outward at all of the people you have blamed for your sour relationships, and affirm you are without blame and consequently without limitations on what you can experience for yourself. That glow you once felt in your relationships, perhaps when you were a budding teenager, was created by your thoughts, not your hormones or the hormones of someone else. Know within that the only limitations you have to magical relationships are those you have imposed upon yourself. You have taught everyone how you are willing to be treated.

    Now you can begin a new school, which has a curriculum of love and respect. That is all you study and share and it is all you will allow into the classroom. *No* limits, nothing but love. That is your mission, and you practice it in your classroom and by seeing the fullness of God in everyone you meet.

    If you meet someone whose soul is not on purpose as yours is, you send them love and move along, trusting and knowing that the right soul mates will show up and meet you at the same frequency you are radiating. This is a very personal path, this journey of real magic and miracles, and it is up to you to have the knowing within that you can accomplish it each and every day.

- *Practice trusting your intuition, that invisible inner voice that guides you in all things, including your relationships.* Surround yourself with people who encourage you to be all that you are capable of being. You will know who these people are. If you sense that someone truly doesn't want you to be around them, then follow that intuitive inclination. Your intuition will give you exactly what you need to know in the way of information about your relationships. Stop forcing yourself to make a relationship work; it cannot be forced. You may succeed in keeping some physical contact, but if your intuition tells you that this is the wrong time and the wrong person, then gently send them love and move along.

There are many soul mates, male and female, who will form spiritual partnerships with you. There are no accidents; these individuals will show up precisely on time. Those relationships that are one-sided have taught you all you need to learn. Continue to give love, but the people around you must be interested in assisting you in your spiritual development as well. Your intuition will tell you who these people are. Don't ignore it unless you want to return to suffering as the way of learning your relationship lessons. You will experience your intuitive dimension in exact proportion to how much you value it. If you reject it, it will not be available to help you, and you will continue learning your relationship lessons the hard way.

• *Ask for guidance in all your relationships by going within to the secret that sits in the center and knows.* You will be guided to give. Do so freely without expectation. You can practice going within and listening daily, but you must be willing to change your belief that this is a "way out" way to get help. Your relationships are what you have created, and only by knowing inside that you have the power to change them can you access the guidance you need.

This very day choose one friend or acquaintance to relate to from this place of inner knowing. Rather than being in your old skin today, give this person precisely what you think they need, based upon how you would most like to be treated. Give to this person without thinking about their reaction to you and without judgment. Forget about what they say or how they react.

Most likely you have been taught to evaluate your actions based on the results of those actions. You have been taught to focus on outcome. The secret that sits in the center and knows cares nothing about outcome. This is your God within, the giving, loving soul that is immune to outcomes.

Next, try the same experiment with a child. Go within and ask yourself, "How did I like being treated by big people when I was a child?" Again, forget about the outcome of your actions, and listen to your soul, to the secret that sits in the center and knows. Give to that child what you as a child wanted from others. Then see how *you* feel, not how the child reacts.

Your relationships all exist in this secret place within you. It is the source you must learn to consult if you want to experience the blessing of real magic in your relationships. Cultivate the magic in that private invisible place, and then send it out. Radiate it toward others and let go of the focus on outcome. Just for today. Then assess in your own private way the difference you experience toward those people.

This is the way to miracles. It will never fail you. There is no failure in the secret that sits in the center and knows. Only loving guidance!

- *Moment to moment, rid yourself of the doubt that you cannot have magical relationships.* Affirm over and over to your-

self, "I know I can make my relationships blissful."
Then, when you are about to be seduced into an argumentative stance, suppress your normal way of relating
and quickly review in your mind what it is you want out
of the relationship. A momentary reflection on how you
want to relate to this person will give you the opportunity to send out love, or to quietly sit in silence rather
than striking out. This is called learning through knowing rather than through suffering or doubting. When
you achieve a silent knowing within you, you will act
accordingly. When you doubt your ability, send out love
or caring, and you will defuse your doubt.

- *Shift from a human marriage to a spiritual marriage.* This
  can be accomplished by deciding what it is that you
  desire out of your marriage relationship. Joel Goldsmith,
  a brilliant contributor to metaphysics and author of *The
  Infinite Way*, spoke these words after a marriage cere-
  mony on November 18, 1959:

  An individual remains an individual, not only from
  birth to death, but actually long before birth until
  long, long after death. . . . We never lose our individ-
  uality; we never lose our uniqueness. . . . Each of us is
  individual, and each of us has individual qualities,
  each of us has individual talents and gifts, and these
  are not to be surrendered in marriage. Therefore in a
  spiritual marriage there is not bondage but freedom,
  but this is not true in human marriage. It is true in
  spiritual marriage; where both recognize that in mar-
  rying they are setting each other free. This is the only
  thing I have discovered in thirty years of this work
  that will make possible such things as happy marriages, peaceful marriages, successful marriages; the
  ability to set the other free and each live with his own

individual life, and yet share with each other without demanding. . . . Neither husband nor wife has any rights; they have only the privilege of giving, but they have no right to demand anything of the other.

This is a wonderful message for creating a spiritual partnership out of what might have been a human marriage with one partner beholden to the other. Live this creed, and you will know miracles in your spiritual marriage. Ignore it, and you will be erecting huge barriers to your bliss.

• *Switch from wishes to intentions in your relationships.* This is accomplished readily with specific affirmations of what kind of relationship you intend to create and how you intend to conduct yourself. The important point to remember is that you cannot intend for someone else to act in accordance with your desires. This will bring you nothing but frustration.

While you may decide to help someone else change, you can only do so "when the student is *ready*." You cannot make someone else ready, but you can take responsibility for *your* readiness. This is within your power, and is what constitutes your intentions. Be ready to give what is necessary, do it with active intention, and then let go of the outcome. Your actions will flow from this intention and you will find yourself much more at peace with your relationships, however they work out in the physical world.

Your intention to have a blissful relationship requires you to act in ways consistent with that intention. That is the secret to making your relationships magical. Even if you cannot intend for others, you will often find that their reactions to this new you will result in having them shift their behavior.

For example, I have witnessed many individuals who are in a "human marriage" to an addictive partner. They despise the drinking or drug use, and feel exasperated in such a relationship. I always advise them that they cannot intend for the other person to stop drinking, but they can have powerful intentions about how they will continue to treat their addictive spouse. "I will send love, but I will remove myself physically from their presence because I am too divine and significant to be the subject of any abuse." "I will teach them with my behavior, not my words, that I am not willing to be their victim any longer, beginning now." "I will offer my help if they are ever ready. I will not send judgment toward them and their choice to be self-destructive, but the most loving thing I can do is to no longer reinforce their addictive behavior. I will be letting them know I am not in bondage to them, and I am going to be leading my own life on purpose, rather than being an emotional slave to their conduct." These kinds of loving affirmations will do more to help those in need than staying around wishing their behavior will change, or that they will someday see the light.

You are here to serve and to love, but that does not mean being a servant. Keep in mind what Abraham Maslow told us: "There is no such thing as a well-adjusted slave." Send out love and let those who continue to abuse themselves, and you, do so to themselves if that is their path, but not to you any longer. This will do more to teach them what you are willing to have in a spiritual partnership than any amount of counseling and intervention you could offer. The great paradox here is that it is just this kind of shock, resulting from your own intention to no longer be a victim, that most often helps those abusers change their intentions from self-defeating to self-loving ones and consequently to a more loving, dignified, spiritual partnership. Your intentions create your reality, so be aware of them, and be willing to put them into practice in your world today.

• *Remind yourself that peaceful loving relationships come first and foremost from your state of mind.* You are in charge of your mind and you create all that resides within you. Once you have this knowing, you can surrender and simply let go of the conflict that exists in any of your relationships. For conflict cannot survive without our participation.

Your decision not to participate in conflict can come in a transformative moment. It does not require years and years of struggle. Satori is available to you right this moment. Instant awakening is a wondrous phenomenon. You can go through the gate and enter that garden of delights in all your relationships right now. If others in your life decide to continue in a conflicted, confrontational mode, you simply "pass" when that angst comes your way: "No thank you," you say inwardly, "I no longer choose to wrap myself in that cloak of negativity. Unless it is love that is coming my way, I simply will not let it into my consciousness." Miraculously, you have just experienced satori. You have created a miracle without changing anything other than your mind.

• *Use the power of visualization to manifest real magic in your relationships.* Keeping in mind that what you think about expands, try visualizing all of your significant relationships as already existing the way you want them to be in your life.

After a recent speech in Oklahoma City, I noticed a woman with tears in her eyes standing in line to talk to me. When the other people left she threw her arms around me saying, "Thank you, thank you, what you are talking about really works." She related how her daughter had not spoken to her for over seven years, simply refusing all contact. About a year before, this woman decided to begin visualizing herself and her daughter, not only back on speaking terms but enjoying the loving relationship that once existed. In her mind she refused to see it any other way, and for one solid year, this was the vision she worked on. She actually began to live each day as if that were the physical reality of their relationship.

She described becoming a happier woman because of this internal picture that she carried around. She meditated on her image and began to smile and live without the suffering that had been tearing her apart for the previous six years.

Then, someone sent her daughter a copy of a book of mine, *You'll See It When You Believe It*, with a note attached to please read the final chapter on forgiveness. Nothing more, simply a gift of a book along with a note, from a friend who knew the daughter was also living in pain. That was six months earlier, and now the two of them had not only reunited, but were in a closer, more loving relationship than existed prior to their falling out.

The mother was crying happy tears as she told me that she believed in the power of her mind to create the physical reality that she wanted so desperately. By acting in her mind first, and then her material world, as if all she wanted already existed, she felt she had created a miracle.

Thoughts are extremely powerful things. Thoughts held unwaveringly, that reflect in advance what you desire, and do not demand an outcome, are the ingredients of real magic. Try it!

- *Pay attention first to your spiritual invisible self, and only secondarily to your physical self.* This will require a dramatic turnabout, a full 180-degree about-face. Suffering does not take place in your invisible self, because that is a dimensionless, boundless, formless part of your humanity. To suffer, you need a body to give your suffering a place to be. It shows up in knotted feelings in your stomach, puffiness in your anguished, crying eyes, pains caused by your ulcers, dryness in your mouth, heavy breathing and sighing in your lungs, and so on.

  Reverse yourself and be a soul with a body, rather than a body with a soul, and play out in your mind first exactly how you want things to go for you. Pay great and exacting attention to those images. They will be the source of what is to be played out in your physical body, and will determine either the suffering or blissful condition of your body. When you pay close attention first to your soul, listening and making contact with it, asking it how it wants to be nurtured, and making that the most significant part of your days, you will find yourself behaving in accordance with those positive, loving, giving thoughts your soul beckons you to maintain.

  The choice is always up to you, and that choice is strictly located in the invisible dimension of your thoughts. It is up to you, in your relationships, and in every aspect of your life. It can either be, "Good morning God!" or, "Good God, morning!" The difference is in how you choose to process your life.

- *Stop pursuing what you do not want.* If you do not want conflict and pain in your relationships, keep in mind you are the one who is experiencing the pain. Assess what it is you are doing to maintain your anguish. If you often insist on being right, don't permit space, make demands you know another person cannot fulfill, or participate in arguments, go to work on your own conduct, which is the only thing you have absolute control over. Keep in mind you can never get enough of what you don't want. You will continue to pursue the pain and struggle you despise—just like the drug addict or the alcoholic continues to chase after what they despise—until you make up *your mind* that you are going to end the vicious circle.

Use whatever strategy you need to free yourself from seeking that which you despise. Practice shutting your mouth if that is what provokes your pain in your relationships. Practice removing yourself physically from potentially hurtful encounters. Take a moment of silent reflection before reacting. Become more intimate and reach out with love where it is an unaccustomed gesture, even if you have to fake it initially. Whatever it is that you do, practice your new strategies in your mind first. See yourself behaving in these new ways, all in the name of putting an end to the neurotic trap of chasing after what you don't want in your life.

- *In your own private, invisible, no-limit mind, ask nothing of those with whom you are in a relationship.* This is one of the quickest ways to create miracles in all your relationships. Simply say to yourself, "I expect nothing, because I know they can only be who they are, not what I think they should be," and proceed to act accordingly.

I find when I remind myself of this with my wife, I immediately release all of the reasons for conflict, and our relationship becomes magical. I always try to remind myself she is in exactly the right place, doing precisely the right thing she is here to do. It is a perfect universe, even if I do not comprehend why everyone isn't behaving as I think they should. There is a lesson for me in any behavior she throws my way, and instead of being mad at her, I take the position of helping her along her spiritual path, and forgetting about my judgments. Only when I remove my expectation of understanding or even agreeing with much of what she does am I able to send her unconditional love.

Even with my children, I can guide them, assist them, hopefully teach them moral lessons and attempt to be a model for what I would like them to emulate, but I cannot expect them to be what I think they should be. I must learn to detach myself from my expectations for others if I am to create real-magic relationships. Of course this does not mean one overlooks outrageous or violent conduct, but I can, and do, control the expectation that it should not be there and the subsequent pain I experience because of that expectation.

You too can rid yourself of those expectations, which ultimately will be the barriers to your own magical relationship. This can be done in a thousand little ways each and every day, with virtually everyone you meet. By sending away the judgments about how others are supposed to be, you create a place within yourself for love, where judgment previously resided. Love of the unconditional variety is what you are working toward in your relationships and everywhere else in your life as well.

* *Finally, meditate each day, and use a portion of that meditation to visualize how you want all of your relationships to be.* Get a picture of yourself acting in these new ways toward everyone, and ask for divine assistance in being a giving, loving, nonjudgmental person. Review in advance how you see other people reacting to this new,

miraculous you. Your meditations will give you peace and serenity for yourself, and will provide you with answers that may elude you otherwise.

Practice the new strategies you see come up on the inner screen of your meditations. You can focus on a divinely spiritual being that is held most holy and perfect in your mind, and literally ask that being what you can do to make your relationships magical and perfect. You will hear guidance coming to you that is motivated out of love and all I have been writing about in this chapter. There are no limits to what you can create in your mind during your meditative hours. You can consult anyone, create their presence right there in your mind, and come to rely upon that guidance at will.

Your meditations will become a special form of assistance to you. Go there often and invite your partner to meditate with you as well. You will never be misled. Your higher self, the divine presence that is always with you, is on purpose and will guide you in the direction you seek once you remove the doubt and make contact.

Much of what you have read here may be difficult for you at first, because all of us are much more comfortable in assessing the quality of relationships by focusing on others in our lives. If only *they* would change (the thinking almost always goes), our relationship would be perfect! The emphasis here has been on your spirituality and your willingness to imagine and create perfectly loving, giving, magical relationships. Thomas Crum's description, from *The Magic of Conflict*, serves as a fitting summary to this subject:

Powerful relationships arise when two centered individuals commit themselves to unconditionally love one another and to support each other's growth toward their full potential. Both give freely, without selfish motives or the desire to lock the relationship into any particular form. There are no boundaries when we fully embrace each other.

Indeed, the boundaries disappear when you commit yourself to miracles. And without boundaries you have no limits to where you can go in all of your relationships. This description is most apt in understanding the spiritual partnership I have been writing about in this chapter. This can be your choice.

If you want to see how this relationship exists in its most natural state, the next time you see a mother nursing her child, know that you have all of the ingredients in that one example. I have silently sat in awe watching my wife unconditionally giving of herself to each of our infant children. A mother doesn't get mothering lessons from any human teacher, she knows in her heart what is required to have that perfect, miraculous relationship. She gives unconditionally of her very own body so that her child might live. She asks nothing in return. She is totally connected to her child on an invisible level, and in awe of the little miracle that she holds at her breast. She knows within exactly what to do—to give without any expectations. She is willing to take the worst that the child has to give and respond only with love and affection. She looks past the inconveniences and the flaws, and has only love to offer. She is on purpose, and because mothers live at purpose we survive as human beings. Without the unconditional love that mothers feel for their young, we would all perish in a few days from neglect.

God has given us the perfect model of how to relate right from our opening moments outside of the womb. Give nothing but love. Send love even when you are sent poopy diapers, loud crying, belching, spitting up, sleepless nights and irrational behavior. Ask nothing in return for your love. Be on purpose. And the great irony is that you would, without question, lay down your life for that little person. That is how important your children are to you. Even without asking anything of them, they give you the greatest blessing it is possible to have. That is your model, and you can create the same magical, perfect relationships everywhere in your world, if you simply follow the natural intuitive awareness that is present within every cell of your being.

5

REAL MAGIC AND
YOUR PROSPERITY

If thou canst believe, all things are possible to him
that believeth.

— MARK 9:23

I guarantee you that this will be the most unusual discussion you have ever read on the subject of prosperity. The central message here, as in the rest of this book, is on rethinking the beliefs you have been taught to treat as sacred. For a moment, put aside the beliefs you have acted upon throughout your life, and imagine in your invisible mind what it is you would like to see in your life. What is your ultimate image of prosperity for your life? How much money, how much total prosperity would you truly like to have?

Now, open your eyes and see what you have created up until now. That's right, you have created your own financial picture, and it is precisely what you have acted upon. This is the hardest part for most people to truly understand. Most of us want to blame others or something outside of ourselves for the way our prosperity picture looks.

But you only need to look inside yourself. You can have all

of the prosperity you are willing to believe in and create for yourself. St. Mark does not say some things are possible and others are impossible. He says *all things* are possible. Keep this in mind as you prepare to create miracles of abundance in your life. Try to imagine a state of unlimited possibilities as being possible for you.

James Allen, in the nineteenth century, wrote the following words, in *As a Man Thinketh*, which I committed to memory as a young man. I have them taped to my bathroom mirror and to the dashboard of my car so I can be reminded of them every day. One simple sentence that, for me, tells it all: "Circumstances do not make a man, they reveal him." Read these words over and over again until you have them committed to memory. The message of this sentence is at the very core of your ability to achieve a prosperity consciousness rather than a scarcity consciousness.

You probably will not immediately agree with this notion of our present life circumstance revealing who we are. It is easier to blame our life circumstances and it only seems proven by the poverty all around us. We feel we would be cruel to say that the circumstances of the poor reveal who they are. Surely those people did not choose such undesirable circumstances.

This well-intentioned thinking, however, allows you to hang onto your scarcity consciousness, and to defend your misery and your inability to transcend your life circumstances. We mistakenly believe that we cannot be compassionate and concerned about those in miserable circumstances while also encouraging ourselves and others to uncover any beliefs that may be contributing to the situation.

Stop and consider for a moment the potential benefits of applying this message for those who are living in the worst of circumstances. Then also consider all of the people who have shifted from a life of scarcity to one of prosperity. When you examine what it was that made the difference, without exception it includes the invisible world of beliefs and attitudes.

A radio talk show host accused me of having a cavalier attitude toward the poor when I described my philosophy on his program. My contention was that being broke is a temporary state of affairs that afflicts almost everyone at one time or another, but being poor is an attitude, a set of beliefs that gets reinforced when we shift to blaming life circumstances for the condition of poverty. One of the incoming calls in response to this radio conversation was from a physician in Washington, D.C., who had grown up in a family of thirteen children in total poverty in Jamaica. He disagreed with the host, saying:

> I lived in dirt-poor conditions all of my life. I mean hungry, starving poverty. But I always had a vision of myself as a doctor. I could not lose that vision, and I would always tell my grandmother about that picture in my head. She was raising all of us on practically no income, and she always told me to never, but never, let the picture become blurred. She told me about the value of that inner picture, and that if I always kept it, and believed in it, I would only have that picture to act upon.
>
> As I got older and finished high school, I applied to several hundred schools in premed curricula, and I was rejected over and over again, but I could not shake that picture that my grandmother helped me to have as a ragtag little boy playing with the chickens in our little hut in Jamaica. Finally I was given a conditional opportunity to enroll in a premed program in Europe, and I worked my way there and all through school.
>
> Today I am a physician with a thriving practice. Without that vision, without that invisible picture in my mind, I could never have escaped the life of poverty that continues today for most of my brothers and sisters

and all of my friends there. They live in poverty and believe that life dealt them a stacked deck, and that I was lucky. But I know better. I am living the life I pictured for myself.

And Dr. Dyer, don't you ever let anyone dissuade you from telling the truths that you know, because you are doing much more to help those in horrible circumstances than those who buy the big lie that their lives are beyond their own control.

I cannot stop telling those truths because I too am a living, breathing example of what I am writing about. I also left a life of scarcity behind me, and I too know the singularly powerful role that my beliefs within my mind played in creating a life of prosperity. Indeed, circumstances do not make a person, they reveal him, and I encourage you to suspend any erroneous belief that this may apply exclusively to Wayne Dyer and a physician in Washington, D.C., but has nothing to do with you.

It has everything to do with you. It transcends individual lives because it involves universal laws and principles that were here long before you showed up in your current physical form. I am just reporting on what I know to be true for myself and many others. If you want to experience prosperity at a miraculous level, you must leave behind your old ways of thinking and develop a new way of imagining what is possible for you to experience in your life.

FIVE ASPECTS OF A PROSPERITY CONSCIOUSNESS

Take an inner inventory and see if the following statements are a part of your consciousness.

- There is not enough to go around.

- You have to get yours or someone else will grab it before you.

- There are only so many fish in the sea.

- You never know if opportunity will knock.

If these and similar thoughts are part of your personal inventory then probably you were taught that you are living in a world of shortages. You have been raised to believe in scarcity. The concept of lack has been embedded into your belief system.

In order to develop an inner vision of prosperity, you will have to shed this old vision of scarcity. The following five essentials of a prosperity consciousness can help you make the shift.

1. *You don't need anything else to experience prosperity.* Getting rid of a scarcity consciousness means changing the inner pictures that reflect a lack in your life. You already have everything that you need in order to experience a lifetime of prosperity. Truly you are not going to get "it" all, you are "it" all already. Prosperity is first and foremost a mind game. It is a set of inner invisible beliefs you carry around with you. You must know you have all that you need right now; you are lacking nothing to gain prosperity for yourself. I have always enjoyed the following story, which perfectly illustrates this principle.

A man who was ragged and appeared to be without anything in a physical sense came upon a road boss and said, "Can you help me? I need work."

The road boss said, "Fine, take that large boulder over there and roll it up and down the hill. If you need work that will fulfill your need."

The man said, "You don't understand, what I really need is money."

The boss replied, "Oh, if it is only money that you need, here is fifty dollars. But you cannot spend it."

Again the man was perplexed. "You don't understand, what I really need is food and fuel and clothing, not just money."

The boss again replied, "If you are sure that this is what you need, then spend the money for food, fuel and clothing, but don't eat the food, or burn the fuel or wear the clothing."

The man was finally forced to look at what he really needed, which was a sense of security, peace and inner satisfaction. All totally invisible, all within the mind. All divine sustenance.

You are led to believe that the material things are reality and are providing you with what you need, while in fact they are only more matter, which is made up of more invisible space. What you need, you already have, and when you know it, and go within and create it in your mind, the divine sustenance you seek in the form of material things or money will be manifested in whatever amounts needed.

You must develop this new inner sense, and trust in the magic of believing. Your beliefs are yours, they originate with you, they are what you use (and all that you have to use) to carve out the circumstances of your physical reality. When you tell yourself otherwise, you are tapping into your scarcity consciousness and creating the very thing you most despise as your physical reality.

Trust in the power of your mind, in the knowing I have been writing about since page 1 of this book, in that divine guidance that is readily available to you, and you will have reached the first step toward manifesting the miracle of prosperity for yourself.

2. *You cannot create prosperity if you believe in lacks.* When you have mastered the ability to become a spiritual being as outlined in the first part of this book, you will begin to understand that who you are is located in that invisible, dimensionless realm that we call your thoughts. You have no boundaries and no limits. Understanding this means knowing that you lack absolutely nothing—all that you need for your life is already here, and was within you when you first arrived here in the physical world.

When you say to yourself, "I don't have enough money," or, "I don't have enough education, talent or strength to experience prosperity," you are operating in your mental world from a position of lack. Hence you are unable to go into the world of real magic.

To overcome this way of thinking, you will have to reeducate, or better yet, dehypnotize yourself from the lie that has been foisted upon you by every strand of our Western culture. Everything that you need, you already have. You are complete right now, you are a whole, total person, not an apprentice person on the way to someplace else. Your completeness must be understood by you and experienced in your thoughts as your own personal reality.

When the time arrives for you to depart this physical world, you cannot say, "Wait a minute here, I'm not ready, I am still in training, I have more schooling to attend to, I am building up my strength, I have to collect more money." You will leave your body, and it will still weigh the same. Your life is not that body, it is not in those boundaries and those limitations. It is invisible and weightless. It lacks absolutely nothing.

Whatever you have created for your physical body in the way of material things is the result of that complete invisible mind of yours. The irony of all of this is that when you know you are already complete, you begin to motivate yourself in a totally different way.

What you have become accustomed to is called *deficiency motivation*. That is, you assess all of the things that are missing or deficient in your life, and then you set up a plan to repair all of those deficiencies. "I need more money, more strength, more power, more beauty, more possessions," and so on. "When I get those things, I will have prosperity." Thus, you set your goals and go to work at becoming prosperous. But this is a gigantic trap. You can never experience prosperity from this mind-set, because you will always be suffering from the disease of *more*.

When you get the money you thought you needed to be prosperous, your mind-set hasn't been satisfied. Your mind-set is focused on more—on striving, not arriving. Thus you upgrade your number, and continue to struggle and suffer and even deny yourself in the pursuit of more. This is a common theme in our culture. Prosperity is simply impossible with deficiency motivation, in which the thought is, "I don't have enough," or, "Something is missing." A central theme of this book is, "As you think so shall you be." If your thoughts are centered on what is missing, then "what's missing," by definition, will have to expand. That will be your experience of this material world. What's missing will be your trademark and your experience of your physical reality.

There is another kind of motivation, called *growth motivation*, and this is the trademark of the individual who experiences real magic in the area of prosperity. With growth motivation, you simply change around the inner thinking, and decide to do your living within a framework of completeness. The inner dialogue goes something like this: "I am whole, complete, total, fully alive in this moment. This is it! I am it all, I need no more to be happy or fulfilled. Yet I know that I will be different tomorrow. My physical reality is always changing. The molecules that made up my material self yesterday will be replaced by new molecules. The physical body that I had ten years ago is completely new in a physical sense today. But I am also something other than a mere physical collection of molecules. I am divine necessity that reaches beyond the physical. I will grow. I will become something new and grand, but no grander than I now am. Just as the sky will be different in a few hours, its present perfection and completeness is not deficient, so am I presently perfect and not deficient because I will be different tomorrow. I will grow and I am not deficient."

With this kind of thinking, lacks are impossible. You begin to be motivated in your life by your own bliss, by your dreams, to live the life that you imagine to be your calling, your divinely specialized mission for being here, and prosperity becomes your very watchword. Abundance rains into your life. The universe begins to provide precisely what you need, and it is not doing so to fill a lack of anything; it arrives in your life in the precise amount necessary to help you fulfill your dreams. When you no longer feel you are lacking something, you can live the life you know is perfect for you, and then, more and more of the symbols of prosperity (money, stuff, power, and so on) seem to arrive in your life. A simplified summary of this is: More is less, less is more.

3. *You are not separated into categories. You are at once the seer, seeing and the seen.* To know true prosperity, you must learn to stop dividing yourself up and separating yourself from your prosperity.

There are not three of you in this world. There is not the observer, the observed, and the act of observing. What you observe is within you. Your observations are within you, and so is the entire process of observing. This is all you. Prosperous thoughts are yours, they are you. So too is what you observe as prosperity within you. And finally, the concept of being prosperous is all located within you as well. This may sound confusing, but it is crucial for you to grasp your oneness in all of this if you are ever going to know and become prosperity yourself. Ken Wilbur, in his fascinating book *No Boundary*, describes it like this; let these thoughts in as you prepare yourself for miracles in this dimension of prosperity:

> The split between the experiencer and the world of experience does not exist, and therefore cannot be found. Initially this sounds very strange, because we are so used to believing in boundaries. It seems so obvious that I am the hearer who hears sounds, that I am the feeler who feels feelings, that I am the seer who sees sights. But, on the other hand, isn't it odd that I should describe myself as the seer who sees the seen? Or the hearer who hears the sounds heard? Is perception really that complicated? Does it really involve three separate entities—a seer, seeing, and the seen? Surely there aren't three separate entities here. Is there ever such a thing as a seer without seeing or without something seen? . . . Our problem is that we have three words—the "seer," "sees" and the "seen," for one single activity, the experience of seeing.

You must learn to go beyond your hypnotized state, which has convinced you that here is first you the thinker, then you the doer, and finally the concept of what it is that you are thinking and doing. All of this is actually one and the same.

This is how prosperity works for those who live it each day. All of what you have previously divided up as prosperity thinking, prosperous behavior and something called prosperity that is located "out there," must be thought of as one. And that one can be you if you elect it! When you understand this, you will stop looking for prosperity as if it were something that you can wrench from its hiding place. You stop saying to yourself, "All I have to do is think prosperous thoughts, and it will come to me." You stop setting goals for your own conduct that will lead you to this elusive thing called prosperity.

What you replace this triumvirate with is a singularity of thought and action, which reflects your understanding that you are prosperity if you believe in it. What you need for a prosperous life, you already are. It is all you, there are no boundaries despite the fact that we have invented different words to describe various facets of how we have chosen to perceive it. Wilber sums up the insanity of this boundaried thinking with this example: "We might as well describe a single water stream as 'the streamer streams the streamed.' It is utterly redundant, and introduces three factors where there is in fact but one."

Now, take this awareness and implant it in your consciousness. You are not going to find prosperity. It will flow into your life only when you grasp this notion of your singularity. When you know it, your actions will reflect it. The very same thing may be said of scarcity. If you think scarcity thoughts, and act in scarcity ways, your life will *be* scarcity. You are what you think about, since that is all you have to act upon.

If scarcity is a word that defines your life right now, understand that it is not something that was visited upon you, it is simply your way of processing your life. You have divided yourself up as a thinker and a doer, victimized by something outside of you called scarcity. But in reality, you are scarcity. The choice of prosperity begins with your refusal to further splinter yourself, and instead to see the oneness that exists as you.

4. *You cannot experience prosperity if you believe that you don't deserve it.* As I've said many times already, you exist as a divine, spiritual being having a human experience. Your essence, your very life, is invisible and boundless. In this

realm, there are no judgments to be made. There is no one in this universe, now or ever, that is any better or more worthy of anything. Those who were born of royal blood are treated as royalty because some human beings have decided to elevate them. But in a much larger sense, through God's eyes, there is no "better" or "worse." It is this kind of thinking that you must learn to employ if prosperity is to replace scarcity as your way of living.

If you believe that you are undeserving of prosperity, that is the thought upon which you will conduct your life. You will not attract prosperity by thinking that you are undeserving, any more than you attract love by viewing yourself as contemptible. Surrender the idea that you are inferior. You are neither superior nor inferior, you simply are. And what you are deserves prosperity!

How can one invisible thought be more or less valuable than another invisible thought? When you view yourself as a spiritual being, when you create a real-magic mind-set of yourself as a thinking being first and foremost, then you stop the incessant comparison that leads you to believe that others are more deserving of prosperity. You are in a partnership with all other human beings, not a contest to be judged better than some and worse than others.

Once again, you have to undo the hypnotized state that led you to this kind of attitude. It began in your schooling, and it continues today. Here is John Holt on this subject, writing in *How Children Fail*:

> We destroy the . . . love of learning in children, which is so strong when they are small, by encouraging and compelling them to work for petty and contemptible rewards—gold stars, or papers marked 100 and tacked to the wall, or A's on report cards, or honor rolls, or dean's lists, or Phi Beta Kappa keys—in short, for the

ignoble satisfaction of feeling that they are better than someone else.

There it is, that business of getting people to believe that they are better than others. You very likely have bought into this big lie in some areas of your life. How could you deserve to think of yourself as a special divine necessity when you didn't measure up to the way others were performing or looking? You learned to compare yourself with others and even to believe that this is only human nature. It is the very thing that has not allowed you to develop a self-concept based upon being valuable, deserving and divine. On this subject of human nature, here is what John Stuart Mill wrote in *Principles of Political Economy*:

> Of all the vulgar models of escaping from the consideration of the effect of social and moral influence on the human mind, the most vulgar is that of attributing the diversities of conduct and character to inherent natural differences.

Indeed it is a vulgar model, one that teaches people to grow into adults who believe that it is only natural to compare oneself with others, and it is therefore only natural to learn to play dirty in order to get ahead of the other guys. And if some do not measure up in physical or material ways to others, that is an indication that they are not deserving. It is a vulgar, obscene system that contributes to the creation of large numbers of people who know no other way to assess their own value other than in comparison with others, and in so doing, it creates many who simply begin to think that they are not deserving of prosperity in any sense of the word.

A competitive culture endures by tearing others down. A cooperative culture evolves by helping each person to appreciate their own value and to feel deserving and spiritually valid. The choice is yours. Even if all those around you choose to be in competition with each other, you do not have to live by that model. You can see that you are just as deserving of prosperity as anyone else on this planet. With that kind of mindset, you will no longer act in nondeserving ways.

5. *Rejoice in the prosperity of others.* When you feel contemptuous, or even a twinge of jealousy, toward the accomplishments or life-styles of others, you are harboring negativity, where love must reside. When you have only love within you, because that is how you choose to regard life, that is all you will have to give away. Thus, you can test yourself by checking how you feel toward people who have acquired a dimension of prosperity that is still eluding you. You cannot attract prosperity to yourself if you are filled with rancor, judgment, anger, jealousy, hatred, fear, tension or the like. This kind of negative inner mind-set keeps you from being on purpose. You cannot be fulfilled and envious at the same time.

If you feel satisfied and happy, that is what you have to give away. Foster an inner belief that anyone who has achieved prosperity is entitled to it, and that their success is not a reason for you to feel inadequate or wanting. Even if a person achieves prosperity through what you consider devious means, it is still not a reason for you to feel anguished and upset. Know in your heart that those who use others will be dealt with by a universe that works on purpose and harmony. But for the most part, those who have achieved their own measure of prosperity deserve only your love.

Try to shift your focus from what others have or don't have to what you are going to do for yourself. Remember, when you evaluate and judge others you do not define them, you define yourself. Do you want to define yourself as a jealous, nonloving being if that is what will then expand in your life?

Rejoice in the great prosperity that you witness in all others. Let go of the notion that it shouldn't be that way. It is that way! That is all that you need to know. So too are you *that way*, whatever that way is in your life. Have a quiet acceptance of what is, send it love and then get on with the business of creating a full, prosperous, loving life for yourself.

These are the five factors that are most crucial for getting to a prosperity consciousness. Once you are working each day on developing this way of being, your higher self will begin to allow you to experience more and more prosperity in your life. This new consciousness will lead you back to that all-important dimension that is a central theme of this book: living your life on purpose.

PURPOSE AND PROSPERITY: YOUR TICKET TO REAL MAGIC

As you've seen throughout this book, you can only experience real magic when you get your life to purpose. When you are focused on learning through suffering or learning through outcome, you are using hindsight as your guide, and consequently you pay a heavy price in your everyday life.

In the area of your work, you may have been spending a great deal of time and energy doing things that you dislike, but telling yourself that it was absolutely necessary because you had bills to pay or a family to care for, or you simply had no other choice. Think about it this way, using numbers as a metaphor: If you are 99 percent invisible (thought and spirit), and only 1 percent form (the physical body that houses your soul), and you are doing something that you loathe, then you are essentially an inauthentic person. Your body is going through the motions, while you continue to think about how much you dislike the circumstances of your life. One percent is going through the motions, and 99 percent loathes the activities of your life. So if what you think about is what expands into action, the action or physical part of your life is loathsome and awful. You cannot experience fulfillment or the opportunity for prosperity miracles while you are living a life of loathsomeness. There must be bliss and harmony within in order for you to know miracles. Thus you must shift from suffering and outcome to purpose.

Getting to purpose in the work that you do, or the daily activities of your life, means knowing that purpose is about giving without concern for the results. When you are able to shift your inner awareness to how you can serve others, and when you make this the central focus of your life, you will then be in a position to know true miracles in your progress toward prosperity. There will be no limit to what you will receive in return for your giving and sharing, when giving and sharing are all that you have to give away.

Prosperity can be thought of as having limitless abundance in your life. You will never get to that point by hoarding, or focusing on what is in it for you. Remember, in a much larger sense, you cannot own anything while you are here, you cannot acquire anything—your life can only be given away. This is the area that you must learn to work on in order to be able to experience unlimited abundance and prosperity in your life.

The moment that you realize that giving is the key to your own abundance, you will also see that prosperity is readily available. It is not that difficult to give yourself away. Or is it? For some, they do not perceive the irony here. They want a life of prosperity, but concentrate exclusively on what is in it for them. Consequently they work, and struggle, and set goals, but they never seem to arrive, they never have enough. But, when you study highly successful people in all fields of endeavor, you find that they are not truly focused on the results that will accrue to them personally. Here is a perfect example, as reported in Srikumar S. Rao's June 1991 article in *Success* magazine titled, "The Superachiever's Secret":

> One day, Mehdi Fakharzadeh, Metropolitan Life's top agent, went to see a policyholder who suffered from heart disease and was filing a claim. There was no prospect of selling him more insurance. Most agents (striving for their goals) would have just handed the man a form and left. Not Mehdi, who had "surrendered to the process" of helping people. Mehdi filled out the form for him. When he found out the man also had policies with other insurers, he got forms from them, filled them out, and made sure the refunds came through.
>
> The man pressed payment on Mehdi, which Mehdi politely declined. But a few days later, Mehdi received in the mail a list of 21 of the man's friends and relatives: names, dates of birth, number of children—with a personal introduction to each. Mehdi sold millions of dollars in insurance to them.

When you constantly remind yourself of the overriding spiritual, social or loving purpose that drives your work, you will find your entire state of prosperity shifting. Uppermost in your mind is how you can serve the needs of those around you by focusing always on their needs and their quotas. Being on purpose generally means that you are at peace with yourself, and that peace is what you have to give away.

My experience writing and speaking throughout the world and my personal contacts with thousands of people have led me to believe that this is the one secret shared by those who are experiencing prosperity miracles in their own lives. What goes around truly does come around. The more you give away and do everything that you do in the service of others, the more that seems to come back. And when it comes back, since you are not interested in hoarding or owning it, you are more inclined to give that away, and the cycle of real magic takes root.

This lesson of prosperity applies to all fields of endeavor. An airline business, for example, which is focused on serving its travelers, will prosper most greatly when the entire fabric of the organization is based on serving others. When that sense of serving is neglected at any level of the business, the entire organization suffers. Boarding an airplane early one time, I overheard the sarcastic voice of a flight attendant say, "Here come the animals." I knew it was only a matter of time until that organization would perish from a scarcity of passengers. Sure enough, they have gone into bankruptcy. Employees need to know in their souls that they are privileged to serve those who are willing to give of their own incomes to use the service. The customers are responsible for their having jobs, and they should be valued and coddled and appreciated. The total emphasis needs to be on serving, forgetting about how convenient or inconvenient it is for the servers. This applies to whatever it is that you do. When you work in a dentist's office, your goal is to serve and help others to improve the quality of their lives. If it is to make money, to get the patients in and out as fast as possible, the entire office will experience scarcity, not prosperity.

But I am not writing this book to an organization, I am writing to you, dear reader. You can shift your consciousness all you want, but you must also shift the emphasis of what you do from outcome and results in your own life, to purpose. Try it! Shift for a one-month period of time, and see if miracles don't start showing up in your life.

Being on purpose in your life activities is simply a matter of changing around your own inner beliefs. You do not necessarily need to change positions or move to another location, for it is in the giving that you will experience this real magic.

In the Bhagavad Gita, God's words to Arjuna, the mighty warrior, are quite simple in this regard: "Strive constantly to serve the welfare of the world; by devotion to selfless work one attains the supreme goal of life. Do your work with the welfare of others always in mind." Notice that the emphasis is on what you have "in mind." God's final words to Arjuna are as follows: "The ignorant work for their own profit, Arjuna; the wise work for the welfare of the world, without thought for themselves."

While this may seem like too lofty a notion for you, I assure you that the benefits of this way of thinking are available for you right now. You do not need to memorize a set of lofty principles. Rather, you must simply get in touch with your higher self, which is always with you, and allow this natural part of you to take over. It turns out to be a very easy and fascinating way to live, and it comes not from trying harder but by relaxing and removing the pressures from yourself.

The less you need to force this new way of being on yourself, the easier it becomes to let it be the guiding principle of your life. A quick look back at the characteristics of a spiritual versus a nonspiritual being shows you that this is more a mental exercise than a physical one. It is about allowing your natural self to flow peacefully and knowing that fulfillment comes from giving, not getting. Letting yourself just flow is a concept that you will want to become quite familiar with as you begin to allow the prosperity that you desire into your life.

GETTING TO "FLOW"

Mihaly Csikszentmihalyi, in his book *Flow*, studied super-achievers—including executives, top athletes and artists—who have gained a life of prosperity. He describes the principle of flow as an investment in ourselves to our limits, in which we experience complete joy in our working present moments. He says that "once we have tasted this joy, we will redouble our efforts to achieve it."

Earlier, in Part 1, I discussed how everything seems to work perfectly in our lives when we are inspired. Flow is that kind of an inspiration, one so powerful that all obstacles seem to be removed and we are in love with what we are doing so much that it seems to just flow without any effort from us at all. You can experience flow in virtually anything.

I experience this effortless perfection when I am so involved in my presentation on stage that time seems to stand still, and hours go by in what seems to me to be minutes. Also, when I am totally involved and inspired in my writing, the typewriter seems to almost smoke as I fill page after page without any effort. Sometimes I feel as if I (the invisible me) am actually watching someone else writing, it is all flowing so perfectly. You have very likely known this feeling during an ecstatically divine lovemaking experience, in which time literally stood still and you knew complete joy. You can also get to flow in your work and in your daily activities, without waiting for those magic moments to appear as if they were directed by someone other than yourself.

Getting to flow in your life means achieving a state of concentration so total that everything else becomes nonexistent. People who experience prosperity in their lives know how to achieve this magnificent state, wherein their activities, instead of being a tedious set of chores to finish, become more like a meditation, only they are active and involved rather than sitting quietly. Flow has a great deal to do with purpose in your activities. When you are able to suspend your physical body as well as your ego, and allow your invisible self to emerge totally into what you are doing, your higher self is directing and producing and your body is merely going through the motions without any judgment from you. When you are in this state, you experience in your body a kind of unattached bliss that is saying to you, "This is why you are here, this is what you are supposed to be doing right now. You are fulfilling your grand mission and nothing else will be in your way." You are literally watching your body do things that are incredible, you are experiencing magnificent joy or bliss, and nothing can get in your way. You are on purpose, and you are having the kind of peak experience that others can only dream about.

There is a way to get to this state of flow. While Csikszentmihalyi describes this process in detail, Professor Rao of Long Island University summed up the process in the *Success* article I've already referred to. His summary points reflect what I have been writing about in this book. They are not only the secrets to becoming a superachiever in the workplace, they are the secrets for producing genuine miracles in your life. Following is a discussion of the five points involved in getting to the state of flow.

1. *Have an overriding spiritual goal that gives meaning to your work.* This means forgetting about yourself and shifting your total energy to how you can best serve others. Make your work a meditative experience, and instead of seeing yourself as doing a particular task, you actually, in your mind, become the task. You shift from a *human doing* to a *human being*. You literally become the ball in a tennis match, you become the report that you are working on, you become the book that you are writing, you become the meal that you are preparing. There is no separation, you and the task are unified, all in the name of that overriding spiritual objective to give of yourself in a purposeful way.

2. *Focus, and close your mind to all distractions.* Your mind is so powerful that it does not need to be continuously distracted by extraneous activities. You can train your mind to focus,

and this is why I have been encouraging you to learn to meditate. Give your mind the same mental training that you give
your body when you want your body to be in maximum physical condition. You need not be a slave to your senses. You can
create an atmosphere in which your mind is clear and free of
distractions, where you tolerate no interruptions.

I am writing in this very present moment while on Maui
with my wife and seven children and their constant flow of
playmates. However, I have chosen to create an environment
for myself within this beautiful chaos that I also treasure. I
have rented a tiny apartment for the summer. I have the only
key. The phone is disconnected. I awake at 5:00 each morning, and after meditating I immerse myself in my writing and
research. There can be no interruptions, no one knows where
to interrupt me other than my wife (who also uses this space
in the afternoons to concentrate on her writing projects). I can
totally focus my mind and subsequently my physical output.

You can create this kind of atmosphere for yourself. You
can train yourself to eliminate the endless mind chatter that
fills your consciousness. You can reach that higher place
within yourself and let all other distractions stay away. When
you do, you will begin to know about flow, and you will also
begin to see real magic appear in your activities. This can be
done on the job, in your home or in a quiet place somewhere
else. Focusing is your natural knowing within. You can either
ignore it, or go there often.

3. *Surrender to the process.* You must resist your impulse to
strive for what you want. (Does this sound familiar? I have
been saying this from page 1!) In the system described in
Flow, the world works with you, so you must be with the
actual process and let go of your learned instinct to strive and
struggle. Surrender to God, or your higher power, the invisible force that is always with you, that is beyond your five

senses. You must let go and surrender to the actual process. Forget about the result, the reward, the money, the trophy, the accolades, and put your mind and your physical body totally into the experience at hand. It is not that difficult to achieve. Read what Robert Coram wrote in *Political Inquiries* back in 1791:

> At every quarterly examination a gold medal was given to the best writer. When the first medal was offered, it produced rather a general contention than an emulation and diffused a spirit of envy, jealousy, and discord through the whole school; boys who were bosom friends before became fierce contentious rivals, and when the prize was adjudged became implacable enemies. Those who were advanced decried the weaker performances; each wished his opponent's abilities less than his own, and they used all their little arts to misrepresent and abuse each other's performances.

So, if you choose to stay with results rather than process, you can produce for yourself envy, jealousy and discord. If you make the shift, you can create flow, which leads to prosperity and the awareness of personal miracles in your performances. How do you surrender? Just let go! Don't strain to achieve; instead, enjoy the process of the work that you are doing. The results will come independent of your striving for them. When your mind is on the result rather than what you are doing, you create inner discord that blocks any and all possibilities for miracles to show up. Prosperity is about process, not outcome. Process is about purpose. Purpose is about loving and giving.

4. *Experience the ecstasy.* This is the automatic result that will flow to you from following the above guidelines. You will

know a kind of inner beatitude and bliss that will be unmistakable. It will sneak up on you and hit you over the head, so to speak, but nevertheless, you will know that glorious emotional peak experience if you get yourself to flow in your life.

It is the exact same feeling I described in the section on meditation in chapter 3. The reason it is the same feeling is because you are actually meditating your way through your work, and the automatic reward that comes without striving is that magical feeling akin to a warm shower running inside of you. It will lift you up and put you in touch with the inner knowing that you are finally on the right path. The ecstasy is its own miracle.

5. *Watch as you see yourself reaching peak productivity without striving.* Your state of ecstasy opens up new vistas of creativity and energy. This natural state of bliss is the key to improving your performance. This is the state that superachievers are able to create for themselves. The irony here is that this increased productivity is the result of having reached the state of ecstasy. The processes of surrendering, focusing and living at purpose lead to ecstasy. When you feel that inner bliss, you simply want more and more of it. The more of it that you are able to create for yourself, the more productive you become.

This is how it goes for me. When I am feeling that inner glow from being purposeful, and not focusing on the outcome, I want to write and write all day. Or I want to stay on stage and give and give, and when a talk is completed, I still want to stay with the people for hours and hours. Long after most speakers are back in their hotel beds, I am still talking to those who want to stick around and continue the process. The more ecstasy I am able to create through this method of flow, the more productive I become, and the paradox is that I am not the least bit focused on being productive and producing results.

I have used the following Thoreau quote in each of my last three books and I offered it as one of the secrets of the universe in my novel, *Gifts from Eykis*. It seems most appropriate to conclude this section with it once more. I cannot hear it enough, and I am trusting that you too want to be reminded of the real magical wisdom that is inherent in these words:

> If one advances confidently in the direction of his own dreams, and endeavors to live the life which he has imagined, he will meet with a success unexpected in common hours.

This happens in that invisible place. The emphasis is on "dreams" and "imagined," both of which are thoughts. Your thoughts create all of this ecstasy and ultimately all of the miracles that are going to come into your life in the form of increased prosperity. Your mind is very powerful in terms of what it can produce in your physical reality, as well as in the physical reality beyond your own borders.

USING YOUR MIND TO MANIFEST PROSPERITY

You are now on a path of working toward reversing scarcity consciousness to one of prosperity. This is largely a mental game. You must convince yourself that you and only you are responsible for the pictures in your mind. You must know how very powerful your picturing process is in creating the material world that you experience.

In sports, those who excel beyond their peers picture in

advance how they want to hit, place and kick the ball. The mental part, the invisible part literally, and I truly mean literally, shapes the way the physical results are manifested. Rickert Fillmore, the son of one of the founders of the Unity Christian Church, was asked if this principle applies to the selling of real estate, and he responded, "If it works at all, it works everywhere."

This is a universal principle. It does not work only on Sunday mornings or only for some people. This is a vital, alive factor of the universe that you are a part of and that is a part of you. Any area of inquiry by any human being is a part of this process. What you can conceive of as a picture in your mind, you can create in the physical world, provided you do not let go of the picture. The more you know this, the more you will see it manifesting in your life. Aristotle said it this way— "The soul never thinks without a picture"—ancient wisdom that applies today in your life.

In sales, the individuals who have their minds made up that they cannot consummate the deal will act on this invisible picture, and proceed to sabotage the closing. Sentences such as, "I've never been able to do this," "I know I am wasting my time," "They are not really going to buy this from me," are all road maps etched within the consciousness leading to fulfillment of that very prophecy. If you shifted those sentences around to reflect your purpose of giving and serving that prospect, your mind would be repeating these kinds of inner sentences: "It is impossible for me to waste my time in helping another person" and "They will receive the fruits of my loving intention." "If anyone can do this thing well, then I too have that capacity." "The intelligence that runs through others runs through me as well." The picturing process is the way to create a prosperity consciousness within your mind. No one can ever take that away from you.

My wife and I are currently having our children take lessons from acknowledged masters in the art of meditating and learning to trust one's inner vision. We do this not to give them an advantage over others, but for the purpose of their knowing that they have something within them that no one can ever take from them, regardless of the material circumstances of their lives. They are learning very early that their peace and tranquillity as human beings is dependent upon themselves, and that they have a special retreat within that is always available to them, once they have learned how to enter that special kingdom. They will learn what the title of a favorite poem of mine means, as they practice it in their daily lives.

The following five stanzas are from this poem, "My Mind to Me a Kingdom Is," by the sixteenth-century poet Sir Edward Dyer (a spiritual relative?):

My Mind to me a kingdom is,
    Such present joys therein I find,
That it excels all other bliss
    That earth affords or grows by kind;
Though much I want which most would have,
Yet still my mind forbids to crave.

No princely pomp, no wealthy store,
    No force to win the victory,
No wily wit to salve a sore,
    No shape to feed a loving eye;
To none of these I yield as thrall:
For why? My mind doth serve for all.

I see how plenty surfeits oft,
    And hasty climbers soon do fall;
I see that those which are aloft
    Mishap doth threaten most of all,
They get with toil, they keep with fear;
Such cares my mind could never bear.

Content to live, this is my stay;
  I seek no more than may suffice;
I press to bear no haughty sway;
  Look, what I lack my mind supplies:
Lo, thus I triumph like a king.
Content with that my mind doth bring.

Some have too much, yet still do crave;
  I little have, and seek no more.
They are but poor, though much they have,
  And I am rich with little store;
They poor, I rich; they beg, I give;
They lack, I leave; they pine, I live.

While the rhyme scheme may seem a bit outdated to those of you used to more modern poetry, the message is indeed provocative. All the luxuries of life bring with them attendant suffering, unless you know that within you is the kingdom of serenity that can create all of the prosperity that you could ever want. You can translate the message of this poem to every single form of human activity. Your mind is that kingdom, capable of creating any picture that it wants. And once you know that the picture you want is one of prosperity, that is what will be attracted to you, based upon the actions that will *flow* from those images.

Two cooks in the kitchen follow the exact same recipe, item for item, following each and every detail in precise order and using the same oven. One has a cake that is grand and delicious, the other experiences something quite the opposite—a flop! Why? Their minds picture what they want to create. One has a picture in mind of a positive outcome, knows within that this is going to be a grand cake, and sees the result in advance, even if it is on an unconscious level. The other has a completely different mind-set, one of doubt and fear, and approaches the entire project from a scarcity image. Even though the second cook follows the recipe in exact detail, the cake is exactly what was predicted: "I am not good at this sort of thing, and I know this won't turn out." Sound like a fairy tale? It is impossible for different outcomes, you say, if both follow the same directions.

I have witnessed this type of thing in my own life over and over. Somehow I learned as a young boy that cooking and drawing were not my fortes. Even when I followed the instructions exactly, such as in painting by numbers, filling in every number with the exact paint that was indicated, my painting would turn out like a disaster and my brother Jim's would end up being framed and hung on the wall. Jim knew that he could produce a masterpiece, Wayne knew that his would be a disaster. Same paint, same brushes, same numbers, same everything, except the knowing and hence the result. This was true also of my cake-baking episodes. I could follow the physical directions, but nothing could shake my mental picture, and my mental picture is what turned out to be the reality. Our beliefs are invisible ingredients in all of our activities.

There is a magic in believing that transcends logic. Prosperity in all things, including money, flows from those pictures. Yes, I am saying that we can actually affect the physical world and all of the circumstances of our lives by the way we use our minds. Money and wealth can and will flow into your life when you follow the principles of prosperity consciousness. It works in athletics, selling, cooking, surgery, taxi driving and even your own personal bank account.

Most of us believe that money-making is a game that is played with forces outside of ourselves, forces such as the economy, the stock market, interest rates, the Fed, government policies, employment statistics and the like. But as you move along the spiritual path and begin to get a taste of the power of your invisible self, you discover that money-making is merely a game that you play with yourself. Creating money is just like creating anything else in your life. It involves not being attached to it, and not giving it power over your life in any way. Authentic power does not come to you from the acquisition of money, because without the money you would then be powerless. Authentic power comes from your soul, that magical place that is always within you.

Prosperity in the form of wealth works exactly the same as everything else. You will see it coming into your life when you are unattached to needing it. You will see it flowing into your life when you are in flow and giving of yourself in a purposeful manner. Money—like health, love, happiness and all forms of miraculous happenings that you want to create for yourself—is the result of your living purposefully. It is not a goal unto itself. If you chase after it, it will always elude you. You will never have enough, and you will suffer enormously as a result.

There are examples everywhere of people who have large amounts of money but are purposeless in their souls. Famous actors and actresses plagued by drug habits, committing suicide at what others thought of as the peak of their careers. Hotshot businessmen plagued by fear, wracked with ulcers, and ending their lives because of business failures. Divorce rates among the very wealthy, skyrocketing along with painful courtroom squabbles over who gets what. Lottery winners plagued with alcoholism and ending up bankrupt or suicidal even though they are in possession of unimaginable bank accounts. When wealth is the reason for your activities, and the quality of your life is based on what you have accumulated compared with others, then prosperity is impossible. You will be back at suffering as your means of enlightenment.

When you are on purpose, doing what you know you are here for, and forgetting about what will come into your life in the way of money and wealth, then money and wealth arrive in your life in amounts sufficient to provide you with a life of prosperity. And this is real magic in action. I can say this because it has always worked for me. When I chased after money, I never had enough. When I got my life on purpose and focused on giving of myself and everything that arrived into my life, then I was prosperous.

Prosperity is not the result of following a strict set of gimmicks and strategies, it is a mind-set, a mind-set that is centered on your ability to manifest miracles. Whatever you have believed to be impossible, shift it around to create an inner prosperity picture.

What follows are guidelines that you can use as you start to befriend your own miracle-making potential. Scarcity can go right out the window, replaced by the abundance that you once believed was only available for those lucky others.

APPLYING PROSPERITY PRINCIPLES IN YOUR DAILY LIFE

Paramahansa Yogananda put it in these words:

> Possession of material riches, without inner peace, is like dying of thirst while bathing in a lake. If material poverty is to be avoided, spiritual poverty is to be abhorred! For it is spiritual poverty, not material lack, that lies at the core of all human suffering.

To create a world of real magic for yourself, keep these words in mind. First and foremost, your objective is to create a kind of spiritual consciousness within yourself. Then allow the universe to take over in all of its perfection.

- *Disdain all disbelief!* Work out a system within your mind that allows you to imagine yourself living a pros-

perous life, with all the material things that are necessary. Send scarcity out of your mind and refuse to have
those kinds of thoughts. When an old habitual scarcity
thought begins to enter your consciousness, simply say,
"Next!" That's right, simply say to yourself, "next," and
it will remind you that the old thought is now finished,
and you are entering a new prosperous thought process.
Using "next" as a magic word will remind you to get on
with the magic of believing, rather than the anguish of
doubt. Commit to paper precisely what you would like
to have appear in your physical life. By seeing it and
reading it repeatedly you will plant that thought more
firmly in your mind and you will begin to manifest that
which you are imaging. I use this writing technique
often, and I place the affirmation in a place that forces
me to constantly read the words of the miracle I am in
the process of manifesting.

- *Keep a corner of your mind focused exclusively on your images of
  prosperity.* Go there often and use the power of your mind
  to sharpen your images of prosperity. Get down to specific details about what is there for you. Remind yourself
  that you deserve this corner of freedom that is uniquely
  your own and that no one can take from you. Don't think
  for a moment that you have to win the lottery or have
  some unusually lucky circumstance show up in order for
  you to have this miracle in your mind become your reality. Just stay with the picture, or that real-magic zone
  that you are creating. You will soon be acting upon those
  images as well as attracting prosperity to you. Here is an
  example of what I am talking about, taken from a fabulous book called *The Magic of Believing*, by Claude Bristol:

  > And this brings us to the law of suggestion, through
  > which all forces operating within its limits are capa-

ble of producing phenomenal results. That is, it is the power of your own suggestion—that starts the machinery into operation or causes the subconscious mind to begin its creative work—and right here is where the affirmations and repetitions play their part. It's the repetition of the same chant, the same incantations, the same affirmations, that leads to belief, and once this belief becomes a deep conviction, things begin to happen.

I have seen this work with my children over and over again. They repeat verbally, "I can do it, I can do it," when they previously experienced failure. I am thinking of my daughter Sommer balancing herself on my hands and falling time after time, until she was urged to say those magic words out loud over and over. Then, after failing to balance herself twenty or thirty times, she suddenly experienced the real magic. Saying over and over again, "I can do it, I see myself standing on Daddy's hands," she had the power to make it happen. This is not fantasy. If it works anyplace, it can work everyplace. You must believe it, and have that real-magic zone within you that never permits doubt to creep in, and where you endlessly repeat the affirmation that will lead to belief that will lead to miracles.

• *Study the world of matter, of all material possessions at the subatomic level.* Begin to note that everything material is nothing more than empty space when viewed from a closer perspective. See the folly of making that material world your master. Just like your thoughts, the material world is limitless. It is without beginning and end, totally abundant and totally available to you if you know what your true purpose here is.

Remember, prosperity, like everything else, is experienced in your mind. If you are somehow able to think of yourself as prosperous, and no one or nothing outside of you can deter you from that belief, then in fact your life is a miracle of prosperity. It is not in how much you have accumulated, unless that is what you choose to believe. The great irony here is that when you see yourself as prosperous regardless of material possessions, and you act on that belief, then the material possessions will arrive in exactly perfect proportions for your well-being.

- *Develop a trust in your intuitive inner voices.* It has been said that those who are classified as lucky are essentially those who go with their hunches, rather than with what others have prescribed. If you feel a strong inner inclination to change jobs, or locations, or to be around new people, or to try a particular investment, then place more trust in that hunch. This is your divine guidance encouraging you to take a risk, to ignore the ways of the herd, to be the unique individual that you are. Prosperity will be your experience of life, if that is how you begin to process life inside. It is inside that counts the most. This is the residence of your intuition, your guiding invisible force that never leaves you. Learn to trust it, and allow your physical body to travel the path that you are feeling within.

My hunches have always guided me in my investments. I can honestly say that the only time I experienced a big loss financially was when I ignored my intuition and invested in "guaranteed municipal bonds" that were for the development of projects that I knew within me were inconsistent with my beliefs. I struggled with the decision, but since the yields were high and the bonds supposedly guaranteed, I went against my intuition. That decision cost me over $150,000 in defaulted bonds. My intuition told me to stay away from such projects and invest in only those things which I believed in strongly, but my lust for higher yields won out. It was a very powerful and costly lesson for me. I have since learned to go with what I am feeling inside, regardless of the advice I receive from others about the wisdom of my choice. I only invest in what I feel to be proper and moral, and that feeling comes from going within and trusting the guidance that I receive. Some call it a silly investment method, but I trust totally in my intuition—and prosperity is the result.

- *Work at replacing thoughts within you that reflect a scarcity consciousness.* If you elect to constantly tell the world what is missing in your life, and how you never can get ahead, it is because you are in possession of an inner space that believes strongly in lacks. Those thoughts of scarcity include hardship, losing, difficulty and so on. These may be the topics that you find yourself discussing and the ways in which you present yourself over and over to everyone that you meet. You can replace these inner slogans that have come to be the logos of your life with new thoughts that include abundance, plenty, bountifulness, profit, ease, sustenance and the like. When you see these thoughts as the way your universe is, and process your world in these ways, the words and concepts will be your way of presenting yourself.

The secret that sits in the center of your being and "knows" is that silent invisible soul that is yours to use as you like. You must begin to catch yourself when you are thinking in ways that subvert your own prosperity. You must monitor yourself all day long, and be sure to catch each and every thought that involves a scarcity consciousness. You can transform those thoughts, but only if you are willing to become your own monitor, and then do nothing more than transform the thoughts. Eventually, you will begin to act on the new thoughts, just as you previously acted on the old ones to create your life circumstances.

• *Develop a conviction in your heart that prosperity truly belongs to you.* To think about prosperity is a great beginning. But you must make those thoughts that you are entitled to prosperity into actual beliefs. You must cultivate this kind of mental conviction if you are to manifest prosperity. This is your intention at work. It is the process of living through *knowing.* Merely wishing for it is not enough, for nothing will be truly in your life until you reach a conviction within you that it belongs there.

While it may sound extreme to you, listen to these words of St. Mark (11:23–24) in terms of this divine principle, and see if you can grasp their significance for your own prosperity undertakings.

Whosoever says to this mountain, "be removed and be cast into the sea," and *does not doubt* in his heart, but believes that those things he says will come to pass he will have whatever he says . . . whatever things you ask whenever you pray believe that you receive them, and you will have them.

Those are the words of miracles. Yet in fact these are the very stepping-stones to your own prosperity in what you are capable of believing, knowing and intending in your life.

• *Trust in the divineness that you are and that is the perfection of the universe.* When you have worked on the above beliefs, monitor yourself for a day, keeping track of how many scarcity thoughts versus prosperity thoughts you have, then surrender and stop fretting about it. Trust in that invisible force that flows through you. Remember— when you trust in yourself, you trust in the wisdom that created you! And obviously when you doubt yourself, you question that same divine intelligence that brought you here! Know within that the universal laws of prosperity and abundance have not been repealed. Know that if they worked for others they will work for you.

Now surrender and relax about it, and you will know what to do. This is satori—instant awakening. You no longer have to worry; prosperity will indeed come to you, and you will be creating it in a magical way, just like the magic that you experience every time you create a thought out of nowhere. Trust in the miracle that you are. Trust that the universal force flows through you—if it didn't you wouldn't be reading these words in this moment. Then get on with your life in a purposeful way.

- *Now act prosperous!* That's right, act as if what you deserve in the way of prosperity were already here. The person who acts prosperous is very generous. Be that way right now. If you're not generous when it is difficult, you won't be generous when it is easy. You must be willing to give to others, even when your coffer is not full, for this is your purpose. Your purpose is independent of coffers. It is spiritual. Act in a spiritual way. Give at least 10 percent of what you see coming into your life to those who provide you with spiritual sustenance.

For me, this principle has always worked in creating prosperity. I have always been a giver, even as a little boy. It was always easy for me to give up what I had in my pocket, even if it was only a few coins. I loved buying things for other people, and helping others of my choice to have more abundance in their lives. I have been giving much more than 10 percent to those I choose to assist and it always comes back to me more than tenfold. It seems to be a part of that invisible law of the divine.

Living as if one is already prosperous is to be a generous person. Giving it away without any expectation is living according to your spiritual self first, and your physical self second. It is the most divine way that you can be, and it is the secret to manifesting your own miracles in this prosperity domain. Kahlil Gibran wrote the following inspiring words on this subject. Study them carefully—they reflect the prosperity consciousness I have been writing about in this chapter.

> And there are those who
> have little and give it all.
> These are the believers in life
> and the bounty of life,
> and their coffer is never empty.
> There are those who
> give with joy,
> and that joy
> is their reward.
> And there are those who
> give with pain,
> and that pain
> is their baptism.
> And there are those who
> give and know
> not pain in their giving,
> nor do they seek joy,
> nor give
> mindfulness of virtue;

they give as in yonder valley
the myrtle breathes
its fragrance into space,
through the hands
of such as these
God speaks,
and from behind their eyes
he smiles upon the Earth.

When God speaks through your hands and smiles upon the earth through you, because you are an unconditional giver, a purposeful being, asking nothing of anyone, prosperity will be your reward.

- *When you have mastered the art of giving to others, then practice the equally important art of giving to yourself.* Take a percentage of all that comes to you in the form of money, and invest it in yourself. Put that money into a savings plan that is yours to monitor. See it as your miracle fund, and be rigidly firm about your contributions to this personal, fast-growing account.

  I have been doing this for my entire adult life. I have put away a certain percentage of what comes to me into my own financial miracle fund. It is automatic with me, and I never ignore this principle. As a result I was able to make myself financially independent at a very young age.

  You will be surprised at how quickly this fund will grow and produce income for you, a specific percentage of which goes right back into your miracle fund. If one does this from as early as childhood, one could be financially independent by the age of thirty. This is nothing more than a physical-world investment in your own prosperity. It is a fantastic policy to teach your children, and it will lead them in the direction of their own financial prosperity.

• *Get rid of the polarity that you may have about money.* You
have perhaps seen money either as God's blessing or as
the archenemy of spirituality. Money has often been used
as a battleground for matters spiritual and matters physical. Thus, if you have accumulated money, you may
have come to believe that this is in some sort of conflict
with your spirituality. Keep in mind that if your purpose involves providing things that require money for
others and for yourself, and if you are uncompromised
about your own commitment to your purpose, then
money will show up in your life to assist you with your
heroic mission. Similarly, if you believe that you do not
deserve money and that it symbolizes all that is nonspiritual, then you will block its arrival into your life.

When you are committed to your own personal highest powers, then a great amount of authentic universal
power will begin moving through you. It may in fact be
symbolized by the arrival of money into your life, and
then you will have to resolve any ambivalence that you
harbor toward this money.

Thus, the denouncing of money is a trap. Instead, see
it as that which is manifesting in your life to assist you
with your purpose. Then, stay on purpose and use that
money—and any other physical abundance that will
begin showing up in your life in larger and larger
amounts—to fulfill your commitment to your purpose.
You can be spiritual *and* have nice things. You can be
spiritual *and* have money flow into your life. But you
cannot be a spiritual being if the arrival of that money is
for the purpose of hoarding it, or using it to prove to
yourself and others that you are in some way superior.
Your authentic power comes from within, *and* you live
in a physical body in a material world as well. Allow
that physical world to be in harmony with your inner

world, and you will have resolved your ambivalence toward money.

I view the money that arrives in my life as the energy that I can use to stay on purpose. It is a blessing and it is used in that context, and as a result it continues to flow into my life in sufficient amounts to meet that commitment of mine to being a spiritual being having a prosperous human experience and helping others to do the same.

* *Realize that you will never get enough of what you don't want.* If money is all that you covet and you want it for the purpose of gaining power over others, then you will never get enough. Your goal is in the invisible realm, that place where you do all of your living. Money and other symbols of prosperity arrive in your life to assist you on that path. If you miss that message, you may see lots of money come into your life, but you will also experience it disappearing. Here is a perfect example of this mentality that you want to shed, expressed by Yogananda:

> I once saw a cartoon drawing of a dog hitched to a small, but well laden, cart. The dog's owner had found an ingenious method for getting it to pull the cart for him. A long pole, tied to the cart, extended forward over the dog's head. At the end of the pole there dangled a sausage, temptingly. The dog, straining in vain to reach that sausage, hardly noticed the heavy cart he was dragging along behind him.

How many business people are like that! They keep thinking, "If I can make just a little more money, I'll find happiness at last." Somehow, their "sausage of happiness" keeps receding from their grasp. As they strain to reach it, however, just see what a cart-load of troubles and worries they drag along behind them!

- *Avoid the trap of expecting your prosperity to arrive in your life through the efforts of others.* You create your own life of prosperity. No one has to change in order for you to experience your own prosperity. This is an inner game, and you must leave behind your expectations of others. Even if you do manage to get others to provide you with the symbols of prosperity, it will all disappear quickly and you will be stuck with that infernal sausage ahead of you, always suffering from the disease called *more.* And then it will be a new cast of "others" that you will seek out, always striving and looking outward. Take responsibility for your own feelings about prosperity and you will eliminate any and all suffering that you experience in this context.

- *Finally, meditate on your prosperity.* Get pictures on your internal screen that reflect you as a prosperous individual. Refuse to let those pictures fade, despite whatever circumstances you may have created in your life. Your meditations will give you an inner script to follow. Use this valuable practice to manifest what you truly want to experience in the physical world.

   Prosperity is something that I know can be achieved by anyone. If I can experience it, having come from my scarce beginnings, then it is hard for me to imagine that anyone cannot make it happen. Looking back on those early days, I realize that even then I embodied a prosperity consciousness. For prosperity is located within.

   I have watched my children grow and flourish. They were all once in little baby bodies. Each of them would cry for a toy or some object of their immediate attention. Something as simple as a rattle that had caught their eye, or a toy that someone else had. They would cry until they received the toy, then they would throw it away and cry for something else.

We leave those baby bodies behind us, but many of us fail to leave that infantile thinking. We want something else to satisfy us. But we do not know how to be satisfied. We continue the relentless pursuit of more, chasing after prosperity as if it were something that resided in objects external to us. To know the secret of prosperity, know that you can never find it. Or to paraphrase Eykis, there is no way to prosperity, prosperity is the way.

6

REAL MAGIC
AND YOUR
PERSONAL IDENTITY

There's only one corner of the universe you can be
certain of improving and that's your own self.

— ALDOUS HUXLEY

You can choose to have the personality that would most
please you, beginning today. Yes that's right, you can
choose your own personality. Why not? You have already
established through a lifetime of choices precisely what kind
of a human being you have wanted to become. In that invisible realm where you make all of the decisions about your
physical circumstances, you have been making choices to
have a certain kind of personality, along with specific fears,
habits, customs, levels of confidence, intellectual abilities
and the like.

If you close your eyes and visualize for a moment precisely
what kind of person you would like to be, what picture
emerges? Try to get an accurate picture in your mind, even if
you consider its fulfillment in reality an impossibility. Is this

your miracle: to reduce your fears? to have a genius IQ? to be able to stand up for what you believe? to overcome your shyness? to be rid of your phobias? to have a positive, loving self-portrait?

Forget for a moment that you have been taught that you cannot help having the personality that you have, that you inherited it from your parents, or that people cannot truly change. Forget the notion that some people have higher intelligence than others, or that talent is inherited and you were shortchanged. Let all of that go in your inner vision, and simply see yourself living and performing at the level of real magic. You must develop within you a new knowing that you have the capacity, through your invisible spiritual self, to create any change that you can conceive of for yourself. That is, if you can authentically believe in it, you can create it.

This is the message of this chapter. You have created your own personality, and thus you have the ability to change any part of it. You can manifest real magic in your own inner life, and become the person you once thought was possible only for others to become. You already have everything you need to make this happen, you do not need anything else.

THE BIG LIE

We grow up believing in so many limitations that after a while our lives actually manifest those limitations. We hear ourselves saying things that we accept as truth, when in fact they are misbeliefs that have turned into our truths. As long as you hang onto the big lie, the "truth" of these misbeliefs, you cannot become a person who experiences miracles. Here are five of those misbeliefs that permeate our culture. Keep in mind that each and every one of these is nothing more than a belief, an inner thought about our own physical world. The more you hang onto these thoughts, and convince yourself and others that they represent the "truth," the more you ensure that this "truth" will inhibit the flow of real magic into your life.

1. *I can't help the way I am; I've always been this way.* I hear these sentiments from people almost every day, and these same people always wonder why miracles never happen in their lives. If you find yourself believing that you must always be the way you have always been, you are arguing against growth. Whatever the state of your personality—be it shy, aggressive, fearful, introverted or extroverted—you must shed the illusion that you cannot help the way you are. You may even read studies that indicate that your personality is outside of your control, it is just what was given to you and you have no choice in the matter. You may tell others that you wish you could change, but this is "just the way I am" and "I've always been this way." This inner picture is a guarantee against creating miracles. In fact, such a change in your personality to become more outspoken, confident, loving, gentle or anything else might be the very miracle that you seek. You must toss this excuse into the garbage and out of your life completely. In the past, you may have always chosen to be a certain way, but you must create a knowing within that you have the power to create whatever kind of person you want to become, in all aspects of your humanity.

2. *It's my nature; I inherited who I am and it can't be changed.* "You are just like your father, he was uncoordinated and so are you." "You got that tone deafness from your grandfather on your mother's side, he couldn't carry a tune either." "Your brothers and sisters were all poor in mathematics, it runs in the family." "She is shy just like her mother and her grandmother's mother." These are the sentiments that help to perpetuate the big lie. Miracles are impossible because you have

come to believe you inherited your limitations and it is impossible to overcome genetics. The scientists will tell you that that code has been passed on to you through your DNA and you have to take what you get and make the best of it.

To enter the realm of real magic you will have to suspend such thoughts, and become a spiritual being first, a being who has no limitations in the inner domain where boundaries are nonexistent. In this place, you can imagine for yourself anything that you desire without anyone being able to take it away from you. In this realm, your corner of freedom, you can be multitalented, brilliantly intellectual, confident, devoid of fears and gorgeous to boot. It is here that you create your limits and it is here that the beginnings of real magic take place.

Your miracle might involve something that you are blocking because of your insidious belief in inheritance. The world is full of people who have gone beyond what their genes might have indicated were their limits. It is up to you to commit yourself to this new intention.

3. *My personality is controlled by my chemistry and metabolism.* This is a lie that we hear over and over again, and it is repeated in some of the most prestigious circles, making it even more difficult to overcome. "How can I change and become what I consider miraculous, when my body chemistry controls who I am?" Articles are regularly published describing how certain enzymes are present in certain kinds of people and therefore they are presumably prisoners to those enzymes. Shy people have shy enzymes, which are a part of their chemistry. Overweight people have fat enzymes, aggressive people have military peptides, musical people have singing endorphins—and you are led to believe that that explains why some people are a certain way and others are not. Scientists explain away miraculous achievements or lack of achievements by the presence or absence of certain chemicals.

While scientists may in fact have a point about body chemistry and the presence of invisible creatures in our systems, what they too often fail to address is what kind of control we have over our own bodies. Obviously our body chemistry controls a great deal of how we conduct our lives, but you must come to an understanding that is fundamental to our humanity: *If we are to have magical bodies, we must have magical minds.* Our body chemistry is always being affected by how we choose to think. Ulcers in a body show up in altered body chemistry, there is no doubt about it, but you must go to the source of the problem to understand how to create miracles. I do not dispute that those little invisible creatures are in our bodies, I simply want you to take a look at the enormous power that you have in your mind for containing those creatures, or retraining them to work for you rather than against you.

4. *My family is responsible for my personality.* "I could never escape from the clutches of my family." "My mother was overbearing and my father abandoned us when I was a child." "All of the girls in our family are this way, we can't help it." These, and thousands of similar excuses, are part of a big lie. These kinds of pronouncements are the very sort of inner thoughts that will keep you from ever allowing miraculous changes to take place in your own personality. As long as you are convinced, even in a small way, that your family is responsible for the kind of person that you are today, you are trapped in that cycle. You must *know within* that you not only have a choice today, but you have always had a choice concerning how you react to the influences of your family. They cannot create the you that you experience, only you can do that. The choice is always yours.

You have the power to reject behaviors, attitudes and beliefs coming at you that you find objectionable. Although you cannot eliminate the influences that were very much a part of your childhood, you and you alone decide whether they will persist. Cultivate the inner knowing that your family and your role within your family influence you today to the extent that you believe that they do. If you do not accept total responsibility for how they fit into your life, then you will not allow any miraculous personality changes to occur. If someone else is at the controls, then you are their victim, even if they seem to be directing you on a positive course. You must become the producer, director and actor in the unfolding story of your life.

5. *I can't escape my culture and times.* This is the lie that encourages you to believe that your habits and customs are the result of that mysterious "culture" that is always shading and shaping your life. The influence of society is a part of the illusion that you are formed by this bigger and better social force. "Society lays down the rules, and we are all the victims of those practices." "We live in a culture that teaches obedience, and I am just one more of those obedient souls who thinks and acts like the herd." "How can anyone get ahead when the government and Big Brother are always telling you what you can and cannot do?" These are statements that reflect an inner vision of helplessness.

If you believe that the culture determines who you are and what kind of person you will turn out to be, then that will be your reality. On the other hand, everyone who has ever made a difference in the world has been an innovator. An innovator does not look at the cultural norms and say to himself, "This is all that I can do." Instead he looks within, and allows his conscience and commitment to a purpose decide who he will become. Society or the culture is not even a part of his personal consideration as he pursues his purpose of serving. If you are going to follow your bliss and make a difference in the world, you will soon learn that you cannot follow the herd.

The old maxim "If you follow the herd, you'll end up stepping in shit" applies here. Using culture or society as excuses will only hold you back from making miraculous changes in your personality. You cannot depend upon the conduct and approval of some amorphous *they* to determine what *you* can become. You cannot blame *them* for what *you* have failed to become.

Once again, it boils down to personal responsibility and a willingness to consult your own spiritual awareness, that higher invisible self that flows through you. Nothing *out there* can control what is *in there*, it is the other way around. As you think, so shall you be. Your thinking is yours, originating with you. The society in which you find yourself is simply the stage upon which you are acting out your own miracles.

These are the five misbeliefs that make up the big lie that was thrust upon you from your earliest moments of consciousness. If you find any of them familiar, and if you are continuing to use them as justification for your lack of self-growth, then you must begin a program to overcome these illusions. This all takes place in that invisible place within you, where you have the choice to rid yourself of these toxic beliefs permanently by cultivating new and transforming thoughts to replace those old beliefs.

OVERCOMING THE BIG LIE

"I am a miracle!" Repeat this over and over to yourself until it is firmly planted in your mind. Be in awe of yourself. Producing miracles for yourself is about knowing within that you are already miraculous. When you know and feel the miracle that you are, you begin to also know and feel that nothing is impossible for you. You begin to sense that you no longer need to hang onto those five excuses outlined above, and in

their place you substitute your new awareness. To overcome the big lie that your misbeliefs are the truth, you will need to equip yourself with new, empowering beliefs. You must come to know that you can choose the life you want to live. You can choose to make your life into a grand, ever-evolving work of art. The key is in your thoughts, the wondrous invisible part of you that is your spiritual soul.

You have come into this world housed for a while in a limited body. But you also have an unlimited mind. This mind of yours is unbounded, formless, and infinitely capable of creating any kind of miracle that it chooses, when it is fully honored and celebrated. It can occupy an ill form, grow up in a dysfunctional family, be in a shy depressed personality, have stuttering behavior, an average or genius IQ, and a host of phobias and fears if it wants, and it can even choose to believe that it has no choice in the matter and convince others of the same.

Or, it can choose something else. It can use this infinite invisible force to create a miraculous purposeful person. With real-magic thinking you can leave behind the old conditioned hypnosis and see that there are those who have surpassed seemingly insurmountable conditions. Then you can use your thoughts to know that if one person can leave schizophrenia behind, and one can overcome manic-depression, and another can become a physician in spite of being told he was dyslexic or even retarded, then whatever force is flowing through them to allow those miracles, you can tap into it and use it to become the personality that you want to be. Real-magic thinking says, "I believe it, I know it, and I will access my spiritual powers to do it. It is my intention!"

If you align yourself with the belief in limitations, then I am sure that you think this is all simply unrealistic optimism. You look at all the suffering in the world and what seems like "God's mysterious anger toward us" and choose thoughts like,

"Look at all those people who are trapped by their circumstances, who have terrible mental afflictions, who live in
abominable family situations. There is no hope for them and
there is no hope for me. People can't change who they are. We
have no choice."

So be it! You can learn to be optimistic or you can learn to
be pessimistic. My philosophy about this is succinctly stated:
"No one knows enough to be a pessimist!" No one!

We have only begun to tap our awareness of the power of
the invisible world that we are immersed in. Our minds, our
thoughts, our souls, are only beginning to be recognized by
those left-brained scientists that I have already mentioned. A
heart starts beating in a mother's womb six or seven weeks
after conception and life as we observe it is under way. And it
is a complete mystery to all of the "greatest" minds on the
planet. Where was that life before, what mysterious invisible
force was present in the joining of those two blobs of human
protoplasm that determines every wrinkle, every hair, every
cell until that body dies? And where was that invisible force
before that life began, and what happens to it after we close
parentheses? All mysterious. All unknown. So how can anyone elect to be a pessimist in the face of what we don't know?

For me, I know the power of that force, and I am positive
that it can be channeled to create miracles in your own personality. You can choose the way of real magic and experience
the kind of person you have dreamed of becoming, or you can
choose to harbor the doubt, and create your life based upon
those doubts. Martin Seligman, a friend and colleague, puts it
this way in his powerful book *Learned Optimism*:

> A pessimistic attitude may seem so deeply rooted as to
> be permanent. I have found, however, that pessimism is
> escapable. Pessimists can in fact learn to be optimists,
> and not through mindless devices like whistling a happy

tune or mouthing platitudes, but by learning a new set of cognitive skills.

The emphasis is on the word *cognitive*. This means to *think*. And this is precisely what you can and will do to create your magical personality with all its unique characteristics. You overcome the big lie—that is, the idea that you cannot help the way you are—by and through magical thinking. That magical thinking will lead you to being exactly the kind of person that you choose for yourself.

CREATING YOUR OWN MAGICAL PERSONALITY

As you now know, this entire program of creating miracles revolves around the simple premise that you become in the physical world that which you create in your invisible world. Here are the six keys to making yourself into the person that you choose for the purpose of fulfilling your heroic mission here.

1. YOUR PERSONALITY What would you like to be able to say about your own unique personality? Create a fantasy in your mind and imagine exactly how you would most like to be. Rather than looking at what you see now, look to what you would truly like to enjoy as your personality. What level of confidence would you like to exhibit as you meet with other people in all walks of life? Would you like to be more assertive? Less inward and contemplative, or more so? More loving and gentle? More or less vulnerable? More tender? Less anxious and nervous? Create in your mind a picture of the kind of personality that would serve you best.

For now, just know that all of these inner imaginings can be translated into physical behavior, for that is precisely what you have been doing all along, ever since you showed up here in the human form that you occupy. You have been imagining yourself as more or less confident, more or less nervous, and so on. Even if you weren't aware of it, that is how your personality got shaped. You are acting upon those inner visions all the time. When you *know* rather than *doubt* that you can elect the personality that is best for fulfilling your purpose here, and you trust in your ability to be that person both in a spiritual and a physical sense, then you will create the real magic that will transform your present life. You will literally become that personality that you could only fantasize about, and you will adopt physical behaviors that will reflect your miraculous new inner vision.

2. YOUR TALENT For a moment, visualize the optimal talent that you would like to have. Simply see yourself in possession of that illusive commodity that we have come to call talent. Talent is thought of generally as some God-given innate ability that allows some to achieve at higher levels than others. Mozart had talent, some mystical gift handed to him by God. Michael Jordan has talent. Baryshnikov has talent. We can agree on those who have this thing called talent, but we cannot define it.

Let's look at it another way. Talent is really a quality that is defined through comparison. Without others to compare Mozart or Michael Jordan with, we have no talent concept. If those two individuals simply performed in their own personal ways, fulfilling their own purpose in their particular areas, and were seen as individuals not in competition with anyone else, then we would not be using a concept like talent to describe them. Talent, by this definition, would apply to everyone.

But it is almost impossible for those of us raised in the West to conceive of such an idea. How else can we judge peo-

ple? And *judge* is the operative word here. You do it to yourself all the time. You judge yourself and the relative merits of
your talents based upon how others around you perform. Your
talent in any particular area is simply what *you* believe about
yourself and how you have compared yourself with the performance of others. You have accepted the lie that some people
are more or less talented than others. But you can shift your
inner awareness to a new level. You can begin to say to yourself, "I am as talented as I have chosen to become, and while I
admire and enjoy the performances of others, their actions say
nothing about what I can or cannot achieve."

A line from *Learned Optimism* describes this awareness: "A
composer can have all the talent of a Mozart and a passionate
desire to succeed, but if he believes he cannot compose music,
he will come to nothing." Mozart, even as a four-year-old,
believed in his ability to compose. Baryshnikov goes on stage
believing first and foremost that he can twirl and move like a
flying angel; Michael Jordan, as he jumps into the strato-
sphere, first and foremost believes that he can soar, and then
his body fulfills his belief. Even more than believing, they all
know, and their miraculous feats flow from that intention of
knowing. This is talent!

Needless to say, the physical body you showed up in will
have an effect on your performance in this physical world.
Your choice to excel in any given area will be based upon your
own personal interests. You very likely are not interested in
being a professional basketball player if you are living in a
five-foot, three-inch body. But if you did have that interest
and knew that you could do it, and even dunk a basketball in
the process, if this were your knowing, then you would act
upon that belief and make it happen. And if you do not
believe me, then have a conversation with Spud Webb, who
won the slam dunk contest in the National Basketball Associ-
ation in just that sort of body!

Your talent, like everything else about you, is a function of the invisible force that flows through your body. It is not in your hands, your genes or any part of your physical apparatus. It is in the force that flows through all of your being.

This is difficult to accept when you have been thoroughly indoctrinated to believe that some have talent and others don't. But you can change the toss of the cosmic dice and create the level of talent that *you* and only *you* need to fulfill your purpose here. Stop structuring your life upon a need to be better than someone else. Instead, examine your purpose in life and then know that you have all that you need right now in the way of talent to create the miracle in your life that you seek.

Read the following words of Jane Roberts from *The Nature of Personal Reality*. They apply to your own personal talent level as well as everything else about yourself.

If you are ill you may say, "I did not want to be sick," or if you are poor, "I did not want to be poor," or if you are unloved, "I did not want to be lonely." Yet for your own reasons you began to believe in illness more than health, in poverty more than abundance, in loneliness rather than affection.

I would add that you may say you want to have more talent, yet for *your own* reasons you began to believe in your absence of talent rather than the talent you do have. When you begin to *know* rather than *doubt* your talent, you will discover the necessary physical abilities to carry out your purpose.

3. YOUR INTELLIGENCE How smart would you like to be? How does the label of *genius* next to your name feel? Would you like to raise your IQ and possess the intellectual skills to

outthink those around you? Would it take a miracle for you to be smarter intellectually than you already are? It is in this area of the imaginary IQ that many people lead a life of illusion. Rid yourself of the belief that some magical number attached to your mind power limits your capabilities and achievements as a human being. The best definition of IQ is: Intelligence is what intelligence tests measure.

You are not a number. You are a soul that is numberless and infinite. The capacities of your inner self are unlimited because it has no boundaries. Test makers and test users of all descriptions would like you to believe the opposite, so they circulate this kind of misinformation within the culture. "You cannot change your IQ, it is fixed and it determines what you can and cannot do in life." But think about this for a moment.

These tests, which supposedly measure something abstract called intelligence, were devised by people who want to sell their instruments, who want to slot people into compartments, who want to restrict people from attending certain schools, who want to set up a practice for the purpose of giving out these numbers to parents. They are physical-world instruments that attempt to deter people from achieving their purpose in life. They are silly, absurd procedures that give people some kind of external number to hold on to and explain their levels of success or lack of success in the material world.

Let me give you two examples from my own life to illustrate this point. I was once invited to take an examination to measure my intelligence in reading skills, and the test makers had used several paragraphs from my book *Your Erroneous Zones*. I was instructed to read the paragraph and then answer five questions based upon my interpretation of the material. I read the paragraph that I had written myself, and then I proceeded to answer the questions. I received a score of 80 percent on the five questions. The only question that I failed to answer correctly was number 5, the "intent of the author." My IQ was lowered because I was unable to correctly identify the intent of the author, when I was the author!

On another occasion when I was still a college student, I took an examination in a course on modern American poetry. The instructor told me that my interpretation of the poem in question was incorrect and he consequently lowered my grade considerably. The poet was alive at the time, teaching at a large Midwestern university. I decided to write to the poet and send him my interpretation of his poem, which I thought was insightful and "correct." I received a beautiful letter in response, and the poet told me that my views on his poetry reflected his own. He indicated that I too had the mind of a poet and suggested I pursue writing my own poetry. I took my interpretation of the poem, along with the letter from the poet, to a scheduled consultation with my English instructor, feeling certain that I would have my "poetry IQ" raised as a result. My instructor refused to raise my grade. His response was, "Sometimes poets don't really know how to interpret their own poems. Your grade stands."

Consider examples such as these as you evaluate your own IQ. Know that there are no accidents in this perfect universe. Know that your purpose is beyond anything that can be measured with scientific measurements. Know for certain that one person's ability to solve the rhyming scheme of an Elizabethan sonnet, and another's capacity for understanding calculus formulations, is simply what it is. There is no need for comparison or sliding scales.

Your IQ is an illusion. You can change that number around drastically by changing around what is on the tests. Is the person who can fine-tune an automobile less intelligent than a person who can solve a quadratic equation? Is the classroom teacher, dressed in a suit and tie, who explains environmental matters from an intellectual perspective, more intelligent than a young environmentally aware person who chooses to learn firsthand by living in the woods? Who decided on this business of IQ? Why should we label everyone in our culture with another number—a number that is misinterpreted by the person receiving the number, and by those who are issuing it as well?

You are as capable as you need to be to fulfill your purpose. Your intelligence is infinite. You must know that there is an absurdity in this assignment of an IQ number to people. Intelligence is about the mind. The mind is without boundaries. But IQ numbers are all about boundaries. There is no way to quantify something that is without dimensions. If you want to experience the miracle of having genius-level intelligence, then change around those inner voices that have convinced you of your limitations because of your intellect.

Almost twenty years ago, in *Your Erroneous Zones*, I redefined intelligence. I stand by that definition to this day: "A truer barometer of intelligence is an effective, happy life lived each day and each present moment of every day." You are a genius! When you know that you have the intellectual capacity to create your own happiness, and when you know whom or what to consult, then you are your own genius.

Certainly you can improve upon your ability to do any intellectual task. You can improve your arithmetic and reading skills. You can learn anything that you put your mind to. What you have or have not learned up until this moment is a function of the choices that you have been making, not some innate incapacity determined by a number assigned to you by those who have their own self-interest at heart in their numbering game. Know this about your intelligence level and keep it uppermost in your infinite, boundless, numberless mind. You are a spiritual being first and foremost. And you cannot put a number on that.

4. YOUR HABITS AND CUSTOMS Would you like to be able to change some of the things that you find yourself doing repeatedly but that do not serve you? Would you like to rid yourself of self-defeating habits? Be free of customs that you dislike and feel a victim of? Use your magical powers of inner persuasion to challenge everything about yourself. Your personality is made up of the hundreds of habitual ways that you conduct the daily physical affairs of your life.

If you are leading an existence of television and inactivity that you dislike, but that you can't shake, you can create the miracle that you seek. You can change around your daily humdrum habits and get yourself fully involved in life, regardless of your income level or circumstances. Remember, circumstances do not make a man, they reveal him.

A neighborhood within a few miles of my home has the highest unemployment rate in the state of Florida. Something close to 75 percent of the people are out of work. Yet, as I drive through the neighborhood I notice broken glass on the lawns, litter everywhere, grass that is not trimmed, houses that are not clean or painted. Why? If 75 percent of the people are unemployed, wouldn't it seem logical that you would see these people at least picking up the trash and broken glass with their abundance of free time? But you don't. You see people sitting around doing nothing. The circumstances of their lives have revealed how they have chosen to live. It costs nothing to pick up and clean up, yet this is not done, because those habits have become the ways of dealing with their circumstances. Your habits reveal you! They say something about how you have chosen to live your life and to use your powerful mind. The same invisible force that runs through those who do pick up the broken glass and manage to work and support their families runs through those who make the opposite choices. It is in every one of us. Some tap into it; others ignore it and then blame their circumstances for the habits and customs of their lives.

Being unhappy is a habit. Being depressed is a habit. Being lazy is a habit. Being limited is a habit. These, and many other personality traits, result from the way in which you use your mind. There are many many people, including this writer, who have spent a large portion of their lives with very little in the way of material possessions, yet their habit was not to be depressed about it. There are many in such circumstances who have a habit of choosing happiness over despair, since these are inner, not outer, processes. And those who do manage to choose self-enhancing habits are almost always those who transcend their circumstances of scarcity and create more abundance in their lives.

Whatever habits and customs you find yourself blindly obeying, you can change in a moment when you become a spiritual being first and a material being second. You have the power to change those things that do not work for you, that you have come to call troublesome habits or customs. If you believe this, and know it within yourself, you will find your physical self automatically following a new course. Learning to think in nonhabitual ways is the essence of overcoming personality traits that no longer serve you. You need not stay conditioned and hypnotized in your current state if it does not serve your purpose.

You may have adopted a habit of allowing others to influence you or push you around, or of being a servant to others at the expense of fulfilling your own destiny. These are habits that you have adopted by teaching others in your life exactly what you are willing to put up with. You can rid yourself of habits that come from allowing others to manipulate you. You can rid yourself of "ingrained personality traits," which are not truly ingrained at all. They are habitual ways that you have chosen for yourself. The way to creating a miracle for yourself in which you are not a victim of others, your circumstances or yourself is in shifting your inner world and creating, in that private space, room for a purposeful, spiritually fulfilled human being.

5. YOUR AGING Imagine for yourself the ultimate miracle, a slowing down or an elimination of the aging process. Now there is an outright, uncategorical miracle! You can have an enormous impact on the state of aging in your body. Here is my friend Dr. Deepak Chopra on the subject in his classic work, *Perfect Health*:

> Aging seems so complicated that it is difficult even to pin down exactly what it is. A typical liver cell performs five hundred separate functions, which gives it five hundred ways to go wrong. All of these possibilities constitute the ways in which it can age. On the other hand, the view that aging is complex may be wrong. Despite the thousand waves that bring it in, the ocean tide is a single phenomenon, driven by a single force. The same may be true of human aging, although we see it as hundreds of waves; disconnected aches and pains, new wrinkles around the eyes and deeper smile marks at the corner of the mouth . . . and innumerable other minor inconveniences.

Try to get this new perspective that Dr. Chopra outlines brilliantly in his chapter titled "Aging Is a Mistake." While everyone succumbs to the aging process, the question of significance is: Do we have to? He points out that DNA, which controls all the cellular functions, is virtually invulnerable to wear and tear. It has survived without even a millimeter of aging for six hundred million years—at the minimum. The very stuff of your being is simply ageless. Yet we age. Why?

The ancient sages called the aging process a mistake of the intellect. Aging is the forgetting of how to make things right within a cell. It is not normal, it simply is a learned way of being. The mistake of the intellect is in identifying exclusively with the physical body and coming to know that one has to experience the aging process. The mind begins to prepare for aging as soon as it is capable of intellectualizing. You have seen it all around you, you have read about it and that is all you know. Therefore you prepare your body for its own self-destruction.

The way out of this trap, the real magic that is available to you, is located, as is everything else, in your invisible self. Your mind. You can absolutely refuse to let an old person into your body. This is your own garage that you use to temporarily park your soul. You can change around your inner perspective and literally affect each and every cell of your body. Your invisible self, your mind, is not located only in your brain. It is your spiritual consciousness and it is in every single cell of your being. The world is in you, so to speak, and if you can work your mind in a genuinely magical sense, you can strongly affect the aging process of the cells composed of indestructible DNA. If, as you read these words, you are filled with doubt about that possibility for yourself, then of course your doubt will affect each and every cell in your body, including the DNA memory for renewing itself.

It is in your mind, where that invisible intelligence works its magic, that you must examine your attitudes toward aging. Do you think old thoughts? Do you believe that you must stoop, and slow down, and lose your memory, and look old? For it is in these invisible formulations that you program your cells to function. That invisible intelligence is ageless and perfect. You can begin to rethink how you feel about having your individual cells deteriorate. And, if you use your mind in a new way, to develop a new knowing within, perhaps you will be able to affect that process that you have come to think of as inescapable. Here is another quote from *Perfect Health*, which I cannot resist putting in:

> If you take your mind to a level of functioning that is beyond age, then your body will begin to be touched by the same quality. It will age more slowly because your mind tells it to, at the deepest level. Seeing yourself as free from aging, you in fact will be.

Rather than rejecting this notion, just let it in and see if you can get it to make some sense for you and the fifty trillion cells that are all working in perfect harmony to maintain your aliveness in that human ageless body of yours.

6. YOUR EMOTIONAL HEALTH You have infinite possibilities for how you can live emotionally. The problem with most of us is that we have restricted ourselves to only a very few choices in the emotional realm of our humanity. When you experience fear, for example, your mind is capable of literally producing molecules that show up as adrenaline. Yes, a mental impulse produces something in your body that is of the physical world. It has substance, is measurable, and it originated in the mind. This is the miracle of the mind at work. Our thoughts produce physical manifestations that we have learned to call emotions. The molecules that make up your emotions derive directly from your mental world. The chemicals that show up in your body are literally created by the invisible mind. This is actually the very miracle that I have been writing about throughout this book, it is simply more obvious in the emotional world. Yes, you and your invisible

mind can create the physical world that you want to create. Yes, your mind is capable of affecting things in the physical world. Yes, you can create miracles for yourself through the magical use of your mind.

Your emotions are physical manifestations of your thoughts. The joy you experience is located in your physical body, and the chemicals that are present when you experience elation can be identified and quantified. The same is true of fear, stress, anger, rage, jealousy, depression, phobic reactions and the like. These are all chemical changes that are taking place within you. You manufacture those chemicals in your own quantum pharmacy that begins with your mind. That mind is capable of literally manufacturing from scratch thousands of "drugs" that show up in your body. Need an antidepressant or a tranquilizer? You need not necessarily go to the drugstore. Your mind can create exactly what your body needs.

You are constantly creating molecules that have many labels and that we have come to call emotions. When you begin to heal the inner you, and consult that inner voice constantly, you begin to literally alter your immune system. Dr. Dean Ornish published a best-seller, *Reversing Heart Disease*— that's right—on *reversing*, not simply stopping, the symptoms. Dr. Ornish and I have appeared together in the media on several occasions and I have been immensely impressed with him and his pathfinding work. I was pleasantly surprised to see that the major focus of his impressive book is on the inner self and teaching people to work on their own physiology by eliminating the distressing signals they are sending to their immune systems from their minds. His entire approach to actually reversing the possibility of heart disease is on learning how to overcome the ways in which our minds create disease.

The emotional reactions of anger, stress, tension, fear and

the like originate with the mind. These reactions create chemical imbalances and actual toxins that cause deterioration of the body. The way to cure these ailments is not to attack the chemicals by sending in a new army of laboratory-manufactured drugs, but to work on the original pharmaceutical machinery that is creating the chemical imbalances. This is the way to cure ourselves of virtually all illnesses, and it is the way to understanding our own emotional condition.

You are the creator of your emotions. They originate with your thoughts. Those emotional reactions are actually physical in nature. Whatever emotions you are choosing with your thoughts will take up residence in your body. This is a most important understanding to have for yourself. Once you know without doubt that you are the one who is choosing your fears, anxiety levels, phobias, ecstasy levels and so on, then you can also be the one to create whatever miracle you want for yourself in this world of your emotions. You may not know precisely *how* you choose to create the toxic molecules that show up in your emotional world. However, simply acknowledging that *you* do, sets in motion the physiological changes you desire.

An old Indian saying expresses these ideas well: "If you want to know what your thoughts were like yesterday, look at your body today. If you want to know what your body will be like tomorrow, look at your thoughts today." Emotions show up in your body as physical manifestations of your thoughts. Keep this in mind as we head toward the path of real magic.

These six categories constitute the inventory of personality variables that you control in your invisible mind. Your attitudes toward your personality, talents, IQ, habits, aging and emotions are the inner baggage that you carry around with you everywhere you go. Your beliefs about them are all yours.

You have selected all of your inner attitudes toward each of these categories.

Your biggest hurdle to reshaping your personality into the work of art that you desire will be overcoming your fears and doubts. You live with those fears and doubts all the time, and they are companions that have kept you from taking responsibility for creating a magical life for yourself.

Before moving on to the strategies that you can employ to bring about real-magic changes within yourself, I feel that it is important to consider the biggest fear of all, the one dread that seems to be omnipresent in all of us.

YOUR RELATIONSHIP TO YOUR OWN DEATH

One thought that you carry around with you for all of your life beyond early childhood is an awareness of your own death. The question that seems to universally perplex us is "Where do I go when I die?" Most of us have a relationship with death that is unresolved. You know people who have died. You have seen others flirt with death. You know that you will die someday. But death remains an eternal mystery. In order to create a life of real magic you must free yourself of the fear and anxiety surrounding this mystery of your body's demise.

Fear of death can be a great inhibitor in your life. It can keep you from living fully and it can make your time here in this human form anxious and sickly. The way out of this dilemma is to face your fear of it directly. Like everything else I have written about in this book, facing it means looking at it from within.

Your fear is a thought. It is invisible. If you live in anxiousness about your own death, your way of processing all that you have seen and heard about death is to make it something

permanent. Death in this thought process is simply the end.
The big void. You are a cosmic accident and life is one giant
terminal disease. There is nothing before, there is nothing
after. Indeed, that *is* one great big scary notion! But something within you in that invisible space tells you that this
cannot be so. You know there is a part of you that is immune
to death, since death refers to endings—your invisible dimensionless soul is not subjected to such delineations as beginnings and endings. You know that your life itself is invisible,
and that it is simply located in your physical body. It is this
awareness that you must become familiar with in order to
transcend your fear of death.

There is an essential immortality that is the birthright of
every human being. To grasp this you must begin to refute
your total identification with your body. Every holy spiritual
teacher (and some who have not been so holy for a large part
of their lives) has given us this message. The Bhagavad Gita
speaks of this life in these words:

> As a man abandons worn-out clothes and acquires new
> ones, so when the body is worn out a new one is acquired
> by the Self, who lives within.

The translator and lifelong Gita scholar Eknath Easwaran
says of these words in the Gita:

> To such an enlightened being, . . . death is no more
> traumatic than taking off an old coat. Life cannot offer
> any higher realization. The supreme goal of human exis-
> tence has been attained. The man or woman who realizes
> God has everything and lacks nothing: Having this, one
> desires nothing further; he cannot be shaken by the
> heaviest burden of sorrow. Life cannot threaten such a

person; all it holds is the opportunity to love, to serve, and to give.

Think about what Easwaran is saying here and what the Gita is telling us. The supreme goal of human existence is attained when we become peaceful with our own immortality and view death not as an ending or a punishment, but as an awakening, a reward, a return to the infinity that surrounds our parentheses in eternity.

In the Christian tradition, Jesus talked of immortality: ". . . and this is life eternal, that they might know thee the only true God." Every tradition speaks of coming to know one's own immortality by achieving a spirituality and sense of purpose. In all the ages of man, from the beginnings of recorded history in every human tradition, there have been similar beliefs about immortality. They have all believed that there exists an invisible world that is a part of every single human personality, and that the purpose of life in one's physical body is to discover God—or however you want to spell that which signifies the invisible intelligence that suffuses all life. But hearing me talk about it, or having spiritual masters convey it to you through their various religious traditions, will not make your anxiousness go away. You must come to know it within, and that is something that you can achieve yourself.

Although I have quoted some of the spiritual traditions and left out hundreds more because of space limitations, you might also be interested in the words of someone who has had no religious training. In fact, his entire life was spent in very nonspiritual pursuits. He had been a linebacker, a tough street kid, a self-confessed cocaine addict for many years, and generally a guy who had very little regard for matters spiritual. His name is Gary Busey, an American actor best known for his portrayal of Buddy Holly in the film about the rock and roll star who died at the age of twenty-two.

In 1988, Gary Busey was riding his motorcycle and was nearly killed in a severe accident in which he received head injuries that put him at death's door. The following words are Gary's from an article by Luane Lee that appeared in the *Long Beach Press* on February 28, 1991:

> The great tragedy is not death, but what dies within you when you are alive. The second part of my life started on December 4, 1988. I crossed to the other side. I went to a room full of lights. I was just the cord that lives within my spinal column which houses the soul. I had three plates of light come up to my face and tell me I was in a beautiful place of love. And I *was* love. I could go with that energy there and leave this body. Or I could go back to this body and resume my destiny. It was my choice.

This is not the talk of a new-age guru, but a brawny Texan who lived life on the raw edge all of his life up until his encounter with the other side. Today, the journalist describes him as tranquil, thoughtful and not trying to impress or convince. To his detractors who find his transformation unbelievable, he responds:

> It doesn't have anything to do with believing. The truth goes beyond belief. It happened. I have nothing to say but that. I was there. Whether one believes it or not doesn't matter because it's the truth.

And this former junkie, whose language was once sprinkled with expletives, concluded his interview with these words: "The most important word that's ever been invented is the word love."

I have heard literally thousands of stories like Gary Busey's. My own sister-in-law, Marilyn Dyer, told me of her visit with the other side after a head-on collision some twenty years ago. She has never feared death since. She knows what she saw and it was joyful and blissful. Some believe her, others are skeptics. So be it. Dr. Elisabeth Kübler-Ross and Dr. Raymond Moody have written volumes about what have come to be called NDEs (near-death experiences). There is almost a universal agreement among those who have been to the edge. They all report blissful lights and an absence of suffering. An eternal welcoming. You can read it and believe, or you can be skeptical. The choice is always yours.

The basic reason for your anxiety about death is your lifelong habit of thinking of your body as *you*. As you learn that you are really a conscious mind dwelling within a body, you will begin to see the folly of such an all-out identification with your body. Soon you will develop an attitude of loving concern for your body but a detached sense of identification.

If you ask the question, "Where do I go when I die?" and you are referring to your soul, the answer is that you do not die. Death is a concept that refers to endings. Endings need boundaries, and obviously your dimensionless self has no boundaries. Your immortality is something that you become very familiar with as you become a spiritual being having a human experience. If you identify your total self with your body, then you must rephrase the question to ask, "Where does my body go when it dies?" Here you are dealing again with two people. The "my" implies an owner or possessor, and the "body" implies that which is owned.

That body which you are housed in has been "dying" every day since you showed up here. You lose some of it each day and you renew it all at the same time. None of the physical cells that you had a few years ago are present in you today. It is a process of renewal and repair. That part of your body which dies must be renewed with living tissue. Several pounds of your body die every single day and are eliminated into the ground in several physiological processes. You then ask the ground to provide you with the renewal material to keep you alive. Had you not been physically dying every day, and you are fifty years old, you would weigh many many tons. The dying process in the physical world allows you to live.

The minerals that constitute your body are used as a part of the perfect recycling system that is the physical universe. They are not you. Those few remaining minerals will be used for the same process ultimately. But your soul has no minerals, it is without form, and this means that it is impervious to death.

Every night you go off to sleep and your body experiences rest. This is a time of renewal. You are building a new body with this rest period. You do this because you are worn out from all of your activity during the day. Ultimately, your current body will wear out (unless you solve the mistake of aging) and it will go into a state of rest. But what about your soul? Ah, the great mystery! I love this passage from Lao Russell's *God Will Work with You, Not for You:*

Everywhere in Nature you see the rebirth of roses, of trees and of grass. Last year you picked an apple from this branch. This year you behold another apple where you plucked one last year, and the next year, and the next you can still pluck one. And if you open one you will find the same apple that you are going to eat all folded up in the seeds of other apples not yet born that will repeat the bodies of apples which have long been born. That is nature's eternal process of repeating eternal life. She divides eternal life into eternal repetitions of life. We call them life and death, but both of them are opposite expressions of life. Is not that a wonderful thing to know? Is it not wonderful to know that every day you live in the visible world of bodies, your every thought and action is also simultaneously repeated and recorded in the invisible world of mind?

As you unfold in the spiritual invisible direction that I have been writing about throughout this book, you will gradually lose your sense of bodily reality. You will acquire a new awakened reality, which has great reverence for the physical body you are living in. This reality tells you that you are capable of creating molecules of physical reality with your conscious mind, that your mind is constantly renewing your physical body and creating your physical world.

Ultimately, you come to the world of real magic, where you can create miraculous happenings in the material universe with your invisible mind. While others will call them miracles, you will know them as your conscious but invisible mind doing what it has always been doing, creating your physical-world experiences—only now they are experiences of bliss and purpose.

As you awaken further and further, you will lose your concern for what happens to your body, and replace that concern with a knowing. Your goal will be to get your body and mind in balance with the universal laws of God, seeing the miracle that you are, and releasing any absurd notion of death. You will discover that those who have died are not gone at all. They are simply renewing themselves just as you have been doing.

PUTTING REAL MAGIC INTO YOUR PERSONALITY

Your personality, with all of the components that I have outlined in this chapter, is your own creation. You can create a miracle in yourself by making that personality all that you are capable of imagining for yourself in your omniscient, omnipotent mind. Here are some of the steps that you can implement to manifest your new way of being, beginning today.

- *Remove all doubt about what kind of person you can become.* This is a mental world that you live in. Everything that you know about yourself as a physical being corresponds to a mental equivalent, or a belief you are holding. If you perceive shortcomings in your personality, then it is because you have the mental equivalent of a shortcoming in your belief system. This is called doubt.

    Constantly remind yourself that all that you have become is the result of all that you have thought. Your intellect, levels of confidence, talents, fears, habits—all are physical-world manifestations of a mental equivalent. The way to change those mental equivalents is by thinking quietly, constantly and persistently of the kind of person you truly want to become. These thoughts will become the seeds that you plant in the physical world. You will ultimately create molecules in your physical world that correspond to the mental images you have. Just as you create ulcer molecules with your thoughts, you can create what you desire if you remove doubt and replace it with belief.

- *Stop using sentences in your material world that reflect what it is that you do not want to be.* If you call yourself limited, clumsy, stupid, tearful and weak, you will be blocking the miracle-creating possibilities that you seek. If your miracle is to be some way you have never been, then you must stop those old tapes.

    Begin a process of affirmations reflecting a consciousness of confidence and strength by talking about your unlimited capacity to learn any new intellectual skill and appreciating the fears you have overcome. Stress how capable you are both in conversations with others and to yourself. Remember, what you think and talk about expands into action. If you are talking about your weaknesses and defending them, then you must be thinking about them as well. Keep in mind that what you are saying to others, even in what seem to be insignificant ways, are reflections of that inner mental equivalent. If you want confidence to expand in your life, you must speak of your confidence, and mention examples of that confidence. If you want fearfulness to expand, then tell others about those fears and all of the gory details that will keep convincing you of your weaknesses. It may seem oversimplified, but it is the way to create a real magical transformation in your personality. Keep that zone of self-assuredness in your mind and practice letting those new miraculous thoughts develop their material equivalent in your daily world.

- *Stay focused on what you are* for *rather than what you are against.* For instance, don't think about not having any further resentments, because then you are still thinking about resentment and subsequently that is how you will conduct yourself in the material world. Instead, think about what you want to expand. Think on health, harmony, love and bodily ease, and you will act on those things. If you think of yourself as lacking in talent or intellect, don't say, "I will not think of myself as ignorant or talentless," because then you are thinking about ignorance and strengthening the mental equivalent of limitations. Instead, use your mind to focus on images such as, "I possess all that I need to fulfill my dreams. I am limitless and a part of the perfection of this physical world. I am not a mistake, I am a divine necessity." These kinds of images will shift your physical-world equivalent behaviors dramatically. You will act upon a new self-image, based upon possibilities, and you will see yourself performing miracles that you previously believed impossible.

- *Remind yourself daily that you are a purposeful being.* When you are living on purpose, giving of yourself in a blissful way, your personality will reflect that bliss. You will manifest the necessary talent and intellect to fulfill your purpose. It will not require a struggle or a detailed worksheet of goals and objectives. Your ability to manifest changes in your own personhood is already intact. You are not going to acquire intelligence, talent, skills and confidence from outside of yourself. These are components that already reside within you. What you want to do is shift to a purposeful state, a state in which you feel inspired and significant. When this is your state of mind, then all that you need in the way of personality characteristics will surface.

  Remember that neither your family nor your culture gave you your personality. You created it! You have manifested precisely the personality that you needed to take care of your life's work up to this point. And now you can reenergize yourself on your life's journey. You do not have to continue to relive and reuse those old variables if they are no longer functional. Maintain your sense of purpose and you will not operate from any lacks in your thinking.

- *Totally trust your intuition for a day at a time.* Your inner voices will insistently let you know that you have the necessary ingredients to get your life to bliss. Your invisible silent conversations will have the allure of a debate:

"I can dance if I want to."
"No, you have always been a klutz."

"I am brilliant."
"No, you flunked geometry in high school."

"I am brave."
"No, you are afraid of your own shadow."

The "I" is your intuition, the "you" is your physical experience reminding you of the absurdity of your claims of real magic. You must learn to not only trust your intuitive voices, but to go with them regularly. It is your divine guidance talking in those silent conversations! When you know that it is there and refuse to believe otherwise you will find miraculous changes taking place within you.

One day while I was running I noticed a couple in a mild state of distress. They had somehow managed to lock themselves out of their rental car while the engine was still running. They were frantically trying to break into the idling car and get to the airport some twenty miles away. Several people were attempting to help them, including two employees from a security truck. I observed them, and my intuition said, "You can probably help them." But I continued to run, ignoring that inner voice.

On the way back from my run, forty minutes later, the couple along with the same small crowd were still unsuccessfully attempting to gain entry to their idling automobile. I ran past them again, and that inner voice was even stronger. "Go back, I am sure that you can help them to solve their problem." I ran about one hundred yards farther, and then I could no longer ignore my inner pleadings. I went back to the car, told the woman who was in a state of panic that I could open her car since this had happened to me several times. I had no idea what I would do, but I *knew* that I was there to help them and that I could do it.

They had been using a bent clothes hanger in an attempt to catch the door lock, which was smooth and tapered, designed to repel such invasions. I told the woman, "Your car is running, you have power locks, so we want to touch the power window button with a long stick." I turned around and there was the perfect stick right there on the ground. I took my room key and wedged the window open just enough, and she put the stick down the opening, and just managed to touch the right button. The window magically opened and they were on their way to the airport.

I left that scene awed by the power of my intuitive voice, and with a new commitment to never ignore that inner voice. It was strong and clear: "Your purpose is to help, you will be guided on what to do, go there and use your intention to help manifest a miracle for those people. That's why you are here in the first place." I have no idea who those vacationers on Maui were, but I know that I am connected to them in a spiritual way. My inner voice, my intuitive divine guidance, provides me with an opportunity to manifest skills that I often don't even know I possess. When I arrived on that scene and announced myself as an expert on getting into locked cars, I was as surprised as they were at my words. But somehow I knew that I could help, and sure enough, all that I needed was there. I didn't have to go to locksmith school, I already had the necessary talent and skills to fulfill my purpose.

- *Know that there is a secret buried deep within your invisible self*. It says to you, "You do not need another thing, you are already all that you need. You have a divine personality, let it come out, and stop judging it. You are multitalented, get on purpose and your talents will all be there for you. You are brilliant, all the intellectual skills that you require for your purpose will surface." You must give up the notion that you are a mistake, or that you got shortchanged in any way.

What you are is all that you are supposed to be. Your inner and outer design is perfectly in balance with all things in the universe. You may have convinced yourself otherwise, and if you have, make this your new reality. Your perfection is not changed, but your lack of belief in that perfection is, and what you believe about yourself is all-important here. The secret in the center of your being is that you are it all already—no accident, no imperfections, simply a divine masterpiece you have allowed to deteriorate in your inner world. Surrender to that secret and you will have everything you need to live a purposeful life. Fight it, and mental anguish will define your life.

- *Inventory the behaviors and characteristics that you exhibited as a child but that are no longer applicable to your adult life.* You sucked your thumb. Now you know better. You struck out at your siblings when frustrated. Now you know better. You dribbled food down your chin and stuck your fingers in the chocolate cake. Now you know better. You wobbled and fell when attempting to walk. Now you know better. You were puzzled by fractions and decimals. Now you know better. This list could go on for volumes. Keep those words, *"now you know better,"* high in your consciousness.

You are in a constant state of change in your life. You are continuously learning how not to behave, and what new talents, intellectual skills and personality variables to use. The old ones no longer work. Certainly you have learned by now not to hit your sister when she takes your things. You don't defend that behavior with sentences like, "I've always been that way, I am just an aggressive person by nature." Now you know better! Use this awareness for developing other aspects of your personality. The key word in this awareness is *know*. You no longer doubt, you *know* better. You have replaced that old behavior with a knowing. You will continue to make this kind of replacement throughout your life when you are on a spiritual path.

Today I know better than to say to myself, "I do not have the talent to do something," just as I know better than to say, "I'm just inferior, I'll never learn to walk. I guess I'll have to crawl for my entire lifetime." Today I know better than to say, "I can't write a book about manifesting miracles and real magic," just as I know better than to say, "I know I'll never learn to add numbers, I just don't get it." Today I know better than to say, "I am afraid of new challenges," just as I know better than to say, "I am afraid of the boogeyman when the lights go out."

You see how silly it is to continue with those old rationalizations. You know better. Trust that you will gain the necessary variables in your personality to create everything you need for yourself, and you will no longer hang onto those infantile descriptions of yourself at an early age.

- *Create an intention inventory for yourself.* Not a wish list, but an inventory of what you intend to create within yourself. The kind of person you want to become, along with the necessary ingredients for creating that person, are all within your power. You must first *know* this. Then shift to your intention stance. "I intend to manifest the necessary talent and intellect to become the kind of purposeful person I am destined to be." This kind of inner commitment to your own excellence is the stuff of which miracles are made.

You will begin to have a better memory, if you "intend" that it will be so. Rather than focusing on how many things you are forgetting, you will concentrate your mind on all that you are able to remember. "I was able to think of that person's name without any difficulty that time. I am truly improving my memory." "I did that yoga exercise without any strain for the first time. I am manifesting a new talent." "I actually stood up for myself with that pushy salesperson. I am creating a self-confident manner." Use your mind to focus on what you are intending, rather than on what you are unable to manifest. In this way, you shift from wishing to action, and you are using your intentions to bring about miraculous personality changes as well.

- *Begin to act in your physical world as if that person whom you would love to be were already here.* Even if you have convinced yourself that you have been afraid of crowds all of your life, or that you are a sickly person, or that you are lacking the intellectual skills to associate with certain people, begin to act as if the miraculous person you would like to become were already here. Yes, I said *fake* it!

Go right out and without ever telling anyone else that you really are a quaking shivering mass of jelly inside, act confidently in a given situation where no one knows you. In that present moment of your life, regardless of what you have convinced yourself of in your mind, you are that new miraculous self-confident person. Act the part that you want to play. The acting is the physical world. The *want* is the inner voice.

There is no one on this planet who is any better in God's eyes than you. You have that spirit of God flowing within you at all times, and you will discover a simple secret: Anything you desire to do you can do. Anything! The key is desire, which is an invisible, dimensionless concept that resides within you. If you truly desire it, and can picture it for yourself, you can manifest it.

The way to this truth for me has been to act as if that which I desired within myself were already here in the material world. When I was applying to graduate school I knew that my test scores on the entrance examinations were not at the top of the scale. But, throughout the admission procedures, I was behaving as if I were already in the program. Every interview was an opportunity for me to do just that. And despite the odds against it, I was admitted. I had already seen it in my mind, and I knew that it would be so.

When I was admitted, I heard that only a small percentage of those who were admitted actually completed the program and the dissertation. But I saw myself completing the program, and I saw myself doing it in three years. I acted this way at all times. I announced from the start, whenever the subject would arise, that I would complete my doctorate before my thirtieth birthday, in three years of full-time study (along with full-time work and parenting as well). On May 4, 1970, six days before my thirtieth birthday, I passed my final oral examination. I had already known it in my mind, and I acted as if it were a reality long before it was manifested in the physical world. Use the technique of first seeing it, and then acting upon that image before the actual event is materialized. It cannot fail you.

- *Learn to preplay who it is you want to be in your mind before you put anything into action.* For example, if you feel that you lack the talent to sing or paint, go within and live out your life on a spiritual basis first, and then try it out in your material world. See yourself at an easel, creating a masterpiece much like you do in your dreams. Effortless, flowing and without judgment. Practice being this spiritual consultant to your physical world on a regular basis. Sing out with perfect pitch in your imagination, glory in the wondrous feeling of joy that you receive from holding nothing back and just belting out your own tune. Forget about anyone in the physical world and what their reactions might be. Simply allow yourself this inner voyage of talent.

  This is how you create the miracle of a talent that you never believed possible for yourself. You live spiritually first; that is, you live it out in your mind—your IQ, your habits, your personality, your health and your fearlessness. Pay the most attention to your inner dimension and know that everything that you have created about yourself as a physical being has that mental equivalent within you. It is in this dimension that you want to be totally accepting of your own greatness. Nonjudgmental, unlimited, simply allowing yourself to swim in your ocean of abundant inner possibilities. You need not share these inner preplays with anyone, they can be your own private journey. They will lead you to real magic if you stay with them unconditionally.

- *Remind yourself that if you have judged yourself to be lacking in any personality variable, you will continue to manifest that lack as long as you focus on it in your mind.* You can never get enough of what you don't want. Your low self-regard will continue to plague you. Your lower intellectual abilities will stay with you as you convince yourself and others of your limitations. Everything about yourself that you see as a lack will keep on being more of a lack until you *know* something different about yourself. And what you know about yourself is yours for the choosing. If you have a choice in what you will know about yourself, then why not know positive things rather than negative? You got to where you are in your self-assessments because of your choices. Keep that simple realization close at hand and it will serve you well in creating miracles for yourself.

• *Seek out no opinions on your own personality.* Ask nothing of anyone in the way of assessment. Forget about looking to IQ tests to determine your abilities. Look instead to your own divine awareness of your unlimited abilities. Forget about what others say regarding your talent or fitness for anything, always consult your own personal observer or invisible guides that are a part of your intuitive awareness. Others may give you "realistic" assessments of your abilities, but you are not interested in having their opinions, either negative or positive. It is enough that you know it and that you pursue your own interests. If you meet with obstacles, so be it. Bless those hurdles as lessons that God has provided, and then move along on your path. Use discouraging words from others as reminders of your determination to get your life on purpose in your own dream. Ask nothing of anyone. Be polite when their opinions come along, send them loving thanks for their thoughts and then proceed to go within.

I have personally learned to avoid the slings and arrows that come my way in my public pursuits. I have millions of books and tapes out there in the marketplace.

Some people love them, others see them in an opposite light. It is enough for me to write and speak from my own position of purpose, knowing within that I am on the proper path. I have learned to ignore the reviews and stay on purpose. I am not trying to please anyone else in my work. I am simply doing what I know to be the right thing for me while always considering improving the lives of others and doing divine work. If my work helps you and others, I am thrilled. If not, I am still thrilled at being able to produce it. I am not focused on the outcome of my efforts. Results are not what motivate me. I am motivated by my inner awareness of having a heroic mission and staying with it, regardless of outcomes. Ironically, since I have been able to get my life on purpose, my writing and speaking seem to flow better than ever. I encourage you too to live this irony. Ask nothing and you will receive much. But if the receiving is your aim, you will be living a life of constant deficiency.

- *Develop your own personal excellence program, first in your mind, and then start putting it into practice in your daily life.* See yourself exercising, eating more vegetables and fruits, drinking more water and less soda and alcohol, reducing your intake of poisons, attending yoga classes, reading life-enhancing books, listening to tapes on spiritual and physical growth and quietly sitting in meditation. Get a picture of yourself actually doing these new kinds of behaviors and visualize the desired results. See yourself trimmer, less out of breath, with lowered blood pressure and cholesterol readings, feeling lighter and ageless rather than aging, attractive and content with yourself. When you regularly hold these mental pictures you will begin implementing them in your daily regimen. You will begin to make time for being healthy and happy. You will find your body responding in beautiful miraculous ways to your mental equivalents.

- *Use meditation regularly to create the inner harmony and peace that will allow you to become the personality that best suits your magnificent, divine purpose here on this planet at this time.* While meditating, experience your own death in your mind. See yourself moving into the light and discarding the robes you have been using that you have come to call your body. Look back from this perspective on all that you are attached to, and realize in your meditation how absurd these attachments truly are. You can see from this vision that you can own nothing, that it is just as absurd to be attached to the items of your life as it would be to hang onto the characters and physical manifestations in your dream, after you have awakened. Awaken in your meditation and know that your eternal formless self is free of attachments and worries. To die while you are alive is an enormously enlightening experience. The experience removes your fears and teaches you who you really are. Discovering that invisible force that is within you allows you to treat this physical world that you showed up in with reverence but without attachment. This will free you to be purposeful rather than chasing rewards and results.

- *Use your meditations to see yourself free from the labels that you have placed upon yourself and to become free of the big lies about your inability to change certain things about yourself.* Get very peaceful about being perfect and having all that you need to live your purpose. Meditatively activate your knowing that you do not need another thing to experience miraculous changes in your personhood. Allow yourself to experience the feeling that you already are everything, including a miracle.

As you contemplate all of the messages in these four chapters on manifesting real magic in your life, think about these words from Hermann Hesse, and work each day to make them apply in your own personal reality.

There is no reality except the one contained within us. That is why so many people live such an unreal life. They take the images outside them for reality and never allow the world within to assert itself.

Your miracles are an inside job. Go there to create the magic that you seek in your life. That is indeed your only reality.

7

REAL MAGIC
AND YOUR
PHYSICAL HEALTH

Our bodies are our gardens, to which our wills are
gardeners.

— WILLIAM SHAKESPEARE

This book emphasizes your unique capacity to create real
magic in your life. The central premise is that you
become what you think about all day and those days become
your lifetime.

It is my belief that you have been *taught* the physical limitations of your own body. You have been taught what it can
do and how well it can do it, how often it gets sick or injured,
how difficult it is to stay at perfect health, approximately
when it will die, and what diseases and addictions it can and
cannot overcome. You have been subjected to what amounts
to an indoctrination on your own limits as a physical being.
This chapter will help you unlearn most of what you have
been taught, for entering the magic garden of miracles means
the emphasis is on developing a consciousness of possibility,

rather than impossibility. To create the miracles that you seek in your physical body, you will need to follow some new strategies.

I will not be writing about what foods you should be eating, what exercise program you should adopt, what nutritional information you will need to consider, how much rest to get, what vitamins and minerals to use and so forth. I do not discount the importance of these things; quite the contrary, I pay close attention to all of them, as should you. Obviously you know that vegetables are better for you than Gummi Bears. You do not need to be told that exercise is better than being a couch potato if you want to achieve maximum physical health and benefits. You know that proper nutrition involves eating more fruit and less fats and sugars, and drinking a lot of water.

If you need to learn more about proper nutrition, exercise and fitness programs or diets that work, there are many excellent books available at your local library or bookstore. My particular favorites are *Perfect Health* and *Unconditional Life*, by Deepak Chopra, M.D., and *Fit for Life*, by Harvey and Marilyn Diamond.

Yet with all this information so readily available, why are so many of us trapped by physical limitations, and why do so few of us attain peak physical health? It is in this area that I choose to write directly to you.

I know that you are already a physical miracle waiting to unfold. I am absolutely convinced that you can have it all when it comes to your physical body, and that you need not experience the limitations that characterize your way of living. I also know that you know what to do about it. You do not need another diet book or another exercise video.

What you need is the ability to translate what your mind already knows into physical reality. And this is all accomplished by realigning yourself along the principles outlined in the first part of this book. Now it is time to get specific about your physical body, and get you started on manifesting miracles in your health and physical accomplishments.

DEFINING YOUR MIRACLE

As you approach this subject of real magic for yourself as a physical specimen of perfection, keep in mind the body in which you have showed up in the first place. You will not be asking yourself to be six foot six inches if you elected to show up here in a five-foot-six body. You do not want that six-foot-six-inch body and you are aware of that. Perhaps next time!

For now, as you consider what it is that would constitute a genuine miracle for yourself related to your physical being, just ask yourself the questions that are truly important to *you*. What would you genuinely like your body to look like? What would you like it to be able to realistically accomplish? What poisons would you truly like to see out of your body permanently? What healings would you love to see take place so that you can truly live the miracle?

After asking yourself these questions, try this terrific exercise. Stand before a full-length mirror and close your eyes. Now envision precisely what you would like this physical body to be *able to accomplish,* how you would like it to look, how healthy and addiction-free you would like it to be. With your eyes shut, get this vision firmly planted in your consciousness. Now, open your eyes and look carefully at the body that *you* have created. Yes, I said that *you* have created. Do you have a *knowing* or a doubt about your ability to fulfill your inner vision?

If you're like most people, you *doubt* your ability to create your miracle. Most people I have talked to about this matter of miracles and their physical bodies define it as the fulfillment of a dream that they know is remotely within the realm of possibility, but that they currently believe to be impossible.

As you go about examining what it is that would constitute a miracle for yourself in this area, keep this thought uppermost in your mind: *Anything that has been accomplished by any other human being in the physical realm is within the field of possibility.* This is a reminder that the universal law that allowed any miracle to have ever occurred in any human being at any time has not been repealed! Do not be afraid to imagine for yourself anything that has ever been accomplished, even if at this time you do not have the confidence that you could pull it off in the body you currently occupy. (You just might have to transform your body in order to make it happen!) At this point just allow yourself to imagine what it is that would constitute real magic for yourself and keep it uppermost in your mind.

Defining your miracle is the first step toward making it your reality. Perhaps it is in having your body look and feel as it once did, even though you have lost that magic feeling and haven't seen it for a long time. Perhaps it relates to an illness that you would love to see removed from your body, but you doubt your ability to heal yourself. Perhaps it is in overcoming an addiction or series of addictions to toxic substances that have dominated your life. Perhaps you would love to complete a triathlon or run a mile, or swim across the lake, or anything that simply has always seemed to be out of your reach.

I am not asking you to walk across that lake, or fly over the treetops, or change the shape of your nose with magic thinking. I am asking you to simply and clearly have in mind what it is that would constitute a miracle for you, and you alone. Get the vision, and just for a few minutes as you read through this chapter, suspend your disbelief and your skepticism and allow yourself to take this journey toward real magic.

Remember, your body is only the physical package that houses the invisible part of you that we call your soul or higher self. How that body functions, its relative state of health, and all of its abilities stem from the mind. As you think, so shall you be. So let's consider what you need to do with your mind in order to create real magic in the realm of your physical body.

BECOMING A WILLING STUDENT

Remember the ancient Zen proverb I quoted at the beginning of this book? "When the student is ready the teacher will appear." If you want to see a miraculous transformation in your entire physical being, a shift to super health and super accomplishments that you once thought impossible, then you must shift your inner world, that invisible self called your mind, from the state of "wishing it were only so," to an intention of willingness to pay attention to whatever comes your way that will assist you in this endeavor.

Become a student of your physical body. In your mind decide that, in spite of present physical health or abilities, you are already a miracle. You are in possession of a body that is filled with the universal flow of life. Just being able to contemplate such an exciting state is miraculous all by itself. You could be a stone, or a cement block, or a tomato plant. But no, you are filled with something that allows you to breathe, and touch, and taste, and see, and contemplate and be alive in the universe.

If you are committed to seeing your physical self with wonder and awe, and if you can know deep within that your invisible self wants the body it inhabits to be as healthy as possible, then you are a student who is ready. However, if you are really only deluding yourself with this kind of thinking, and somewhere in that invisible higher self that occupies your body you are filled with doubt, saying, "I would like to max-imize my physical body and experience this real magic, but I know that I can't do it because I've never been able to do it before, and basically I am weak and I will give in to the very first temptation that comes along," then you are not a stu-dent who is ready. Instead you have some real work to do in the invisible realm that is your very essence here in the mate-rial world.

Let's assume that the nagging doubt is still there, and you are in a position of wanting to experience real magic in the physical body you occupy, but you seriously doubt your abil-ity to do so. What will happen if this is your story (and it is indeed a very common one)?

The answer is in the Zen proverb: "When the student is ready the teacher will appear." What you guarantee with mental doubt is that you will not receive the guidance and assistance that you need. In other words, you have refused to let the teachers appear who can assist you in this endeavor. It's not that the teachers are not there, and unwilling to assist you. It's that you are unable to allow them to come to your aid. Your mental doubt, those thoughts which direct the machine called your body, are sending real magic away. If this is what you have believed, then you are substituting real tragic for real magic. Make no mistake about this. You create the absence of real magic with intentions that doubt your abilities. The tools you have used to create your physical self are your thoughts, those that have been imposed upon you as well as those you have decided upon as your way of processing your universe. I am assuming that you are still in a doubting mode, otherwise you would have experienced that real magic of perfect health. It is incumbent upon you to examine how to change those thoughts around so as to give yourself the opportunity to create real magic in your physical being.

Dr. Elisabeth Kübler-Ross, in a passage from *Healers on*

Healing, explains how she had to unlearn some of the things that she had been taught throughout her career:

At one of my workshops a huge man, weighing perhaps four hundred pounds, suddenly and unexpectedly went into an acute homicidal rage. I could see that I had to rescue a woman who was much too close to him. I stepped forward and pushed her away, but in the process the man brought a rubber hose (which was supposed to be used to take out anger on a phone book) down on my bare toes with all his strength, crushing them.

I could not stop to focus on the pain. I capped my big toe with my hand, ignoring the pain, and focused all my energy on the enraged man in order to push him even further into the depths of his rage, so he could go all the way through it and get it out. Then, suddenly, he was over it and the group was safe.

I found myself wondering why I was sitting in such a strange position, pulling my right knee up and holding my big toe. Remembering what had happened, I took my hand away to look at my toe, expecting the worst. To my amazement, there was no trace of any injury. It had been instantaneously healed.

I have had several other experiences of spontaneous physical healing in emergency situations. In each case, the reason I was able to heal myself was that I did not have time to think. As a physician I have been trained to believe that such instantaneous healing cannot happen. But in emergencies, when we have to focus totally on the situation and have no time to think, we do not block our innate potential for self-healing—a potential that I believe each of us has. If we would develop more trust and faith in our own inner healing ability, spontaneous physical healing could occur more often.

Although this passage focuses on physical healing, Kübler-Ross's conclusions apply to all aspects of one's physical well-being.

If you are a student truly getting ready to be ready, you will assume responsibility for all that you have created. Your body's relative state of health, your physical attractiveness, your addictions or bad habits that serve to restrict you from experiencing perfect health—these are all the results of your intentions over a lifetime. Your first step is to accept complete responsibility for all of this. Then, reexamine how you have used your mind to create the physical body that houses your soul on this glorious spiritual journey here in human-beingdom.

In order to remove nagging doubt and transcend the old way of thinking and creating your physical body, take an honest look at how it has been working and then commit yourself to a trial period of change. Once you have firmly entrenched a new way of processing the creation of your physical life, your teachers will begin to show up just as they have all along, but now you will be in a position to accept the assistance they will provide.

SEVEN STEPS TO MANIFESTING REAL MAGIC IN YOUR PHYSICAL BEING

You *can* learn to develop more trust and faith in your body to heal itself and stay healthy. How? Begin with a review of the seven beliefs for achieving real magic that I presented in chapter 1, as they apply to your own physical body.

1. *Recognize that there is an invisible life force within you.* Have you recognized the all-powerful invisible life force that is within you? Even though you can never experience it with your five senses, learn to tap into this life force when you are

trying to understand the physical workings of your body. When you make contact with this life force in a positive, believing way, you will begin to act automatically upon what that force within you dictates. For example, if you have convinced yourself that you are incapable of being physically fit, that you are too weak to accomplish certain tasks such as swimming or running long distances, or that you are sickly and unable to transcend the diseases that run in your family, this is the direction that your body has taken. Others have very likely taught you to believe in such pronouncements and you do not know any other way. Each day you look in the mirror and you see a flabby body, or a weak body, and tell yourself how unfortunate you were to have inherited big bones, or genes that don't allow you to be healthy. Then, the life force that is always within you works at reinforcing your thoughts.

In order to be a student who is ready, begin to reexamine those inner voices and, at the very least, start to challenge them firmly. Just as Dr. Kübler-Ross realized the amazing ability of the body to practice self-healing instantaneously, so too must you convince yourself, at least in your mind, of the power of your body to heal and strengthen itself.

2. *Know that your thoughts originate with you.* Rid yourself of the belief that you are not in control of your body. Shakespeare, in the quote at the beginning of this chapter, referred to our "wills." Yes, your will is the gardener that tends the garden called your body. That will is totally invisible, but nevertheless it originates with you, and only you. Give yourself permission to use that invisible will in a way that opens up your physical world to what has seemed impossible. Know that your thoughts originate with you and that they control all of your physical experiences. Although you may not be able to create a world-class body-building physique that will win you an Olympic gold medal, you do have the capac-

ity to be grandly, divinely healthy and capable within the body you have.

If you truly believe and act to heal your body of diseases and conditions that you believed beyond your control, you will discover real magic. But the willingness to use trust and knowing will come to you only through your thoughts. And when you have that knowing, and believe in it, and go to it often in the ways I am suggesting here, you will be unable to go back to doubt.

3. *Realize that there are no limits.* Begin reinforcing within your trusting mind that there are no limits existing within the physical world to your achieving real magic in your life. There is nothing to stop you from converting your illness to wellness. *Nothing!* If you are reading these lines and saying to yourself, "He is wrong, he doesn't know about my condition," then that is what you will be using to create your physical body as you read along right now. Your limits will be what you defend and believe, and you can only act upon what you think, even in the creation of the physical body that you occupy. That body is constantly being re-created each and every moment of your lifetime. The tools for recreating it, and reproducing the new cells that will replace the old, are all within your invisible self, your mind. Regardless of what any medical team may have convinced you of, regardless of what you experience of addiction to substances such as nicotine or caffeine or alcohol, regardless of your eating disorder that you so religiously hang on to—all of these conditions of your body, *all of them*, are capable of being reversed in some miraculous way. But only if you know and understand that the limitations that you experience are the result of limited thinking and limited believing. The very least you can do, rather than hanging on to your limitations, is to shift around how you are going to process your thoughts toward your body. Maybe, just

maybe, those physical limitations that you know and experience are the result of your thinking.

As you toss away your limited thinking, the teachers that have long been absent in your life will begin to appear and to guide you to miracles. But remember, thinking that you must have limitations is like putting a barricade in front of you that will not permit those teachers to appear in your life.

4. *Know that your life has a purpose.* It is very likely that your physical body has been as purposeless as your nonphysical self. Everything on the planet has a purpose, including your visit here as a human being. It is part of the perfection of this inexplicably divine and perfect universe. You must get your body to purpose as well.

The question "What is the lesson here?" must now be applied to your physical self. Seriously seek to discover the lesson embedded in your inability to accomplish certain tasks, the physical breakdown that you are experiencing, or the addiction to substances that you suffer. You can then switch from focusing on suffering to learning what you can from your illness, accident or addiction. Remember this method? I described it as the path of enlightenment through outcome in chapter 1. It is the path preceding that of purpose. First comes suffering, second is outcome, and third, purpose.

At purpose, you no longer need to be focused on what the lesson is, because you know that your entire life is about giving and serving and reaching out to others. When you truly know that your life has a grand and heroic mission, you have realigned yourself as a spiritual being having a temporary human experience. Consequently, in order to fulfill your mission and stay purposeful, you will automatically provide your body with all of the most powerful fuel and love that you can muster for fulfillment of your purpose.

You will find yourself wanting to exercise frequently and you will do it with love and appreciation for the perfection that your body represents. You will treasure your physical being as a vehicle that houses your soul, and you will be in awe of its perfection and beauty. You will not have any judgmental, ugly thoughts about it ever, because you will know in your heart that your purpose is about love and serving, and this means having harmonious, giving thoughts toward everyone and everything, including your body. When you align yourself with your purpose, so too will your body.

It will be a joy to feed it properly, remove the poisons, heal it naturally and appreciate its perfection. Your life has a purpose! Don't forget those important words. When you know it, act on it and live it daily, the teachers will begin to appear with regularity and guide you to real magic in your physical being.

5. *Overcome weakness by leaving it behind.* Learn to practice leaving self-defeating habits behind you, rather than trying to outthink or outmanipulate them. It is amazing how quickly you can leave negative habits behind when you realign yourself as a spiritual being. It is like walking through a gate to a garden of health and happiness. What seems so difficult when you are thinking in terms of limitations is now miraculously simple to achieve. When you leave your old ways of thinking behind, your old ways of being remain back there as well.

I was shocked at how easily I quit nicotine and caffeine. When I knew unconditionally that I no longer wanted those poisons in my body—and when I believed that quitting didn't have to be difficult—I was easily freed from those substances. The addiction was my way of *processing* what I thought about addictions! Once I believed in myself, and saw my soul and body as divine and precious, I was automatically converted to a being who could create the miracle of ending my addictions. And believe me, changing from a person who smoked heavily and consumed gallons of caffeinated soda pop daily, to a person free of those substances, feels miraculous.

I have had temptations placed before me countless times, but I never feel tempted. I have left that part of my life behind me, and it takes serious recollection to make me believe that I was once an addict to those poisons.

One simply leaves those behaviors in the past. Going back is just as impossible as returning to crawling when one knows how to walk. You will leave behind those impediments to your journey automatically when you decide to proceed with the steps that I am outlining here.

6. *Examine what you believe to be impossible, and then change your beliefs.* If you think that cancer is incurable, you will come to know there is no truth in this position for you. If you think you are relegated to a lifetime of addiction or disease or discomfort, you will reexamine that belief and begin to apply real-magic thinking in its place.

The words "It's impossible" are symbols for thoughts. The notion of impossibility is not a reality separate from our thoughts. Technically, in thought, which is dimensionless and formless, nothing is impossible. Your body, which appears to you to be a solid mass, upon closer examination is empty space, or consciousness. In fact, as we've seen, empty space dominates all matter, and the more powerful the microscope, the more you can see that, all the way to infinity, matter is composed of empty space. Or you'll recall, as Robert Frost poetically described it, "the secret that sits in the center and knows."

As you go through your life, keep in mind that every cell in the universe, including those in your body, is composed of an invisible force. Forget about how to pronounce what it has come to be called, or how to spell it or label it. Know it is there, and that nothing is impossible in this dimension, including your ability to use that life force to make of your life in the physical sense all that you want it to be. Miracles can only happen when you get rid of that concept of impossible and allow yourself to experience the magic of believing.

7. *Go beyond logic.* Abandon heavy reliance on your rational mind as your guide. Your rational mind plays tricks and deludes you. You cannot logically explain your own mind, where it is located, where it was before you showed up here in form, or where it goes when you leave.

There's a long list of things that defy rational explanation. What is a thought? How are thoughts connected to each other? How can mothers know what their babies are thinking? What allows geese to fly in formation without any training? How can a salmon get back to its spawning place? If we cannot even begin to explain what life is, let alone how we think, then why should we rely so heavily on that rational left-brained side of our humanity for what can and cannot be accomplished?

Every cell in your body has the entire energy force of the universe located within it. Instead of perceiving yourself as one human in the vastness of the universe, try the reverse. Try imagining that the world is within you. In every cell of your body the world and all of its magic is present and available to you. If you use logic and rational analysis to try to explain miracles, you will soon be back thinking how impossible all of this is. You will trap yourself in your old patterns, helpless and hopeless about what is possible for you.

Allow yourself the luxury of believing in the divinity of your own soul. Allow yourself to know that every thought you have is a miracle incapable of being explained away by logical, scientific discourse. Know that you, body and soul, are a miracle and that nothing you can imagine in your mind is impossible. Even the creation of life itself comes from that invisible dimension of thought.

These are the seven steps to real magic, revisited for the benefit of applying them to your physical self. The way to the actual creation of that new self, as with everything you have to learn, begins and ends in your invisible self, that place with no boundaries where all of your actions are first set into motion—your magical mind.

CREATING HEALTH AND HEALING MIRACLES

José Silva, the founder of the Silva Mind Control method, is a man I've admired for a long time. I have used the Silva method of visualization for many years. It has helped me over- come illnesses and accidents and avoid surgery. I was able to heal myself of a hernia that I had been advised would require surgery. Obviously I have a great deal of faith in the power of the mind to heal and assist us in creating higher and higher states of health.

The following quote is from the preface to Silva's powerful book *You the Healer.* I concur totally with his statement. This man has helped millions of people tap into their minds to cre- ate perfect health. I urge you to look for his books and tapes and even attend his training sessions around the country.

You need not live a life of sickness.
You need not die from ill health.
It is your natural state to be healthy.
It is your right to live a perfectly healthy life
right up to the day you die of natural causes.

Strong, powerful words. What else could you possibly want for yourself in your physical body? Simply to be healthy, happy, fully alive and free from sickness. Yet so many of us are not even close to accomplishing this.

Several years ago my wife and I spent some time on the island of Bali in the South Pacific. We were fascinated by the way the people there related to each other. They had very little in the way of physical possessions, living mostly on an average family income of less than fifty U.S. dollars a month, but it seemed to matter little. There was a noticeable and much appreciated silence about the people, even in the large families where the children slept on dirt floors under straw roofs, and they looked into each other's eyes rather than each other's wallets. But what we didn't realize until we returned home was how unhealthy we Westerners appear contrasted with the Balinese.

After arriving in San Francisco to catch another flight to the East Coast, Marcie and I simultaneously looked at each other as we sat down on the plane, with the identical reaction. We were jolted by the appearance of most of the passengers. The people all around us, for the most part, showed evidence of anxiety in their skin and eyes and they looked so overweight. We hadn't seen any of this on Bali, where, though the people lived in poverty, there was abundant healthy food thanks to its location in a lush rain forest climate on the equator. We saw not one overweight body and no one who appeared to be physically out of shape.

We were struck by how our fellow passengers seemed unable to look each other in the eye and exemplified the Western inclination to look past each other into wallets and possessions. That attitude, combined with the evidence of physical deterioration, presented a sharp contrast to the people we had seen on Bali. It seemed clear to me that the Balinese and the Westerners were displaying physical evidence of their inner mind-set.

Yet, most of those people on the plane would never for a moment consider that their physical appearance had anything to do with their inner thoughts. If asked why they felt so bad, or fatigued, or had so many colds and flu attacks, or spent so much time and money on painkillers and antibiotics, they would most likely attribute those conditions to the stresses of modern times. But it need not be that way. Your own health and healing capacities are located strictly within you.

Silva presents numerous case studies of people who were told their physical ailments were beyond their control. One of those that he writes about is a man who had been a quadriplegic for eighteen years, with total paralysis on one side and 8 percent paralysis on the other. He had been diagnosed with multiple sclerosis, an incurable progressive disease. This man learned to go to the alpha state that I discussed in the section on meditation in chapter 3.

On the first day of his training, he noticed some feeling in his little finger. From there, he began to set physical goals for himself that originated in his newfound power of healing with imagery through the alpha state of higher consciousness. Within eight months of daily alpha meditation training, he was able to drive a car even though he was still restricted to a wheelchair. Then he decided he wanted to climb stairs and walk on his own. He created his own miracle in fourteen months of deliberate mind training, and walked up those stairs.

What is relevant here is how this relates specifically to you. The message I wish to impart is that you are capable of picturing the highest state of physical health for yourself within the confines of your mind. And it is these pictures, these mental movies, that are the very stuff of which miracles are made.

The stories of people who have been able to manifest physical healing miracles are legion. One of the most profound books of this kind that I have read is *The Cancer Conqueror*, by Greg Anderson. It is a parable based on the truths Greg learned during his two bouts with cancer and his release from the hospital supposedly to die. Told he would not live beyond the next thirty days, Greg's experience led him to a new respect for the power of the human spirit in overcoming illness.

The book is presented as a parable, but his own personal story is real and offers dramatic testimony to what I am writing about manifesting miracles. It is not a wait-and-hope-that-things-will-get-better approach to miracles. As Greg puts it, "You become a cancer conqueror not because you go into remission. . . . Instead, you become a cancer conqueror because you choose to become a new person."

He discovered how powerful fear, anger and distress are in affecting the immune system. He discovered also that unconditional love, inner peace, giving away love, reducing expectations of others and tuning into the powerful effect of meditation and visualization were the seeds for defeating the cancer that was raging in his body. He had to shift his entire consciousness from a nonspiritual to a spiritual mode, and in the process he was able to magically restore his own healing capacity. His is indeed an incredible journey. I recommend that you read his wonderful book and share it with anyone you know who is diagnosed with cancer.

The key to miracle making is not in reading a book or listening to another's words, however. The key is knowing, when you are told that you have some kind of physical affliction, that you can either prepare to suffer or prepare to heal. This is not meant as a disparaging commentary on the medical community. In fact, they have made enormous strides in eradicating the disease process for many conditions. And in recent years they have been instrumental in conducting research on the power of the mind and teaching people how to tap their invisible selves to treat their illnesses.

One of my favorite people and a person I think of as a dear friend and soul mate also happens to be a fantastic medical doctor. He is Deepak Chopra, a man I've referred to already. His exciting books include *Perfect Health, Quantum Healing, Unconditional Life, The Return of the Rishi*, and *Creating Health*. Consider the following from Dr. Chopra from *Perfect Health*, as he discusses how we can become healers, or what I call miracle workers:

As we probe deeper into the pathogenesis of disease, however, a primary truth comes to light: all disease results from the disruption of the flow of intelligence. When people speak of intelligence, they refer almost automatically to the intellect and its dealing in concepts. Intelligence is not simply in the head, though. Its expression may be at the subcellular level, at the cellular level or tissue level, or at the level of the central nervous system. . . . Although all these levels of intelligence can be located, intelligence itself cannot. It permeates each level of its expression; it is all pervasive in us and universal in nature. Intelligence is mind . . . its scope embraces the cosmos. We would be rash to suppose that it operates from the confines of the brain alone. In that sense, all disease processes originate on this vaster stage of Mind. So also does health.

This is a mind-boggling notion indeed for those who are not yet schooled in the belief of miracles and real magic. Your health is the result of an intelligence that is in every cell in your body, and that intelligence is neither visible nor identifiable. That invisible intelligence is not local in nature. It is not just in your brain, it is in every cell, every neuron, every hormone, every antibody that is a part of you. Indeed, your very essence is that invisible intelligence. In order to create perfect health for yourself you need to understand that the mind is the place where you process it all, and decide about the physical reality you will experience.

You needn't feel guilty about your ailments, since guilt will only immobilize your immune system and help to shut down your ability to achieve a higher state of health. Instead of feeling guilt, try asking the questions, "What do I have to learn from this disease, or this lack of health? What is the lesson here?" Then begin to apply your new awareness about the power of your mind to alter that debilitating state you have previously accepted as your destiny.

Dr. Abraham Maslow devoted a large portion of his life to the study of what he called self-actualizers. In *The Sky's the Limit* I wrote at length about the qualities of such people. One characteristic that stood out in looking at the lives of these very special people was that when faced with seemingly insurmountable problems they always looked inward for a solution. Those who lived at the peak of health and well-being found the answers to life's problems within their minds. They refused to look outside of themselves either for blame or the magic elixir of healing.

In *Creating Health*, Deepak Chopra writes, "The possibility of stepping onto a higher plane is quite real for everyone. It requires no force or effort or sacrifice. It involves little more than changing our ideas about what is normal."

I have chosen not to include a long series of case studies of people who have overcome incurable illnesses because that is not my purpose in writing this book. I am writing to you, to that invisible intelligence that permeates your body. If you are *not* a believer that you can create a miracle in your physical health, then a million such stories will not convince you. If you *are* a believer then you need no further reminders of others who have preceded you on this path.

For now, keep alive the vision of what it is that would constitute your own personal health miracle, as you explore the realm of miracles in your physical abilities. At the end of this chapter I will provide you with a review of how to set your mind for miracles in your body.

CREATING MIRACLES IN YOUR PHYSICAL ABILITIES

What are the things that you have always dreamt about accomplishing, but know would take a miracle to make happen? Once again you must shift your inner consciousness to a place of limitless possibility. And as before, a miracle is awaiting you in this realm of your life. I promise!

When I was twenty-eight years old, the idea of running a marathon, twenty-six miles, was simply unheard of. It would have taken a miracle for me, at that time of my life, to be able to run for almost four hours without stopping. Since then, however, I have run seven marathons, and have passed the fifteen-year mark of running for a minimum of eight miles per day without ever missing a day. Yesterday's miracle is today's reality. Today's miracle will be tomorrow's reality.

So how did I run for twenty-six miles without stopping? By having the thought in my mind that I could do it, and then refusing to doubt it or be afraid of it. The rest was a piece of cake. I didn't need to go out and get instructions, or have someone else show me the way. Once I had the idea in my mind, it was simply a matter of aligning myself so as to keep the vision. The body will do what it is willed to do with that ever-present gardener Shakespeare was talking about.

It is also significant to point out that you have created whatever reality your physical body is capable of accomplishing on this date as you sit and read these words. All that you are capable or incapable of achieving flows from what you have decided within that invisible sphere called your mind, where all of your thoughts originate, and where your physical reality ultimately originates as well.

This story appeared in the *Maui News* on Sunday, June 23, 1991, in the sports section. It was written by Hal Bock, an Associated Press sportswriter.

The statement deserves at least a drumroll, but Jim Law doesn't say it in any dramatic way, just rather matter-of-factly, really.

"I'm not sure I'd be alive today if it were not for the Senior Games."

Just like that. A simple matter of life and death. Law is a professor of psychology at Johnson C. Smith University in Charlotte, N.C. Five years ago, when he was 60, he got involved in the Senior Games—nothing terribly strenuous, just table tennis—and went to his doctor for a routine checkup. It was then that he learned that his cholesterol count was 322.

Three hundred, twenty-two.

Normal is under 200. Borderline is 200–239. High risk is over 240.

Jim Law was at 322 and he knew why. "Ice cream, fast foods, red meat, smoking," he said. "All the tasty things. And a sedentary lifestyle."

Sounds like your average American diet.

Suitably alarmed, Law started exercising and eating right. He began running and switched from fats to fruits, from red meat to green vegetables. He quickly lost 20 pounds and his cholesterol tumbled to an entirely acceptable 188. But he wasn't through. "In four months, it was down to 127," he said.

"I began to feel better as I lost weight. If I didn't exercise, I felt bad. I made the time because it was for a good cause—me!"

Law's wife, Aurelia, is 63 and she runs with him. "One time she was huffing and puffing in a race," he said. "A man, I think he was 73, took her by the arm and said, 'Don't worry. As long as we get in by sundown, it'll be all right.' "

Law gets in well before that. Running the 100, 200 and 400 in the 1989 Senior Games, he won three golds and set three records for his age group. His best times outdoors are 12.71, 26.10 and 59.39—the first two American records, the third a world record.

How strong is his zest for this competition? Well, senior runners are divided by five-year age groups. The day after he turned 65, Law couldn't wait to take a shot at the next category and drove 700 miles so that he could run in an event.

Imagine that. A man in his sixties totally transforming his life. From the perspective of being overweight with a cholesterol reading of "panic," he went to work in his mind and created a life that he once knew was impossible. When he knew it was impossible he acted on his thoughts by eating ice cream and watching television. When he knew something else was possible in his mind, he acted on those new thoughts and a miracle occurred in his life.

You have the inner capacity to imagine for yourself anything that is in the realm of real magic. Anything! Once you have that vision, you will be able to use the steps provided throughout this book to make that miracle your reality. And, you will receive all of the divine guidance that you need in the process. This goes for virtually anything you can visualize for yourself as an accomplishment that now *seems* impossible. The same strategy for manifesting miracles in your physical accomplishments applies to all other areas of your life. Real magic can be accessed only if you shed the doubt and fear, and convert yourself to a spiritual being.

Let me tell you about one experience I had in this area of getting to a level I had never before experienced, one that I thought was impossible to achieve for myself until I became an authentic spiritual being having a human experience.

I was playing a tennis match against a very fine tennis player and we had been battling each other in the hot sun for over three hours. I had won the first set and Tom had won the second set, and then something very strange began to happen. I sensed there was a presence with me on the tennis court telling me something. I had been meditating for several years at the time, and I was completely convinced that one could access divine guidance, or what we tend to call intuition. Of course no one can explicitly define inner knowing or intuition, but we all know whereof we speak when it is mentioned.

The strangest thing began to happen. I could not score one single point, yet I was playing outstanding tennis. Tom seemed to be in what experienced tennis players call a zone and what others call "flow," as discussed in chapter 5 (others call it being unconscious). He could not miss a shot and even balls that I hit directly at him at a high rate of speed when he was retreating to protect himself would somehow bounce off of his racket and land in my court for his winner. It was as if my invisible guide were somehow laughing at me, and soon I began to laugh out loud at what was happening.

At one point Tom hit a high lob over my head that was heading for the fence. I looked up and knew it was going out of bounds by six feet at least. Suddenly, out of a stillness, a wind that wasn't there a moment earlier picked the ball up way above my head and literally blew it back and it landed smack on the back baseline for a winner. I was dumbfounded. This kind of miracle making had gone on for game after game, and an inner voice was saying, "Lighten up Wayne. Don't take this so seriously. Don't want it so much. Relax, have fun, and everything will work out exactly as it should."

I began to know I wasn't alone out there and that I was being taught a valuable lesson. I lost five consecutive games at the beginning of the third set, yet somehow knew if I kept my poise, stopped fighting and being frustrated and sent love and congratulations to Tom it would be fine. I was behind 0-5, and yet I had been playing excellent tennis.

As we changed courts to play out the match, I was literally told, "Meditate your way through the rest of the match. Let go, and treat this game as a meditation." I could not believe the transformation that took place.

I let go of everything in my physical world, I mean everything. The surroundings, the sun, the people gathered around watching the match, the court, my racket, everything. I went totally into my mind and began repeating my mantra. My brain went to alpha immediately and I felt that incredible lightness of being I described earlier when writing about meditating. I could not even see my opponent. I actually became one with the ball. Everything turned around. I could not miss a shot. I felt as if I could fly even though we had been playing in the hot sun for hours. My legs felt strong and I had the internal knowing that I could get to any ball.

When we changed courts I simply repeated my mantra over and over silently and felt a wonderful, euphoric high. I won seven straight games without losing more than a few points.

Tom said to me at the conclusion of the match, "What happened to you out there? You even looked different. I've never seen you concentrate like that, you seemed so confident and so peaceful. I don't even feel bad losing after being ahead 5-0 because I played great but you somehow transcended yourself for seven straight games."

That experience happened a few years ago. I was not alone, and I knew something magical was taking place. It was the same lesson I had to learn while meditating under the tree trying to remove that flower from the branch. "Don't demand anything, loosen up and be willing to allow a miracle to happen without any insistence and then everything will come to you that you need." The flower landed in my hand and gave me the message I needed, when I let go.

I believe this is true for all that you want to accomplish in your life. Send out love and harmony, put your mind and body in a peaceful place, and then allow the universe to work in the perfect way it knows how to. My body was in total harmony with my mind during those seven games. I substituted doubt and fear with knowing and trust and allowed myself to perform at a higher level than I had ever achieved before by seeing that tennis match as a meditation rather than a contest.

Those miraculous moments some call zoning or being unconscious can be accessed in any area of your life and are part of an ageless philosophy, as the words of Lao-tzu, written more than two thousand years ago, attest:

> Even the best will in the world, when forced,
>   achieves nothing.
> The best righteousness, when forced,
>   achieves nothing.
> The best good-form, when forced,
>   does not come out right . . .

Your great physical accomplishments that are yet to come are indeed miracles for you as you contemplate them today. Go within to the peaceful solitude of your mind. Access the higher part of yourself and know you are not alone. Stop competing with others and use your mind to allow your physical self to go to its highest level. Follow the guidelines for creating a miracle mind-set that I have presented at the end of this chapter.

A WORD ABOUT ADDICTIONS AND MIRACLES

If you have spent a portion of your life addicted to something that is toxic to your body, I am sure that, in your mind, freedom from that substance or activity would constitute a miracle. If you have been a victim of an eating disorder, or spent time in which you knew your body was out of shape because of some behavior on your part, a miracle for you would be to be free from that condition. If you have found yourself addicted to nicotine, caffeine, marijuana, cocaine, alcohol or even harder drugs, and simply have been unable to shake your reliance on these substances, then being clean and physically free from these substances would indeed constitute your miracle in the physical realm.

Most people have built up a defense system for their particular addictions, and they argue for and defend their habits. They find themselves trying to convince others that their addiction is not really a problem, that they could quit if they wanted to, or that they could transform their lives if they so chose. "What's the point in living if you can't enjoy yourself?" is their defensive credo. Addicts (which includes almost everyone on some level) really want others to believe they do not have a problem.

Inside, in that invisible place where truth keeps smacking one in the face despite external denials, all addicts know they have a problem, and that they would rather not be poisoning themselves. They believe they just need more courage or strength or will to change.

You can get all of the help that is available to you, join the right support groups, get the best medical and psychological attention available in the world, and still, when you change your old habit and experience the miracle of ridding yourself of an addiction, you must do it alone. You must make that decision with your mind, and then carry it out in the physical material world. No one else can do it for you. And neither will you if you see yourself as only a physical being. It has to come from that invisible place, from within.

It is important to remind you, once again, that the universal law that has allowed anyone to ever overcome a serious addiction has not been repealed. It does not matter how far down you have gone. You have within you the ability to make a miracle of your life and rid yourself of addiction.

Here is one letter, written to me a while back, from a woman who put her life back on "health" and created a miracle. When the student was ready, truly ready, the teacher appeared. This is not a fictional story. I have met Kathy and appeared with her on national television where she had the courage to tell her story to millions.

Dear Wayne:

After reading your books, listening to your tapes, (ALL OF THEM at least a thousand times!), and finally getting the opportunity to see you speak in person last May here in Seattle I am ready to write to you. Ready I say because when I first heard a tape of yours years ago I gathered everything I could find on you to feed my painful "crush" on you, the crush that turned into awe, the awe that turned into admiration, and the admiration that turned into an understanding that for whatever reason you have become a mentor in my life. I do not want to bore you with the detailed story of how you literally saved my life, I'm sure you get letters like this by the hundreds . . . but I want you to know where I came from to understand how far I have come and the impact you have had on my life.

In 1982 I was just finishing a year in my life that had thrown me into the utter depths of my own reality. A prostitute with a thirst for vodka and cocaine, I had been married at 17, divorced at 22, had four abortions, and attempted suicide twice. I met my present husband, who had a strong attraction for prostitutes and a serious cocaine habit, just about this time. We began feeding each other's nightmares and our despair doubled. Our lives began a fast track of staying "up" for days on end drinking and doing drugs. I remember waking up one morning and thinking to myself, "I won't live to see 30 years old. I'm going to die."

One day I was in a bookstore purchasing a book for my sister's birthday when I noticed some cassette tapes on a stand. For some reason I was intrigued by these cassette tapes on "how to change your life." I saw your face on the front of one of these cassette boxes and moved toward it. I know how strange this sounds, but from that moment on my life totally changed. I bought every tape the bookstore had available by you and purchased all your books. I asked my husband to listen to them and together we listened to tapes day in and day out. Somehow, I found the Nightingale/Conant series and ordered all of those! Slowly our lives began to change. Without going to one rehabilitation center, AA, or one support group we have been drug and alcohol free for over five years now.

We are living a life we thought would be beyond our wildest dreams! We have a beautiful home, we own a corporation and two separate companies, and we are in the process of starting our family. We are in total control of our lives and feel limitless! I have longed to see you in

person, which I did last May. Then I wanted to thank
you. It's impossible to explain why someone I have never
met became such a strong force in my life, but it really
does not matter. The point is, our lives are changed forever and the one thing I have learned is that there is
nothing more flexible than the human spirit and we may
never know what moves us toward any direction. (Good
or bad.) I want to thank you from the bottom of my
heart for just doing what you're doing! Putting information "out there" that is more needed than you could ever
imagine. You are changing lives, Wayne, by the thousands! Thank you for listening to your higher self and
sharing with us.

Warmest personal regards, Kathy

For Kathy—who now is a proud and beautiful mother, a
happy, successful businesswoman, and in a very spiritual marriage and partnership—her life is a miracle. Who could have
thought back in 1982 such an outcome was a possibility?

Miracles in your physical world, whether they be healing
yourself or achieving maximum physical health, ridding
yourself of an addiction or accomplishing a longed-for
achievement, all depend on how you as a spiritual being
choose to use your invisible mind and the guidance that is
available to you.

Here are some specific suggestions to make this your own
personal reality in a brief review of the miracle mind-set necessary for creating miracles.

MANIFESTING MIRACLES IN YOUR PHYSICAL REALM

The formula for allowing miracles into your life includes taking an active role in reprogramming yourself to create what

you previously believed impossible, and using the following miracle mind-set guidelines adapted from chapter 3.

- *Reserve judgment and disbelief by practicing affirmations.* As a part of your daily agenda, practice these affirmations, which will help you remove the doubt and judgment that keep you from moving to the next level on the physical plane.

  - I am in the process of creating the miracle that I deserve.

  - I am willing to release that which has inhibited me up until now.

  - I trust that I am not alone and that I will receive guidance when I am ready.

  - I am ready.

  - I know that I have the capacity to accomplish anything that I conceive of in my mind.

  - I am willing to do what it takes to make my dream a reality.

  Use these and any others you can write for yourself. When said aloud and repeatedly they will help you dislodge disbelief.

- *Create a real-magic zone by listening carefully to your body and all that it is telling you.* This is your private real-magic zone that you needn't share with anyone else. If you feel bloated, sickly, tired, anxious, lethargic, achy or any other physical symptom, say to yourself, "What is my body saying to me? What lesson do I have to learn here?" Simply listen and take notice of what you are hearing. Before long you will get the message your body is delivering.

"Exercise me. I hate sitting around and getting flabby."

"Pay attention. Stop putting so much food into me."

"I hate sugar and that's why I give you headaches."

"I love it when you give me large amounts of clean, filtered water. It helps me flush out the poisons."

"Use those oils and creams on me that keep my skin fresh."

"Stop with the drugs please! Why do you think I respond with hangovers, sniffles, lethargy, muddled thinking, slurring, anxiety, blood pressure increases, increased heart rates, congestion, coughing and so on?"

Listen to your body and it will tell you exactly what you need to know. Every cell in your body has infinite universal intelligence within it. Nurture that intelligence. Revere it and treat it with the sacredness that it deserves. Miracles will be your reward.

- *Affirm yourself as a no-limit person by practicing new areas of activity.* Note what it is you absolutely were certain you could not accomplish one year ago. Let's say, for example, it is being able to run one mile without stopping. Or to go one full year without having a cold, or twenty-one days without having a drink. Or to go for a week reducing your fat intake by 50 percent. These examples are quite specific for you to have a mind-set of being able to go beyond self-imposed limitations.

  Choose one limitation and literally see yourself in your mind going past it one day at a time. Create your own personal challenge to go to a new level. One mile, one day, one year, but all a day at a time. You will be amazed at the results, which started with a thought. You will find yourself believing there is nothing you cannot accomplish if you put your mind to it and believe it. This is the inner circuitry of a miracle worker.

- *Trust those inner hunches and intuitions concerning your physical body.* Pay attention to whatever seems to be a forceful dramatic inclination within you. Listen and follow those inner dictates. Your inner voices will tell you what to avoid, whom to seek out, what to read, whom to trust, what to eat, when to exercise and when to rest. Certainly you want to seek out the help of knowledgeable others, but be wary of those who tell you what is impossible for you. Or at least, see their negativity as a great lesson for you and use it to go beyond the limitations they are attempting to impose on you. Know you are not alone and trust you will be guided in the proper way. Fill yourself with awe and wonderment at the vastness and mystery of the nonphysical transmitting messages concerning your physical self. You will find yourself experiencing the miracles I am writing about.

- *Begin to trust the secret that sits in the center and knows.* Though you may not yet have accessed your highest self, it is a part of you. Trust in the silent invisible intelligence that flows through your form. Go to it often in meditation and simply ask, "How may I give my life to others?" "How may I serve?" "Guide me to be the best and most purposeful person I can be."

You will discover that in order to give of yourself in a life-time of purpose, you will want to be as healthy, positive and confident in your own divinity as is possible.

This will help you to get on the path of physical miracle making and real magic.

After every meditation I always feel I can accomplish anything, and I am filled with enormous love and awe for everything I encounter in the physical universe. I notice the shape and color and beauty of trees, and I literally feel that way about myself as well. I am in awe of being alive and I want to treat my body well. I have touched a place within me that is love and harmony, and this place allows me to go beyond anything I ever thought I could accomplish before. Since I have been meditating and greeting that secret that sits in the center and knows, I have reduced my own body fat considerably, and returned to the weight I was when I graduated from high school in 1958. I feel free from disease and addictive substances and I find myself accomplishing more than ever before. My speaking and writing have gone to new levels, and I have never felt better in my life.

All this from a willingness to know that I am something far more than a body with a soul. As a soul with a body, I know I can live healthier so my soul will have an exquisite container for its heroic mission. I believe the same is possible for you. I know you can make miracles happen within your body, but you must go within and make contact and then all else will fall into place.

- *Substitute knowing and trusting for doubting and fearing.* In everything you examine in your physical life, and all you would like to see happen for you, just for a short period of time replace doubting and fearing with knowing and trusting. All of your doubts are obstacles inhibiting your entry into the kingdom of real magic. Just know and trust! And let the doubts others offer serve to solidify your own knowing.

Look at the lives of the doubters and ask yourself if that is what you want as a model for what you can achieve. Then look at the lives of the "knowers" and see the difference. The knowers are out there making a difference in their lives—exercising, being healthy, and shocking the world with their grand accomplishments. The doubters generally are sitting around behaving in their accustomed role of critic.

• *Affirm that your intention to make yourself healthy creates your reality.* Once you have put your new ideas into focus and gotten a clear picture of what you are going to accomplish, and you believe in your capacity to make them happen, shift into high gear, which is called intention. Reaffirm your intention to make yourself healthy. "I am healthy and capable of achieving what I set out to do." "I will heal myself." "I am not smoking today." This is intention.

My wife, Marcie, does this with amazing results. She once was diagnosed with a nodule on her thyroid, which three doctors said required surgery. Her response? An intention, "I will shrink that nodule and remove it from my body," not a wish. Nothing could dissuade her. No agonizing, no worry on her part. A simple intention that was followed by her putting those intentions into action. She spent a week at Dr. Chopra's Ayurvedic health center in Lancaster, Massachusetts, learning about diet and how it affects the thyroid.

Her nodule is now almost gone. Her doctors still are expressing disbelief at this miracle. It all came about because Marcie's inner voices told her how to proceed in her treatment.

- *Experience satori in your body.* Instant awakening is available. It isn't going to take a long period of suffering for you to get miracle making in your body. Once you know within that you are on the right path, you will find yourself in possession of the will and strength you need. Be open to the possibilities of it happening in a moment. Encourage the sudden flash of insight, "I can truly do this." Then you are a new person, looking back on what you used to tell yourself. That old addict is not only gone, but you can't even find him any more in your mind. The person who always had colds and fevers has disappeared completely, replaced in a moment with a flash of knowing. Going through the gate happens in a present moment, the very working unit of your life. Be prepared for it. Watch for it. Go with it when it arrives.

  I left behind so many self-defeating behaviors without, it seems, even trying. In a moment I decided, and while that moment was transpiring, I was outside of my body watching as I was making those declarations. Satori! Instant awakening. It is available and will come into your life. It happens first in your mind, and then you will carry it out with ease in whatever physical activity you need to manifest. Miracles come in moments. Be ready and willing!

- *Behave in your body as if it were already what you want it to be.* That's right. Fake it! If you see yourself in your mind as svelte and capable of new and dramatic accomplishments, then act right now as if that were your reality. When you understand you are what you think about, and you act on what you think about, you can see the wisdom of thinking of yourself as fantastic and powerful. The more you treat yourself to this kind of belief the quicker your body will react to the image.

If, on the other hand, you think vast miracle improvements in your physical being are going to be very difficult and time-consuming and you are going to spend a lot of time suffering, you will act on that image. I would wager that that is precisely what you have been doing for a long period of time. Act on the image that you want right now. Behave as if it were already here. If you see yourself as healthy and attractive in your mind, and you believe it firmly, then when you sit down to eat you will act according to that belief. This is the key to manifesting miracles.

- *Remind yourself that your spiritual self has primary importance.* Realign yourself so that your spiritual self has primary importance and your physical self will follow. Treat your entire being—body, mind and soul—as one great big spiritual package that cannot be separated. Your pancreas, lungs, eyes—every organ in your body— have infinite intelligence within them. Be a spiritual being first.

  See in your mind in advance what your physical results are going to be. Then surrender and let your divine body do what it already knows perfectly well how to do.

- *Remember each day that you can never get enough of what you don't want.* Look at all of your addictions, minor and major. Remind yourself that when you are pursuing poisons, you can never get enough of what you don't want. Your body doesn't want that addictive substance or that excess food. But you can never get enough. Why? Because you are operating from a physical self first and a spiritual self second. This is a self-sabotaging strategy to keep you from experiencing real magic. The more you poison yourself, the more you convince yourself that you cannot overcome the addiction. This fills you with doubt, coupled with fear, and lo and behold, there you are, incapable of getting past your addictive behavior.

If it is true that you can never get enough of what you don't want, then it is time to stop pursuing what you don't want, and get onto what you do want. When you pursue what you do want, you don't operate from scarcity. No need to chase after more. No need to look outside of yourself for miracles. Everything you need for perfect balance and health is already within you. You don't need another body, you need to trust in the divine intelligence inhabiting the one you already have.

- *Ask nothing of anyone in terms of helping you to get better.* Do not expect assistance from anyone in your physical world. If help comes along accept it and be grateful, but know in your heart that only you experience this human life in its physical form called *you*. It is all taking place in your invisible self where you process everything in the physical world. Send out love to others, radiate your divineness out there, but know that no one else can do it for you. And if you know that no one else can do it for you, then it only makes sense to expect nothing of them as you create your own miraculous existence.

- *Begin to develop authentic power, which is not located in the physical body.* Your power and authenticity as a person will not be measured in duration, but in your donations of love. This is authentic power. Seek miracles in the physical body you occupy so that you can be even more purposeful, not so that you can control others. If your power is in your strength, then it will leave when your strength dissipates. That is inauthentic power!

To know real magic in the physical sense, you must want that miracle for the purpose of being able to distribute love and harmony wherever you go. When this is your motivation, you will see that whatever you accomplish within your body, or whatever the condition of that body, it will be authentically powerful and you will not be attached to it like you used to be. You will not need it to look a certain way to please some external standard of beauty. Your goal will be how healthy and serving it is, rather than in how strong and attractive it is to others. You will not need to primp and preen and fragrance it for the benefit of attracting others. You will know that you are not that body, and that the real measure of your humanity is in your soul housed in that body. Your sense of self will shift from being totally identified with your body, to being identified with your invisible self. This will give you an incredible power like that of holy people who are said to affect the consciousness of an entire room simply by their presence. Go for authentic power, and you will see your physical body going along nicely for the ride.

• *Meditate daily.* Finally, and most importantly, meditate every day or as often as possible. Use the guidelines offered on pages 120–29, or any method you choose from the many that are available. Accustom yourself to going within and seeing your physical self accomplishing all you know will constitute a miracle for you. When you create the picture in your mind and know it there through meditation, it will come about in the physical domain as well. Everything comes from the invisible intelligence that is our spiritual nature into the physical world.

There it is, the world of real magic for you in your physical body. That perfect divine physical specimen appears to be solid, but always, as you look from a new perspective, it is silent, empty, invisible. That is the source of your miracle, or, as Hermann Hesse put it in his wondrous novel *Siddhartha*, "Within you there is a stillness and a sanctuary to which you can retreat at any time and be yourself." That "yourself" is a miracle. Know it!

Part III

RADIATING REAL MAGIC TO THE WORLD

8

REAL MAGIC
AND THE SPIRITUAL
REVOLUTION

Never doubt that a small group of thoughtful,
committed citizens can change the world; indeed,
it's the only thing that ever has.

— MARGARET MEAD

Just as the state of your life is a reflection of your state of
mind, so too is the state of the world a reflection of our collective state of mind. All that you see in the physical world
has a mental equivalent in the minds of each of us. We act
upon what we think about personally as individuals and col-
lectively as a people. Understanding this leads to knowing
that we are capable of creating a *world* of real magic in the
same way that I have been encouraging you to create real
magic in your individual life.

The universe we live in works in exactly the same way as
the universe that is within us. It is a perfect interconnection
of infinite systems, working in harmony to create a whole.
Within you are trillions of subatomic particles, making up

atoms, making up molecules, making up cells, making up bones and arteries, and on and on into the physical system that is you. Everything that makes up the visible you that is reading these words has a quantum invisible equivalent and is created and directed by that invisible force that is also you. The molecules of your physical body have an invisible component that allows them to be manifested in the physical you that sits there right now reading these words. The words are there on paper, but the thoughts that process the words are in another realm. You cannot separate any part of you from the whole, nor can you separate you from the whole that is your physical world. Interdependence between mind and body rules the cosmic order. And so it is with your relationship to the physical world you find yourself in.

You can be a messenger of miracles to the world. You do not need anything else to create this universal miracle. You are already all that you need to make a world of real magic. You must keep in mind that the world as you see it through your senses exists only because you process it to exist. For instance, when you go to sleep at night you completely leave this physical world and create another world with your mind. The world of your dreams becomes your reality for the entire time of your sleeping state. That is *all* that there is for you, nothing more. You create the cast of characters that will play out their roles in your dreams. You create the physical reality that you require for your dreams, including a reality in which you can fly, or breathe underwater or defy aging. You create a world in a formless dimension of pure thought when you are dreaming that is every bit as real as your waking world when you are not dreaming.

In order to create a world of real magic then, it is necessary to know within that this is your job to accomplish. You cannot give your responsibility for your efforts to anyone else. You cannot resign in anguish if others refuse to see the light.

Know that you can radiate outwardly all of the messages in this book and create the kind of real magical world that you envision.

If some of the cast of characters refuse to go along with your vision, send them love and then ask yourself what you can do to make their presence a part of the perfection that you envision. No matter how tempting, judging or blaming must be left outside of your consciousness. One of your biggest challenges may be in refusing to make them wrong and yourself right. To sit in judgment of those things which you perceive to be wrong or imperfect is to be one more person who is a part of judgment, evil or imperfection. The perceived inequities in the world are truly part of the perfection of the universe, *and so is your desire to end them.* Those whose purpose does not match yours are not wrong; they have their mission, and finding their own purposeful way may involve many detours and acts that seem destructive.

Read these words of Yogananda, from *The Essence of Self Realization*, speaking to that universal purpose that I am introducing here:

> The fundamental instinct of life, then, may be summed up thus: as a desire for continued, conscious existence in a state of perpetual enjoyment. . . . Thus do all beings reveal their divine nature. . . . Complexities arise because soul-joy is forgotten, and because people substitute for it the fleeting pleasures of the senses. All things, however, came from Bliss, or God. Eventually, all things must evolve back to that Bliss-state.

When you understand these words and are able to live them for yourself, you will come to know that ultimately what all people seek is this eternal bliss. The complexities that have arisen on a personal and on a worldwide scale all derive from pursuit of the fleeting pleasure of the senses. It is here that we can see that the world, as we know it within, and as we perceive others within, can in fact reach the blissful state. In fact, if you stand way back in your mind, and look carefully from that distant invisible perspective, you will note that a revolution of spiritual dimensions is taking place right now.

WE ARE IN AN AGE OF SPIRITUAL REVOLUTION

Back in 1974 I was a university professor in the divided city of Berlin. I stood at Checkpoint Charlie and saw how the barbed wire and guards with vicious dogs kept the city divided. The wall was built to last a thousand years, yet today it is nothing more than a relic of an ancient, nonspiritual past. That shrine of tyranny is but one of many that are toppling faster than we can update the history books.

There is a new collective consciousness in the minds of people, and a new spiritual awareness is spreading throughout humanity. Nothing can stop it, for nothing is more powerful than an *idea* whose time has come. An idea is a thought—individual or collective—that, once spread to enough souls, manifests in physical changes. If the collective thoughts are of war, hatred, divisiveness and fear, those seeds are manifested in our physical reality. And indeed, we have seen those seeds blowing in the wind for a long time.

Now we see a new reality, a reality that comes from a new way of thinking, and this is the context of our spiritual revolution. This new way of thinking is consequently a new way of being for humanity. It may not be fast enough to suit your desires, but it is moving along at precisely the right speed. The leaders that are emerging from this new consciousness will be in the forefront of this spiritual revolution. You can be one of those leaders and be part of the changing paradigm that you are witnessing.

Consider some of the remarkable changes that are presently occurring. The Iron Curtain has disintegrated. In Eastern Europe, virtually all of the countries whose governments trampled individual rights have been transformed. The dictators have fled or been forcibly removed. It began with an idea in one country and spread rapidly across the entire region.

Communism, which insists upon atheism from its subjects, has been declared an international failure. No one can tell the people that they must disregard their spiritual nature in favor of a doctrine imposed upon them. Rulers can remove the outer places of worship, but the inner place, that invisible corner of freedom that is ever present in each of us, cannot be legislated. The inner voices of these spiritual beings having a human experience are connected in an invisible way.

We have witnessed miracles taking place all over our world recently. A playwright in Czechoslovakia, imprisoned for his radical ideas on the dignity of man, is elected to the presidency of his country only a few years later. A man imprisoned for his views on solidarity in Poland is elected to the presidency of his country. Dictators are forcibly ousted from Romania. The Balkan people declare their freedom from tyrannical rule to a listening world and attempt a rational discussion instead of violence. The top leader of the Soviet Union declares communism a total failure for the world's ears to hear and report, and now that same union is a relic of the past. Wasn't it not too long ago that one of those leaders pounded his shoe on a desk and said, "We will bury you"?

Each of those scenes is miraculous! They exemplify that thought in the shape of ideas can spread like wildfire through the universe. It does not need a physical vehicle to carry the message, it transcends such mundane methods. It is invisible, this idea, and it is spreading without any vehicles or carriers.

In China, where more than a billion souls are temporarily residing, one million of those souls faced tanks to demonstrate their desire for freedom. And while the messengers can temporarily be imprisoned, the message cannot be halted. In South Africa, all vestiges of apartheid have been declared to be illegal. In one miraculous instant, a man who had been imprisoned and kept from the public eye for more than a quarter century is suddenly released, with no conditions. Black people are playing on beaches in front of signs that say Whites Only. In Central America, a dictator is replaced by a housewife in an election of the people. In South America, a poet runs for national office.

These changes are all taking place in the minds of individuals and spreading to others to form a collective consciousness. Once the ideas become present in a large enough number of us, they become our reality. This number is called a critical mass.

According to the laws of physics, when enough electrons line up within an atom to form a position, then all the rest automatically line up in a similar fashion. This is called *phase transition*, and it is easily observable in the proper laboratory setting. What is the invisible force present within that atom that allows all the rest of the electrons to move into a new phase? It is nameless at the subatomic level, and it is nameless at your level of awareness. It is invisible, and since you are made up of those subatomic particles, it is not too big a stretch to say that you have some of the same properties.

Our world is experiencing phase transition. The invisible force that aligns the electrons within an atom, that spiritual intelligence that flows through all form, is reaching critical mass in a large enough number of humans, and the results are being manifested in our world. The force cannot be stopped.

Some will try, but they will be swept away by the power of an idea whose time has come. It works in our personal lives and it works in our collective world as well.

We become what we think about all day long. When enough of us believed that we needed larger and larger weapons of destruction, we created a collective consciousness that forced us to act upon those invisible beliefs. We built bigger and bigger atomic weapons, and the madness of nuclear proliferation described our world conditions. When enough of us began to believe that a nuclear holocaust was too horrible to permit, we began discussing disarmament. The miracle of cooperation rather than competition is the beginning phase of a transition to a more positive, safe, loving world. It is an idea. It will catch on in the physical world if enough of us choose to so align ourselves in this spiritual manner. It cannot fail. It is in our atoms and molecules, so to speak.

The changes in the world are not restricted to political realignments and new nuclear policies. A new spiritual consciousness toward our environment has manifested itself into action as well. Earth Day, which had been overlooked for two decades, celebrated the new consciousness toward our planet. A miracle! The idea that we should treat the earth with sacred reverence is being translated into physical realities.

New legislation to reduce every kind of pollution imaginable is being mandated, along with penalties for those who violate these new laws. Automobiles that will not pollute the atmosphere are being mass-produced. Smokers can no longer pollute airplane interiors with nicotine. We have known for decades that it is immoral to force people in a restricted environment such as an airplane to inhale other people's cigarette smoke if their personal choice is not to use cigarettes. Why is it now being outlawed with legislation and enforcement? An idea whose time has come. A miracle? Lawmakers are listening to the voices of those who are thinking in new ways. Those thoughts are invisible, but their physical-world equivalents are quite observable.

You are seeing the fruits of those thoughts blooming everywhere. You are seeing No Smoking sections in restaurants, where they were not even considered a few years ago. You are seeing rivers and lakes, once so dirty that swimming was outlawed, being cleaned up and revitalized with a new consciousness as the driving force behind these moves. You are seeing noise-abatement legislation to eliminate noise pollution around airports and even at public beaches. You are seeing new regard for the dignity of animals. You are seeing labels on all of your food purchases so that you will know how much fat and how many additives you are consuming. All miracles.

These new laws and practices all originated in the minds of people, and those invisible minds created a new physical-world reality, a reality that is more spiritual in nature. The rights of an individual to live peacefully, in harmony, lovingly and on purpose are all reflections of a new way of thinking.

All of the changes you see taking place around you that reflect growing concern—for the individual, for a peaceful, safe, harmonious world, for the right to be able to choose life, liberty and the pursuit of blissful happiness—are part of a glorious revolution that is taking place first and most importantly in our thoughts. You are a part of that process. Whatever thoughts you have can and will be spread to those around you. You influence the physical world with your thoughts; of that you should be most convinced if you have read this entire book.

Your thoughts create either prosperity or scarcity in your life. Your thoughts create either joyous or miserable relationships. Your thoughts create your personality, and the very physical circumstances of your life. Those same thoughts affect others around you. The pure thoughts of a spiritual being affect the physical conditions of the environment; they literally raise the consciousness of the people around that spiritual person. You and your thoughts, and the millions of others who are selecting similar spiritual inner thoughts, are creating a phase transition that has brought into being this fabulous new spiritual revolution.

If this revolution, this new way of being, is to take hold and overcome all of the remaining nonspirituality that infects the world, it will have to reach critical mass in all areas of our existence. When enough of us align in each and every area of human activity, then the phase transition will take hold.

In 1988 I was invited to write a piece that was published in *Time* magazine as part of an advertising campaign. I wrote a letter to the people who will be occupying earth in the year 2088. I had no restrictions placed upon me by the advertiser or the magazine. Here is that letter as it appeared in the October 17, 1988, issue of *Time*. It reflects the message that I am offering in this book.

A LETTER TO THE NEXT GENERATION

As I prepare this message for people living in 2088, I find my thoughts are not about futuristic or scientific wonders you enjoy. My curiosity is not about your ability to travel to outer space. My curiosity has to do with this: Have you evolved into a higher human being than those of us on earth in 1988?

My message to you centers on the hope that you are more humane than we are now. I wonder if you are practicing the vital lessons a few of us in 1988 believe humanity will some day master. I wonder if you have been able to move beyond distrust, fear, and hostility. My message of hope is addressed to you in the form of four questions. Your answers will describe where you are in the evolution of this higher human being, now stirring to life here in 1988.

1. *Have you learned that your humanity lies beyond the boundaries of the body?* Do you know and live the idea that a person is much more than a pile of bones, blood, gristle, and skin? Do you recognize that within all form is an invisible intelligence? Is there general acceptance and delight in knowing that persons are much more than their packaging? Is it "socially acceptable" to develop the invisible aspect of yourself as we do today by choosing aerobics or jogging for physical development?

Can you see yourselves as spiritual beings having a human experience, rather than human beings who may be having a spiritual experience? This is what I mean: My three-year-old daughter presented me with a make-believe meal on her plastic toy dishes. On that level, it was a physical, form-only interaction that could have been considered unimportant. On another level, the invisible, the formless part of her was expressing, "Daddy needs to eat something warm, and I want him to have a special dinner. I love my Daddy, and I want to take good care of him." My awareness of that invisible part of her, her thoughts and feelings which are pure love, transformed the plastic toys and make-believe food. I could almost touch those beautiful caring thoughts in back of her actions.

2. *Have you learned and adopted the understanding that we are all connected?* Here on Earth, in 1988, we seem to know intellectually that we are living in the same house, and that when you live on a round planet, you

can't afford to choose sides. But we continue to choose sides. Do you live with the awareness that each human being is a "me that is we"? Do the majority of people see that one cell within an organism, which has no reference to the whole, will destroy adjacent cells, eventually killing the entire being while destroying itself in the process? Are you guiding your young people to develop serenity and ease within themselves, so they will cooperate with the cells adjacent to them? Are your nations at ease within, or are they still acting out their aggressive images on their neighbors? Are you in 2088 seeing and experiencing the belief that each human being on our planet is just as interconnected as geographic neighbors, and that the total being called human being cannot function harmoniously when the components are in conflict?

3. *Do the majority of you see that what you think about expands?* As I write, some of us are nurturing these ideas like seedlings:

- The power of thought is enormous.
- We can create thought.
- Out of thought comes the entire direction of our lives.
- We act on our thoughts.
- We become what we think about all day long.
- In the dimensionless world of thought, everything we think is here.
- We have the ability to turn any thought into form with the power of mind.
- Thought is a formless energy which comprises our essential humanity.
- Our lives are what our thoughts create.

We are just beginning to recognize the importance of thought as the most powerful force in the universe. There is a new awareness and application of these ideas. Instead of being *against* terrorism and war, we are shifting our thoughts to being *for* peace and cooperation. We are beginning to recognize that a war on drugs, poverty, hunger and crime is not as effective as being for an enlightened, educated youth, a higher standard of living for all, and respect for each other's rights and possessions. Do you understand that what we think about expands into action? And therefore, cultivating thoughts of what you are for results in a healthier, happier and more peaceful society. Do you recognize that being *against* anything weakens you, while being *for* something empowers you?

4. *Have you discovered the other side of "I'll believe that when I see it"?* In 1988 there is an awakening to the idea that the development of a higher human being is a process involving the understanding that *you see what you believe, rather than you believe what you see.* Has this belief system led to the development of a higher human being? In 1983 I wrote a parable in which a higher human being named Eykis visits our world. She brings gifts in the form of thoughts to assist us in transforming ourselves and our planet. Her message proclaims, "You'll See It When You Believe It." Did these beliefs which Eykis describes move you toward this kind of thinking in 2088?

- Quality rather than appearance.
- Ethics rather than rules.
- Knowledge rather than achievement.
- Integrity rather than domination.
- Serenity rather than acquisitions.

If the answer is "Yes," then indeed a higher human being is in process, and the trend toward destroying this being called human being has been reversed. My connection to you is pure, formless, dimensionless thought, and so too is your link back to me in 1988 and forward to infinity.

YOUR PLACE IN THIS SPIRITUAL REVOLUTION

Throughout this book I have reminded you of one central theme: *Your thoughts create your physical reality.* Your relationships to those in your life are essentially located in your thoughts. If you see love in those around you, that is what will expand in your experience of others. This is also true of your worldview. The physical universe that you see is all in your mind. When you turn your mind off, or become unconscious, the physical universe, for you, disappears. Then, when you awaken your consciousness, the universe reappears magically. Quite simple really—no thoughts on your part, no physical world. As Walt Whitman succinctly stated: "The whole theory of the universe is directed unerringly to one single individual—namely to You." Without your mind to process it, the universe simply disappears into nothingness.

The most important question to ask yourself as you seek your place in this spiritual revolution I have described is, "How do I see the world I live in?" Keeping in mind that thoughts are yours to create, and that your mind is the repository for all that you experience, take a good look at how you use that mind.

If you want, you can deny that spiritual revolution I have described, and instead see a world that is slowly but surely deteriorating into a nonspiritual morass. You can cite crime rates, starving populations, natural disasters, greedy politicians, inconsiderate young people, increased drug dependence and so on, and you can make a strong case for a nonspiritual environment. If you choose to use your mind in this way, that will be your experience of the world you live in. That is what you will see each and every day. In other words, *you will see what you believe*. You will explain away the changes that are of a positive nature by insisting that they are only exceptions to the rule. And for you, that rule is whatever you have convinced yourself is the true nature of where humanity is headed.

Not only do you become what you think about, but the world also becomes what you think about. Those who think that the world is a dark place are blind to the light that might illuminate their lives. Those who see the light of the world view the dark spots as merely potential light.

Where is your place in the spiritual revolution? Fundamental changes are taking place in the collective bosom of mankind. If you believe those changes are negative and destructive, that will be your place. You will think it, convince yourself of it, and create the intentions to verify it for yourself repeatedly. On the other hand, you can choose to know that for every act of unkindness, there are a million kind acts, that there is a network of good guys out there who are truly making a difference, and that the spiritual changes, while slow, are still present and observable. That then will be your place in the spiritual revolution.

The changes are taking place first in the collective minds of men, and then in the outer world as well. You are here, on purpose, to help make those changes manifest more profoundly and permanently into the consciousness of all mankind. Trusting yourself means that you are trusting the wisdom that designed and created you in the first place, and knowing that you are on purpose, you know that the universe is also on purpose. You are trusting in the divine intelligence that flows through you.

I personally attempt to remove myself from the bad news that is thrust at me in a thousand different ways. I want to be a part of the solution, not part of the problem. Obviously, I am aware that there are still wars being waged, crimes being committed and poverty and suffering in the world. My thoughts are not on judging those problems or being mad at them, or wishing they would go away. My thoughts, which will expand into action, are on doing something about those problems by convincing those in powerful positions to direct their resources toward fixing things; by writing about and teaching these principles to those who need them the most; by sending books and tapes to needy institutions and the like. When I am focused on what I am for, rather than what I am against, I am empowered. This is true in my individual life, and it is true in my larger role here on this planet.

Your place in this revolution will solidify if you fill yourself with love. You cannot be sustained by tension, anxiousness, fear and doubt. These are inhibitors rather than empowering emotions. To become a part of the spiritual revolution, you must be able to radiate outward all that you are gaining in your spiritual consciousness. You have the power to do just that if you make that choice.

RADIATING YOUR NEW CONSCIOUSNESS OUTWARD

What do you have to give away? Keeping in mind that your purpose is always about giving, loving and serving in some capacity, regardless of what vocation you have chosen, this question of what you will be able to give away as your purposeful mission is paramount. It does not take any extra special intelligence to know this simple truth: *You cannot give away what you don't have.* If you don't have any money, obviously you can't give money away. The same principle applies to your contribution to the spiritual revolution.

If you don't have love, harmony and peace within you, then you simply cannot contribute these qualities. Consequently, you will be among those who are watching this revolution take place either wondering why they are not part of it or being part of the resistance. If you have anxiety, stress, fear, anger and tension within, that is all that you will be able to give away. That is what you will be radiating outward, and obviously that is what you will be seeing all around you. The choice, as always, is yours, based upon how you choose to process your world.

The components of anxiety, stress, fear and anger do not exist independently of you in the world. You cannot go out with a bucket and bring home some of these things. They simply do not exist in the physical world, even though we talk about them as if they did. But there are people acting stressfully, anxiously, angrily and fearfully in the world. Those actions stem exclusively from a way of thinking. Thus, if you have those elements within you, it is because that is how you have chosen to process the events and circumstances of your physical universe.

Those who choose to take up weapons against others are operating from fearful thoughts. The presence of those thoughts is justified by an inner processing system that verifies this behavior. These people believe that the world is a suspicious, dangerous place, on both a personal level and a collective level.

If you are a person who would like to discontinue this kind of behavior, then you will be required to change those inner voices. As Albert Einstein put it: "The significant problems we have cannot be solved at the same level of thinking with which we created them." Thus, all of the major problems that we humans face were created by our way of thinking. And a man who is considered one of the brightest intellectual lights of our century reminds us that a new way of thinking will be required to change them.

We cannot go on thinking in divisive ways if we want to bring about unity on our planet. We cannot go on thinking in militant ways if we want to bring peace to our world. We cannot go on thinking in hateful ways if we want to bring love to our world.

Each thought that develops into a helping, purposeful, loving act is your contribution. It matters not what others say or do— they have their own destinies to fulfill. When someone sends you criticism or hate, you can respond only with what you have inside. If harmony and peace reside because that is how you have chosen to think, then that is what you will have to give away. In that moment you have made a difference. You have manifested a miracle into the world and radiated outward the real magic I have been describing.

As you do this on your own personal and local level, you will find yourself expanding and reaching more and more people. That is precisely what has been happening with all of the spiritual revolution changes you see around you. The green movement started in the minds of individuals, and is now a worldwide phenomenon. Giving the Nobel Peace Prize to the Dalai Lama, Tibet's exiled spiritual leader, a man whose very life reflects a spiritual consciousness and reverence for all living things, started in the mind of one person and ultimately became a reality. The end of apartheid, just like its beginning, was first an idea. The ideas in your mind are just as powerful.

The words of Michael Jackson, "We are the world, we are the children, we are the ones who make a better world so let's start giving," reflect a truly spiritual message. And those words have helped eliminate a large portion of hunger and starvation on our planet.

You truly are the world, and your thoughts do make all the difference in this world. Have reverence for your mind. Treat your invisible inner reality with sacred blissful appreciation, and know that you are capable of bringing about real magic in our world, and that every thought you have of love and harmony is one more atom aligning itself toward the phase transition that is inevitably occurring even now as you read these words.

HOW YOU CAN CREATE A MIRACLE IN OUR WORLD

In all that I have written in these pages about creating real magic, nothing is more important than your coming into contact with the higher part of yourself. At first, you will very likely reject this notion of yourself as a miracle worker in the worldwide realm of real magic. Yet as William James once wrote, "A new idea is first condemned as ridiculous and then dismissed as trivial, until finally, it becomes what everybody knows." Many will consider the idea of performing miracles as ridiculous or impossible, and will continue leading lives that reflect their beliefs.

Increasingly, however, people are believing in their own divinity and trusting in the divine wisdom that created them. They are helping to create the spiritual revolution that is now occurring. More and more people are using their invisible thoughts to visualize a better, safer, cleaner, more responsible, more loving world. They are making an impact in the political, ecological and spiritual realms of our planet. They know the wisdom to be found in the following words of Chief Seattle, who in the 1800s wrote a letter in response to the govern-

Be a person who accepts
no limits in your mind.
None!

---

you will not be punished
for your anger, you will
be punished by your anger
           Buddha

So live that you wouldnt
be ashamed to sell the
family parrot to the town
gossip
        Will Rogers.

'as you think, so shall you're'

Circumstances do not make
a person, they reveal him

ment's offer to purchase tribal land. Read Chief Seattle's letter and consider how we have treated the environment we inherited from our forefathers. His words are probably more relevant today than ever.

The President in Washington sends word that he wishes to buy our land. But how can you buy or sell the sky? The land? The idea is strange to us. If we do not own the freshness of the air and the sparkle of the water, how can you buy them?

Every part of the earth is sacred to my people. Every shining pine needle, every sandy shore, every mist in the dark woods, every meadow, every humming insect. All are holy in the memory and experience of my people.

We know the sap which courses through the trees as we know the blood that courses through our veins. We are part of the earth and it is part of us. The perfumed flowers are our sisters. The bear, the deer, the great eagle, these are our brothers. The rocky crests, the juices in the meadow, the body heat of the pony, and man, all belong to the same family.

The shining water that moves in the streams and rivers is not just water, but the blood of our ancestors. If we sell you our land, you must remember that it is sacred. Each ghostly reflection in the clear waters of the lakes tells of events and memories in the life of my people. The water's murmur is the voice of my father's father.

The rivers are our brothers. They quench our thirst. They carry our canoes and feed our children. So you must give to the rivers the kindness you would give any brother.

If we sell you our land, remember that the air is precious to us, that the air shares its spirit with all the life it supports. The wind that gave our grandfather his first breath also receives his last sigh. The wind also gives our children the spirit of life. So if we sell you our land, you must keep it apart and sacred, as a place where man can go to taste the wind that is sweetened by the meadow flowers.

Will you teach your children what we have taught our children? That the earth is our mother? What befalls the earth befalls all the sons of the earth.

This we know: the earth does not belong to man, man belongs to the earth. All things are connected like the blood that unites us all. Man did not weave the web of life, he is merely a strand in it. Whatever he does to the web, he does to himself.

One thing we know: our god is also your god. The earth is precious to him and to harm the earth is to heap contempt on its creator.

Your destiny is a mystery to us. What will happen when the buffalo are all slaughtered? The wild horses tamed? What will happen when the secret corners of the forest are heavy with the scent of many men and the view of the ripe hills is blotted by talking wires? Where will the thicket be? Gone! Where will the eagle be? Gone! And what is it to say goodbye to the swift pony and the hunt? The end of living and the beginning of survival.

When the last Red Man has vanished with his wilderness and his memory is only the shadow of a cloud moving across the prairie, will these shores and forests still be here? Will there be any of the spirit of my people left?

We love this earth as a newborn loves its mother's heartbeat. So, if we sell you our land, love it as we have loved it. Care for it as we have cared for it. Hold in your mind the memory of the land as it is when you receive it.

Preserve the land for all children, and love it, as God loves us all.

As we are part of the land, you too are part of the land. This earth is precious to us. It is also precious to you. One thing we know: there is only one God. No man, be he Red Man or White Man, can be apart. We *are* brothers after all.

This consciousness Chief Seattle so lovingly describes is available to you to share and expand with your thoughts. You, one person with a vision, are like a pebble in a stream, moving ever outward to infinity, impacting on all who come into contact with that ripple, which creates the spiritual world I believe in so strongly.

You make all the difference in the world. Your presence here is a divine necessity. Perfect and purposeful. Your inner silent invisible mind is the director of your world and the world you find yourself immersed in. This is your miracle making in action. These words of St. John of the Cross, found in *The Perennial Philosophy*, by Aldous Huxley, should give you confidence in your ability to produce real magic.

God does not reserve such a lofty vocation (that of mystical contemplation) to certain souls only; on the contrary, He is willing that all should embrace it. But He finds few who permit Him to work such sublime things for them. There are many who, when He sends them trials, shrink from the labour and refuse to bear with the dryness and mortification, instead of submitting, as they must, with perfect patience.

You will see a miracle-laden world when you embrace, rather than shrink from, responsibility for creating it. All that you know of the world is in your mind, and you create the thoughts that occupy that inner space. There are many things that you can do on a daily basis to bring about the Eden that is your birthright. But whatever it is that you find yourself doing in the physical world, you must know that it is all driven by that divine invisible soul that has temporarily settled itself in your body.

By aligning yourself with your spiritual side first, before your nonspiritual side, you will radiate out that peace that is within. You will see those who are still on the side of war and destruction as tests to determine your own resolve to not join that way of thinking. You will not be dissuaded from your mission just because others are not with you. You will stay focused on what you are for in all areas of your life.

The bad news, the gossip, the emphasis in the media on tragedy and pessimism will not capture your attention. You will note these as areas for improvement, but your inner divine self will be noting also how many acts of healing, kindness and friendliness outnumber those of suffering.

You create a world of real magic when you alone decide to use your divine, miraculous inner intelligence to make it happen. It is within you and within all of us to be wise. If you see the world in this magical way, then you have created it. It is not illusional thinking, it is real for you, inside, in the only place that you can live. Here is Jehovah, speaking through the mouth of his prophet: "If I am here, everyone is here. If I am not here, no one is here." And so it is with you. You are the be-all and end-all of real magic in this world.

As I approach the last paragraph of this book it thrills me that I have been able to create this work on real magic from within my mind. I have been guided to write it throughout every stage of its development. It has been a magical journey for me. I live to radiate this miraculousness I feel within me, and I know that this inner voice is capable of creating real authentic magic in many forms. But even more than knowing the magic that I have created in my own personal life, with my glorious family, I shiver inside with the awareness that it can make a difference in your life and in the entire physical world we are all immersed in. My closing quote on this subject comes from the ancient writer Philo:

Households, cities, countries and nations have enjoyed great happiness, when a single individual has taken heed of the Good and Beautiful. . . . Such men do not only liberate themselves; they fill those they meet with a free mind.

You are that single individual, becoming a spiritual being and taking heed of the good and the beautiful. You will indeed fill yourself and those around you with a new freedom in your minds, the freedom to create real magic.

INDEX

ABOUT THE AUTHOR

Wayne W. Dyer is the author of twenty books and has a doctorate in counseling psychology. He lectures across the country to groups numbering in the thousands and appears regularly on radio and television. Dyer lives with his family in Southern Florida.

HarperCollins*Publishers*

Books by Wayne W. Dyer

Coming in Hardcover September 2001:

THERE'S A SPIRITUAL SOLUTION TO EVERY PROBLEM
ISBN 0-06-019230-5 (hardcover) • ISBN 0-694-52426-3 (audio)
ISBN 0-694-52563-4 (audio CD) • ISBN 0-06-621406-8 (large print)

Dyer shows how we can rid ourselves of problems through spiritual solutions.

Quill

YOUR ERRONEOUS ZONES
Escape Negative Thinking and Take Control of Your Life
ISBN 0-06-091976-0 (pb) • ISBN 0-06-109148-0 (mm) • ISBN 1-55994-432-3 (audio)

From self-image problems to over-dependence upon others, Dyer provides the
tools needed to break free from the trap of negative thinking and enjoy life fully.

PULLING YOUR OWN STRINGS
Dynamic Techniques for Dealing with Other People and Living Your Life as You Choose
ISBN 0-06-091975-2 (pb) • ISBN 0-06-109224-X (mm) • ISBN 1-55994-433-1 (audio)

A guide to preventing ourselves from being victimized and manipulated by others.

YOU'LL SEE IT WHEN YOU BELIEVE IT
The Way to Your Personal Transformation
ISBN 0-06-093733-5 (pb)

Using examples from his own highly successful experiences, Wayne Dyer will
convince you that you can make your most impossible dreams come true.

WHAT DO YOU REALLY WANT FOR YOUR CHILDREN?
How to Raise Happy Kids – An Invaluable Guide From the Man Who's Helped Millions!
ISBN 0-380-73047-2 (pb)

Straightforward, commonsense advice about raising children of all ages.

Available wherever books are sold, or call 1-800-331-3761 to order.

✒Quill

REAL MAGIC
Creating Miracles in Everyday Life
ISBN 0-06-093582-0 (pb) • 0-06-109150-2 (mm) • ISBN 1-55994-667-9 (audio)

Dyer reveals seven beliefs central to working miracles in our everyday lives.

YOUR SACRED SELF
Making the Decision to be Free
ISBN 0-06-093583-9 (pb) • ISBN 0-694-51526-4 (audio) • ISBN 0-06-109475-7 (mm)

Your Sacred Self reveals a three-step program to help us understand our place in the world and develop a sense of satisfaction with ourselves and with others.

MANIFEST YOUR DESTINY
The Nine Spiritual Principles for Getting Everything You Want
ISBN 0-06-017528-1 (hc) • ISBN 0-06-109494-3 (mm) • ISBN 0-06-092892-1 (pb)
ISBN 0-694-51778-X (audio) • ISBN 0-694-52547-2 (audio CD)

Through the art of meditation and his own Nine Spiritual Principles of Manifesting, Dyer illuminates the path to achieving our truest and greatest goals.

WISDOM OF THE AGES
60 Days to Enlightenment
ISBN 0-06-019231-3 (hc) • ISBN 0-694-52055-1 (audio) • ISBN 0-694-52546-4 (audio CD)

Dyer interprets the wisdom of time's greatest thinkers, relating their ideas to today.

Also available from HarperAudio:

THE DR. WAYNE W. DYER AUDIO COLLECTION
ISBN 0-694-51621-X

THE WISDOM OF WAYNE W. DYER AUDIO COLLECTION
ISBN 0-694-52206-6

Available wherever books are sold, or call 1-800-331-3761 to order.